STAR TREK

The Cultural History of Television

STAR TREK

A Cultural History

M. Keith Booker

ROWMAN & LITTLEFIELD
Lanham • Boulder • New York • London

Published by Rowman & Littlefield
An imprint of The Rowman & Littlefield Publishing Group, Inc.
4501 Forbes Boulevard, Suite 200, Lanham, Maryland 20706
www.rowman.com

Unit A, Whitacre Mews, 26-34 Stannary Street, London SE11 4AB

British Library Cataloguing in Publication Information Available

Library of Congress Cataloging-in-Publication Data

Names: Booker, M. Keith, author.
Title: Star trek : a cultural history / M. Keith Booker.
Description: Lanham : Rowman & Littlefield, [2018] | Series: The cultural history of television |
    Includes bibliographical references and index.
Identifiers: LCCN 2018005381 | ISBN 9781538112755 (cloth : alk. paper) | ISBN 9781538112762
    (electronic)
Subjects: LCSH: Star trek (Television program) | Popular culture—United States—History.
Classification: LCC PN1992.77.S73 B66 2018 | DDC 791.45/72—dc23
LC record available at https://lccn.loc.gov/2018005381

∞ ™ The paper used in this publication meets the minimum requirements of
American National Standard for Information Sciences Permanence of Paper for
Printed Library Materials, ANSI/NISO Z39.48-1992.

Printed in the United States of America

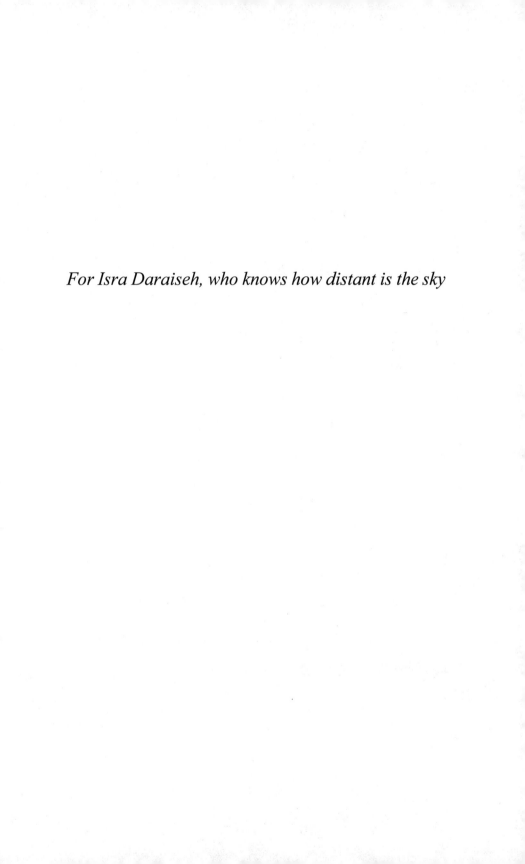

For Isra Daraiseh, who knows how distant is the sky

CONTENTS

THE *STAR TREK* FRANCHISE (WITH ABBREVIATIONS USED IN THE TEXT)

TELEVISION SERIES

Star Trek: The Original Series (*TOS*), 1966–1969
Star Trek: The Animated Series (*TAS*), 1973–1974
Star Trek: The Next Generation (*TNG*), 1987–1994
Star Trek: Deep Space Nine (*DS9*), 1993–1999
Star Trek: Voyager (*VOY*), 1995–2001
Star Trek: Enterprise (*ENT*), 2001–2005
Star Trek: Discovery (*DSC*), 2017–

THEATRICAL FILMS

TOS Cast

Star Trek: The Motion Picture (*TMP*), 1979
Star Trek II: The Wrath of Khan, 1982
Star Trek III: The Search for Spock, 1984
Star Trek IV: The Voyage Home, 1986
Star Trek V: The Final Frontier, 1989
Star Trek VI: The Undiscovered Country, 1991

TOS and *TNG* Cast

Star Trek: Generations, 1994

TNG Cast

Star Trek: First Contact, 1996
Star Trek: Insurrection, 1998
Star Trek: Nemesis, 2002

Abrams Reboot

Star Trek, 2009
Star Trek Into Darkness, 2013
Star Trek Beyond, 2016

INTRODUCTION

Star Trek—Past, Present, and Future

The original *Star Trek* television series, which ran on NBC for a mere three seasons from 1966 to 1969, would go on to become arguably the single most important work ever produced by American popular culture. This series—now often referred to by fans and critics as *TOS* (for *The Original Series*)—addressed serious issues and ideas in a way that had seldom been seen on American television, while boldly taking viewers on outer-space adventures in parts of the galaxy where no one had been before. Moving into immediate syndication after its original broadcast run, *TOS* developed a cult following, becoming more and more popular in the subsequent two decades, until its audience finally began to fade slightly only after the premiere of its own sequel series, *Star Trek: The Next Generation* (*TNG*), in 1987. In fact, the original broadcast run of *TOS* proved to be just the tip of a multimedia iceberg, spawning a wide range of products that were eagerly consumed by a fan base that continued to grow in both size and enthusiasm over the next half century.

In addition to its own reruns in syndication, *TOS* and its vision of a high-tech, socially enlightened future inspired the most extensive and impressive sequence of sequel and prequel series in television history, from *Star Trek: The Animated Series* (1973–1974, often abbreviated herein as *TAS*) to *Star Trek: Discovery*, which premiered on the CBS All Access streaming video service in September 2017. *TOS* also became the inspiration for one of the most important film franchises in the history of

American cinema, at this writing comprising thirteen films, beginning with *Star Trek: The Motion Picture* (*TMP*) in 1979 and extending through the three "reboot" films produced by J. J. Abrams from 2009 to 2016. Along the way, the ideas, events, and characters of *TOS* became the inspiration for a series of novels and comic books, as well as the center of one of the most important fan cultures in the history of fandom, paving the way for (and continuing to be a crucial part of) today's ubiquitous culture of conventions, cosplay, and merchandising.

No one, given the inauspicious beginnings of the original *Star Trek* series, could have predicted this ultimate degree of success. Not only did the series, from its beginnings, have trouble drawing enough ratings to stay on the air, but it had significant difficulties getting on the air in the first place. When presented by series creator Gene Roddenberry (via Desilu Productions, with whom Roddenberry had signed a development deal) first to CBS, the idea for the series was turned down altogether. NBC was interested enough to commission a pilot in 1964, scenes from which would later be edited into the first-season two-part episode *The Menagerie* (November 17 and 24, 1966). The pilot itself was rejected by NBC, but the network was sufficiently intrigued to order a second pilot, with only one character, the now-iconic half-Vulcan Mr. Spock (Leonard Nimoy), carried over from the first pilot to the second. Only Nimoy and Majel Barrett (who would remain a presence through most of the subsequent series and films as the voices of the ships' computers) were carried over from the original cast. This second pilot clicked with NBC management, and the new show was ordered by NBC for the 1966–1967 season, setting in motion a cultural phenomenon whose significance would resonate through the decades.

In retrospect, though, it is easy to see why *Star Trek* had so much trouble getting on the air. The series was simply unlike anything that had been on television before—and television executives are notoriously hesitant to air anything genuinely new or unfamiliar for fear of alienating viewers or (more importantly) sponsors. That was probably even more the case when Roddenberry began to try to sell the series back in 1963, a scant two years after Commissioner Newton Minow of the Federal Communications Commission (FCC)—in a speech delivered at a 1961 meeting of the National Association of Broadcasters—had famously declared the content of American commercial television to be a "vast wasteland," consisting essentially of a nonstop stream of mindless programming, punctuated by even more mindless commercials. [1]

There was little room in this televisual wasteland for a thoughtful—one might even say cerebral—series such as *TOS*, so it is little wonder that Roddenberry famously attempted in his initial pitch to the networks to describe *Star Trek* as a sort of "*Wagon Train* in Space," thus aligning the show with a previous one that had been highly successful (*Wagon Train* had reached number one in the Nielsen ratings for NBC in the 1961–1962 television season). This description also linked *TOS* to the whole genre of the Western, still highly popular at the time, as witnessed by the fact that NBC's *Bonanza* held the top spot in the Nielsen ratings from 1964 to 1967. Perhaps most importantly, though, the *Wagon Train* analogy was also an attempt to link the potential new series with the entire legacy of westward expansion, one of the most popular American national narratives.

Still, *Wagon Train* analogy or no *Wagon Train* analogy, *TOS* simply wasn't much like anything viewers had seen on television before. Many viewers clearly did not know what to make of the unusual show, just as NBC's management did not really know how to market it. The show premiered at 8:30 on Thursday night, September 8, 1966, preceded by *Daniel Boone*, a series about a pioneering adventurer, thus suggesting that their programmers at least took the *Wagon-Train*-in-space description seriously. But the folksy, nostalgic *Daniel Boone* was anything but a true sister series to the progressive, future-oriented *TOS*. And there was really nothing else on television that *would* have been an effective predecessor to *TOS* in the Thursday-night lineup, just as the show had no direct forerunners in American television in general. Largely because of the difficulty with producing the special effects necessary for science fiction (SF), the genre had never been prominent on television. The only previous series that successfully treated science fictional material with anything like genuine seriousness was CBS's *Twilight Zone* (1959–1964), but that series was only partly science fiction and generally had very little in common with *TOS* (other than featuring *TOS* star William Shatner in one of its most memorable episodes).

Of course, it is also the case that a certain segment of the viewing audience was attracted to *TOS* precisely because it *was* so different from what they were accustomed to seeing on television, providing a thrilling sense of freshness and newness. For one thing, the series' willingness to explore important political issues in a serious way clearly appealed to some viewers amid the politically charged climate of the late 1960s. For another thing, the series simply *looked* different, a fact that no doubt turned off some viewers but appealed to many others. In particular, science fiction fans clearly appreciated the advanced technologies that the series presented to viewers—including the sleekly decorated interior of the USS *Enterprise*, faster-than-light warp drives, force-field defensive shields, phasers, scanners, tricorders, communicators, replicators, and (perhaps most memorably) transporters. Indeed, these technologies (whether or not they had a sound basis in science) provided, for an entire generation of Americans, the most important single vision of what future technologies might look like.

Ultimately, though, these shiny, high-tech trappings were just a bonus. Some SF devotees might have been drawn to the series primarily because of its representation of technology, but the biggest reason why *TOS* attracted such a devoted (if small) early audience—and why it maintained its attraction over the decades—lay in the characters and their relationships—and especially in the way these relationships modeled a utopian twenty-third century in which the social problems of the twentieth century had been solved, opening the way for human beings to pursue their true potentials without having to struggle against other human beings for the right to do so. Of course, audiences in the 1960s were not entirely ready to comprehend such a future, which is one reason why *TOS* features characters who are, by and large, not much different from people of the twentieth century. With the exception of the ultra-logical, selfless Spock (who provides a sort of peek at the direction in which Roddenberry imagined humans evolving), the characters of *TOS* are still driven largely by individualist passions. Nevertheless, they are able to establish genuine bonds that point the way toward a more collectivist future that would be more fully realized beginning with *TNG*. This was especially the case with the core trio consisting of Shatner's Captain James T. Kirk, Nimoy's Mr. Spock, and DeForest Kelley's Dr. McCoy, all of whom became, over time, well-developed individual characters. More importantly, despite their differences in character and their frequent disagreements, these three characters developed a genuine three-way bond that provided one of the most powerful visions of friendship and partnership in the history of American television.

The supporting cast of *TOS* was also crucial in delivering its message of multiracial and multicultural harmony in the utopian future. Characters such as the chief engineer, Mr. Montgomery Scott (James Doohan); the helmsman, Mr. Hikaru Sulu (George Takei); the communications officer,

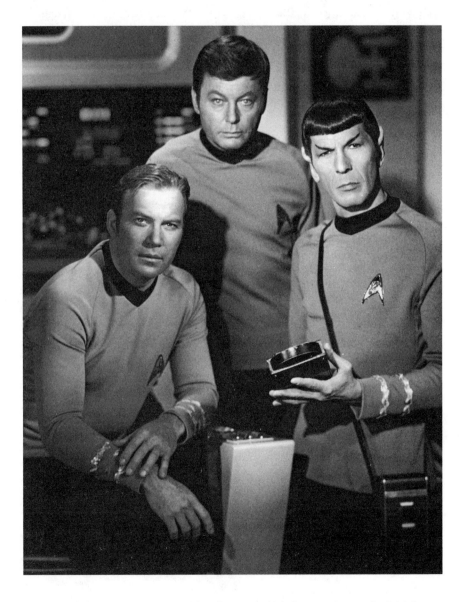

The friendship that grew among Kirk, Spock, and McCoy was key to the initial success of the *Star Trek* franchise. **NBC / Photofest © NBC**

(Nyota)[2] Uhura (Nichelle Nichols); and the navigator, Pavel Chekov (Walter Koenig), might have been secondary to *TOS* itself, but all have become among the best-known characters in the history of American popular culture. As a group, these characters formed a closely knit community that made the *Enterprise* a sort of microcosm of the larger society (the United Federation of Planets) of which they were all equal citizens.

Interpersonal relationships—especially the three-way relationship among Kirk, Spock, and McCoy—were also central to the first six films of the *Star Trek* franchise, each of which could draw upon the history of the characters in *TOS* to provide character and relationship development that is not normally available within the framework of a two-hour film. This aspect of the film franchise made it particularly stand out in relation to other science fiction films, which have not historically been especially good at character development. Indeed, while films such as the 1956 classic *Forbidden Planet* could clearly be seen as direct predecessors to *TOS* and its successors, American science fiction film, which exploded

The bridge crew of the original *Enterprise*. Paramount Pictures / Photofest © Paramount Pictures

**Kirk, Spock, and McCoy prepare to beam down for another adventure. NBC /
Photofest © NBC**

on the scene as a major element of *American* popular culture in the 1950s,
had relatively little in common, as a whole, with *Star Trek* going into its
1966 premiere. SF film of the 1950s had been dominated by anxious Cold
War–driven narratives of alien invasion and nuclear apocalypse. In
contrast, *Star Trek* presented a bright, optimistic vision of the future, a
utopian vision in which virtually all social and economic problems of
twentieth-century earth had been solved, primarily through the beneficial
effects of advanced technology. As a result, the human race of *TOS* was
liberated from the everyday concerns of scrambling to survive, freed to
explore its true potential—not to mention the rest of the galaxy. As such,
TOS—so different from the SF film and television of its time—had much
more in common with many of its predecessors in the *written* science

A typical Original Series landing party. NBC / Photofest © NBC

fiction of the Golden Age of SF (going back to the 1930s), which were filled with similar utopian energies and a similar faith in the power of technology.

Chapter 1 of this volume will trace the evolution of the *Star Trek* franchise over time, with particular emphasis on the various television series that followed *TOS*. And evolution is the proper word here. The *Trek* series that began with *TNG* and ran through *Deep Space Nine* and *Voyager* are all set in the twenty-fourth century, and *TNG* in particular features characters who have evolved beyond the foibles of most of the *TOS* characters, all moving away from passions of a Kirk and toward the rationality of Spock.[3] Indeed, one of the unique features of the *Star Trek* franchise is its ability to portray, over the course of a century or so, genuine changes in the human species. This chapter will also consider the development of the *Star Trek* film franchise and the expansion of the *Star Trek* brand as a whole beyond television and film to include printed formats such as novels and comic books. This expansion into so many different media helped to produce a complex multiverse effect long before it became popular to talk about this effect with regard to the Marvel Multiverse and other multimedia narrative systems that have been so prominent in the American popular culture of the early twenty-first century. Various adaptations of the *Star Trek* concept to comics have been produced (by a variety of publishers) almost continuously since 1967. There has also been a continuous stream of related novels, many of them produced by well-respected science fiction authors (such as Joe Haldeman and Vonda McIntyre). Nevertheless, though they have attracted a number of enthusiastic fans among readers, the novels have, as a whole, received less critical respect than they deserve, a phenomenon that will also be considered in chapter 1.

The points of contact between Golden Age SF and *Star Trek* will be a focus of chapter 2, as will the place of the entire *Star Trek* franchise within the wider world of science fiction film, television, and literature going forward into the twenty-first century. For example, this chapter will discuss the flurry of science fiction television series that appeared about the same time as *TOS*, while noting some of the reasons why *TOS* would go on to be so much more successful than any of its contemporaries. It will also place *TOS* within contemporaneous developments in written science fiction, including astrofuturism and the New Wave, and will then discuss the future development of the franchise in connection with developments such as the science fiction film boom that began with *Star Wars* in 1977 and the rise of cyberpunk science fiction in the mid-1980s.

Chapter 3, on the other hand, explores the extensive dialogue between the *Star Trek* franchise (with a particular emphasis on the Cold War setting of *TOS*) and the wider world of American society over the more than half a century spanned by the franchise. After all, despite its seemingly remote setting in time and place, *Star Trek* has (like all of the best science fiction) always been primarily about the here and now, maintaining an especially close contact with contemporary reality, however far out its ideas and locations might seem. In this sense, it is important to note that, even if *Star Trek* debuted as an outlier in the world of American science fiction television and film, it was from the beginning very much in tune with the real world of 1960s American society, despite all the science fictional elements that made it so different from anything else on American television at the time. For one thing, it is no accident that *TOS* appeared during the final three years of the space race to land a man on the moon, when public interest in space travel was at an all-time high. Indeed, the famous evocation of "Space: The Final Frontier," with which Shatner's voice-over narration opens each episode of *TOS*, is clearly a direct reference to President John F. Kennedy's 1962 speech at Rice Stadium in Houston, Texas, at which he declared the intention of the United States to win the race to the moon by envisioning space as a new frontier to be conquered, on the order of the Western frontier that was conquered in the process of building the modern United States.

That race, of course, would be won by the Americans with the giant leap of the Apollo 11 moon landing on July 20, 1969—just weeks after the broadcast of the last new episode of *TOS* on June 3, 1969. The space race, though, was part of a much broader Cold War context that would extend for another two decades, well into the initial run of *TNG*. This context is crucial to the cultural history of *Star Trek*, which was centrally informed by a strong message in support of international tolerance and cooperation that was unsurpassed by anything else in American Cold War culture. At the same time, if *Star Trek* was both very international and very American, it also operated in complex and ambivalent relation with the Cold War. For example, while its vision of a utopian future was in many ways more socialist than capitalist, it was also so overtly American that it could easily be interpreted to imply the ultimate triumph of American ideals over all others. Moreover, *TOS* in particular often seemed (even if inadvertently) to support American Cold War rhetoric in general, as when its portrayal of the dangerous and sinister Klingons appeared to many observers intended to make these archenemies of the United Federation of Planets serve as thinly veiled stand-ins for the Soviets. Meanwhile, it is significant that—amid the unusually diverse and international (by the standards of the 1960s) nature of the crew of the USS *Enterprise* in *TOS*—there was even a young Russian officer. But it is also the case that the ship was helmed by the very American Kirk and that the Russian, Pavel Chekov (*American* actor Walter Koenig), was often depicted as naïve and misinformed, often in ways that echoed American Cold War stereotypes about the Soviets. For example, he seems to have absorbed from his childhood education an inflated sense of the centrality of Russia to the history of the earth.

The treatment of the Cold War in the *Star Trek* franchise will be a part of the exploration, in this chapter, of the franchise's overall engagement with its social, political, and historical contexts over the half century of its history. This chapter will propose, for example, that at least part of the success of *TOS* was its complex interaction with its context within the Cold War, while part of the success of *TNG* was due to the fact that it was an ideal series for its end-of-the-Cold-War context. The chapter will also examine the ways in which *TOS*, despite failing to escape the gravitational pull of American Cold War attitudes, also resonated in important ways with the progressive political movements that made the 1960s such a special decade: the anti–Vietnam War movement, the civil rights movement, and the women's movement. For one thing, the optimistic political vision of *TOS* was very much in tune with the belief in the possibility of building a better world that drove all of these political movements. In the future world of *Star Trek*, the political oppositions and social problems of twentieth-century earth have seemingly been overcome, making the future earth of the twenty-third and twenty-fourth centuries the enlightened center of a vast, benevolent, and noncolonial United Federation of Planets that encompasses much of the Milky Way, welcoming new planets that are sufficiently advanced (both socially and technologically) to join the Federation, but never imposing its will on weaker planets.

In addition to sharing this fundamentally optimistic vision of the future with the progressive political movements of the 1960s, *TOS* also engages with a number of specific issues that were central to those movements, using its setting in the twenty-third century to create a distance that potentially creates fresh new perspectives on those issues. But the engagement with these issues was again complex and sometimes problematic. For example, while the crew of the first *Enterprise* did include many women among its number, none of them are in high-ranking positions and most are clad in skimpy miniskirts. Similarly, while overtly conveying a message of peace, *TOS* equips the *Enterprise* with powerful, high-tech weaponry as it goes forth on its voyage of discovery, meanwhile organizing the structure of its crew based upon what are clearly military models. Finally, while *TOS* was probably strongest (and most unequivocal) in its anti-racist message, it could often be at its most heavy-handed in the delivery of this message—as in the notorious third-season episode "Let That Be Your Last Battlefield," which features the irrational antipathy between two alien races, one of which is half-white and half-black, the other of which is half-black and half-white. In addition, the legacy of racism and genocide that accompanied the conquest of the

American frontier immediately complicates the *Star Trek* vision of space as a new frontier, waiting to be tamed.

A central emphasis on social issues is one of the most distinctive features of the *Star Trek* franchise. But the franchise has also contained elements of "hard" science fiction all along. That is, the portrayal of advanced technologies has always been a crucial part of *Star Trek*'s vision of the future. Indeed, it is the universal affluence brought about by technological advancement that enables *Star Trek*'s utopian world of the future. Chapter 4 of this volume will consider the role of technology in *Star Trek*. In particular, it will consider the significance and implications of the technologies that are represented in the series, but will also discuss the ways in which *Star Trek* has engaged in dialogue with specific real-world technological advances during the half century of the existence of the franchise. For example, this chapter notes that, despite its generally enthusiastic endorsement of advanced technologies as a pathway to a better life for all, *TOS* tended to be highly suspicious of computer tech-

Deadly racial enemies in "Let That Be Your Last Battlefield." Paramount Pictures / Photofest © Paramount Pictures

nologies, which were, in the 1960s, still so new and still (to many) so threatening. Yet in the time between *TOS* and *TNG*, it was in the area of computers and electronics that technology made its most important advances, making computers a familiar part of everyday life. This change is clearly reflected in the greater acceptance of computer technologies and artificial intelligence shown in *TNG* relative to *TOS*, with the android Mr. Data standing as the most important example of this new attitude.

Finally, no cultural history of *Star Trek* would be complete without a consideration of the phenomenon of *Star Trek* fandom. Chapter 5 examines this *Trek* fan culture, which has in many ways only gained momentum over the long history of the franchise. Rooted in a science fiction fan culture that goes back to the 1920s, *Star Trek* fan culture has itself influenced the growth of fandom in general, a thriving phenomenon that has become an increasingly important component of American popular culture in the twenty-first century, partly because of the greatly enhanced and expanded communication among fans that has been enabled by social media and other online resources. But in-person contact has increased as well, and convention culture has also seen explosive growth in this century, with comics-oriented conventions leading the way. But contemporary American fandom has its roots in the science fiction fan culture that arose in the 1930s, with fans of science fiction participating more in the growth of SF than have the fans of any other genre. It is thus perhaps no surprise that *Star Trek* has generated such an active and enthusiastic fan culture, though the devotion that *Star Trek* fans have shown to the franchise has been unusually intense—beginning with the 1968 write-in campaign that ensured renewal of the program for a third season after it appeared in danger of cancellation after the second.

Together, these five chapters compile a narrative of the place of the *Star Trek* franchise in the cultural history of the United States from 1966 to 2017, with a special emphasis on the role played by the initial series from the 1960s. The changes undergone by various products of the franchise reflect not only events in American history as a whole but also changes in American film and television. Indeed, the *Star Trek* franchise provides a unique window onto American cultural history over the more than half a century of its existence because no other franchise has remained so prominent for so long in so many different media. Finally, the unusual intensity of *Star Trek* fandom has played a central role in the development of fan culture as a whole, extending the importance of the franchise well beyond the bounds of its own actual products. All in all, *Star Trek* has, in its many manifestations, become such an integral part of American culture that a cultural history of the *Star Trek* phenomenon is virtually tantamount to a cultural history of the United States over the past half century.

I

STAR TREK AND THE HISTORY OF *STAR TREK*

The original *Star Trek* series was very much a work of its time. As much as any other series on American commercial television, *TOS* reflected key aspects of the texture of American life in the 1960s in its basic vision and worldview. Moreover, though *TOS* is set in the twenty-third century, its visual style immediately identifies it as a work of the 1960s—from the brilliant colors that supersaturate nearly every scene, to the faux-futuristic design of the *Enterprise,* to the now-notorious miniskirts of its female crew members. One of the most surprising aspects of *TOS,* then, is its ability to remain an important part of American popular culture for what is now more than half a century, despite being so firmly rooted in its own time. Not only has the original series demonstrated amazing staying power, but *TOS* has inspired a wide range of direct successors, creating a massive transmedia empire that now extends to an animated television series, five additional live-action series, thirteen feature films, a wide range of comics, and a vast variety of novels. This chapter explores the ways in which this array of *Star Trek* products tells the story of the franchise itself over time; subsequent chapters investigate the ways in which the evolution of *Star Trek* reflects and participates in changes in science fiction as a genre and even in American society as a whole.

In a sense, the first sequel to *TOS* was the syndication of *TOS* itself, a phenomenon the success of which marked a milestone in the evolution of the American television industry that, in retrospect, can now be seen as the beginning of the end of the total domination of that industry by the major broadcast networks. After its initial run during the heady years of 1966–1969, *TOS* remained on the American cultural map due to the concerted efforts of its devoted fans, efforts that will be examined in more detail in chapter 5 of this volume. Given the ongoing intensity of fan interest, it should perhaps come as no surprise that *TOS* was such a success when it went into almost immediate syndication after the end of its broadcast run,[1] despite the fact that its seventy-nine episodes fell a bit short of the one hundred episodes often felt to be the minimum for successful syndication.

STAR TREK: THE ANIMATED SERIES

The growing popularity of *TOS* (as well as continuing fan activity) kept *Star Trek* on the American cultural radar, even if the commercial broadcast networks were not ready to give it another try beyond its initial three-year run. The franchise did return to NBC, however, in the form of an animated series that aired in their Saturday-morning children's block, beginning in September of 1973. Produced by Filmation in much the same low-budget, limited animation style that they used in other period cartoons, such as *Fat Albert and the Cosby Kids* (1972–1976), the animated *Star Trek* (now generally known as *Star Trek: The Animated Series* or just *TAS*) was nevertheless much more serious than the typical animation fare. The writing on *TAS*, much of it by writers who had written for *TOS*, was particularly good, helping it, in its second season, to win a Daytime Emmy Award for Best Children's Series—even though the series was never really pitched to children. Indeed, the mismatch between the tone and content of the series and the typical audiences for Saturday-morning animation was a big reason why the series only ran for two seasons, one of sixteen episodes, the other of only six.

Filmation proposed the animated series to Gene Roddenberry, rather than the other way around, and Roddenberry, who was seemingly unable to take animation seriously, was reportedly never truly devoted to the project. Consequently, he served only as a consultant on that series, not as showrunner. Other principals were more enthusiastic, however, and all of the most important members of the *TOS* cast returned to voice the animated versions of their characters. A particularly important returnee was Dorothy Fontana (credited as "D. C. Fontana"), who had written several episodes of *TOS* and served as a story editor during the first two seasons. Fontana served as both story editor and associate producer for *TAS*, for which she played a very active direct role, while also serving as a sort of liaison to Roddenberry who meanwhile devoted most of his energy to other projects.

The continuity between *TOS* and *TAS* often went beyond personnel and basic concepts, extending to direct links between specific episodes, with several episodes of *TAS* serving as sequels—or at least spin-offs—of corresponding *TOS* episodes. Perhaps the most direct example of such links occurs in the first-season episode "More Tribbles, More Troubles" (October 6, 1973), which is a direct sequel to the second-season *TOS* episode "The Trouble with Tribbles," one of the most beloved episodes of the original series (figure 1.1). The continuity between these two episodes is further strengthened by the fact that both episodes were written by noted science fiction author David Gerrold, who endowed both episodes with a comic tone that is unusual (but certainly not unique) in the *Star Trek* franchise. Interestingly, another near-sequel, the *TAS* episode "Mudd's Passion" (November 10, 1973), was also largely comic. This episode features conman Harry Mudd (voiced by Roger C. Carmel), who has very much in common with Cyrano Jones, the huckster who trades in the lovable but dangerous tribbles in both "The Trouble with Tribbles" and "More Tribbles, More Troubles." Mudd, of course, had been featured in not one, but two episodes of *TOS*, "Mudd's Women" (October 13, 1966) and "I, Mudd" (November 3, 1967). Stanley Adams, who played Jones in *TOS*, voices the character in *TAS*, just as Carmel had played Mudd in the two *TOS* episodes in which he had been featured. It is also worthy of note that, in "Mudd's Passion," Mudd is hawking a love potion—the effects of which are temporary but powerful enough to cause the normally stoic Spock to fall madly in love with his longtime admirer Nurse Chapel, thus echoing the turn to romantic passion that Spock had displayed in the *TOS* episode "This Side of Paradise" (March 2, 1967), scripted by Fontana.

Despite being widely perceived as a "light" version of *Star Trek*, *TAS* actually went beyond *TOS* in a number of ways. For example, the first-season episode "The Lorelei Signal" (September 29, 1973) provides a seeming departure from the male-dominated world of *TOS* when the male officers of the *Enterprise* are rendered ineffectual, forcing the female officers (with Lt. Uhura in command) to take over the ship. Moreover, the

Figure 1.1.   Captain Kirk beneath a pile of tribbles in "The Trouble with Trib-bles." NBC / Photofest © NBC

women are highly effective and the crisis is successfully resolved. The episode thus serves as a seeming nod to the burgeoning women's movement of the time, perhaps even more so because it was written by a woman, Margaret Armen. However, the feminist message of this episode is tempered by the nature of the crisis in the first place. The reason the male officers cannot function effectively is that their energies have been sapped by a race of beautiful women who periodically project a musical signal that lures spacecraft to their remote planet in the Taurean system so that they can replenish their own energies by feeding on those of men. The episode is thus a modern, science fictional take on the Greek myth of the Sirens, though the title of the episode specifically refers to a nineteenth-century German version of this story. But this suggestion that women use their seductive powers to ensnare and then take advantage of men is clearly problematic from a feminist point of view.

One key characteristic that *TAS* shares with *TOS* is the use of high-concept science fiction, occasionally sprinkled with elements of fantasy and mythology. For example, in "The Magicks of Megas-tu" (October 27, 1973), the *Enterprise* crew is transported into another dimension where the rules of physics are completely different, making magic a routine occurrence. Moreover, they learn that the magical aliens once lived on earth until the hostility of earthlings to magic caused them to flee the planet. They are also told that the red-hued, cloven-hoofed, horned alien who transported them there (who calls himself Lucien) is actually the Lucifer of earth lore. Kirk, however, scoffs at this information, declaring, "I'm not interested in legend," which could mean that he does not believe Lucien is really Lucifer, but it could also be taken to mean that Kirk regards the Christian story of Lucifer as unworthy of being taken seriously. *Star Trek*, after all, is typically quite skeptical of religion, coming down firmly on the side of science as a means of understanding the universe—and of technology as a means for improving the lives of the inhabitants of the universe.

Technology often goes wrong in the *Star Trek* franchise, however. Indeed, the very next episode of *TAS*, "Once upon a Planet" (November 3, 1973), centers on a recreational planet where visitors can go to rest, relax, and live out their wildest fantasies with the help of the highly sophisticated computer that runs the planet. The machine comes to resent its role as a servant to humans, however, and things go dangerously haywire, in a mode reminiscent of the similarly premised film *Westworld* (itself the beginning of a whole pop cultural franchise). That film, incidentally, premiered on November 21, 1973, two and a half weeks *after* the broadcast of the episode, so there does not appear to have been any influence of either robots-gone-wild work on the other—but both are perhaps reflective of anxieties afoot in the 1970s. "Once upon a Planet" was, however, clearly influenced by the *TOS* episode "Shore Leave" (December 29, 1966), written by science fiction master Theodore Sturgeon and featuring a trip to this same recreational planet. Both episodes end well: In the *TOS* episode, the dangerous situations in which the crew were cast on the planet were all a big misunderstanding; in the case of the *TAS* episode, Kirk manages to talk some sense into the computer and convince it that it is in its own best interest to be friendly to humans. In both cases, though, there is a strong sense that overreliance on technology can be foolish and dangerous. As pro-technology as it might be in many ways, *Star Trek* as a franchise is consistently humanist in its orientation.

RODDENBERRY ATTEMPTS A COMEBACK

This humanist orientation is one of the reasons why *TOS* was so character oriented. It is probably also one reason why the animated series never really quite worked—both the short lengths of the individual episodes and the animated format were ill-suited to telling serious stories of genuine human relationships. Roddenberry, though, remained committed to telling such stories, struggling throughout the 1970s to get his vision back on live-action television. Even before *TAS* was on the air, for example, Roddenberry was in the process of developing the postapocalyptic series *Genesis II*, which at one point seemed headed for CBS until CBS decided to go with the (disastrous, as it turned out) television series adaptation of *Planet of the Apes* instead. At first glance, *Genesis II*, with its vision of a twenty-second-century earth struggling to recover from the effects of an apocalyptic world war, would seem to be dramatically at odds with the famed optimism of *Star Trek*. However, even *Star Trek* has postulated that human civilization would go through some very difficult times before finally emerging into utopia by the twenty-third century. Moreover, *Genesis II* is not actually as dark as a brief description of the premise sounds, containing strong utopian energies as well.

Roddenberry developed story concepts for a number of episodes of *Genesis II*, but the only one that was actually produced was the pilot. Still, one can already see the outlines of these utopian energies in that single seventy-four-minute episode, which aired on CBS as a TV movie (and scored strong ratings) on March 23, 1973. In this pilot, protagonist Dylan Hunt (Alex Cord) is a scientist who is engaged in research into suspended animation in 1979. Not heeding the science fiction/horror tradition in which scientists experimenting on themselves always leads to dire results, Hunt tries out an experimental procedure on himself, going into suspended animation just before a rockslide buries his laboratory, which just happens to be located in Carlsbad Cavern. His lab buried beneath tons of rock, he thus stays in suspended animation until he is discovered in 2133 by citizens of Pax, one of the insular communities into which civilization has fragmented in the wake of a devastating war. The episode stipulates that the fall of human civilization has had a beneficial environmental effect, showing that nature has largely now recovered from centuries of abuse at the hands of humans. Hunt, meanwhile, splits his time in the pilot between Pax and the relatively nearby city of Tyrania. Apparently paying no attention to the names of the rival communities, Hunt basically spends the pilot attempting to determine who are the good guys and who are the bad guys in the rivalry between Pax and Tyrania, ultimately concluding that the peaceful and loving (but somewhat puritanical) community of Pax is the preferable of the two. Pax, in fact, with its strong emphasis on respect for all human life and its emphasis on enrichment of that life through culture and the arts, emerges as a utopian enclave. In the dystopian Tyrania, on the other hand, the mutant ruling class maintains a relatively elevated lifestyle on the backs of human slave labor, with the slaves kept in line through the use of handheld devices that can deal out intense pleasure or pain at a touch.

Thus, *Genesis II* actually resembles several episodes of *TOS*. Its post-apocalyptic collapse of civilization into rival factions quite directly recalls "The Omega Glory," for example, while the stratified society of Tyrania clearly recalls that seen in "The Cloud Minders." Even the "sleeper wakes" premise that propels a man from the 1970s into this future world is anticipated in *TOS* in the classic "Space Seed" episode (figure 1.2). Finally, the central female character of *Genesis II* is a rather scantily clad Tyranian named Lyra-A, a character who might have stepped directly out of any number of *TOS* episodes. She is even played by Mariette Hartley, who had also been featured in "All Our Yesterdays," one of the last episodes of *TOS*.

The collapse of *Genesis II* did not dissuade Roddenberry from pursuing the project, and by April 23, 1974, a second pilot based on another of Roddenberry's story concepts for *Genesis II* aired on ABC as *Planet Earth*. Here, several of the characters are recast, including protagonist Dylan Hunt, who is now played by John Saxon. Meanwhile, Lyra-A is missing entirely, but a key female role is played by Diana Muldaur, another veteran of *TOS* (and a future regular for a brief time on *TNG*). The basic scenario is unchanged, though there is even more emphasis on the restoration of nature after the fall of humanity. Meanwhile, this second pilot introduces two new communities with which Pax must deal. First are the warlike "Kreegs," vicious thugs who drive souped-up armored vehicles and live by preying on others. They are minor players in the episode, however, interesting primarily for the way they anticipate the road warriors of the *Mad Max* franchise. The real focus of the episode is on the "Confederacy of Ruth," an enclave ruled by women, where men function strictly as slaves, kept obedient by secretly dosing them with a

**Figure I.2.   Kirk and Khan in "Space Seed." Paramount Pictures / Photofest ©
Paramount Pictures**

drug that renders them terrified of displeasing their mistresses. Unfortunately (in a motif that might be taken as suggesting that feminism can be
emasculating), they are rendered so afraid of disappointing their women
that they are generally also impotent, which means that the birth rate in
the Confederacy has dropped nearly to zero.

As Hunt wonders when he first learns of conditions in the Confederacy, "Women's lib? Or women's lib gone mad?" Indeed, at first glance,
Planet Earth would seem to be projecting a patriarchal fantasy of what
might happen if women ever ruled. The overtly stated point, however, is
that both patriarchy and matriarchy are bad and that, instead, the two (and
there are only two in this world) genders should have full equality. Conditions are dire in the Confederacy, but these conditions could be seen as a
mirror version of patriarchy designed to help viewers see the flaws in
patriarchy in a new light. That reading, however, might be overly generous, and the overall impression created by this episode is that rule by
women would simply be ridiculous—a reading reinforced by a comedic
seduction scene in which Muldaur's character (frustrated by the impo-
tence of the men in her community) attempts to seduce Hunt, who plays

along in order to distract her so that his friends can have an opportunity to administer an antidote to the drugged men of the Confederacy. [2]

In the meantime, Roddenberry had brought the pilot for an entirely different series to air (this time back on NBC) on January 23, 1974. *The Questor Tapes* features an android (the "Questor" of the title, played by Robert Foxworth) with a damaged memory who is on a quest to find his lost creator and thus to restore the lost portion of his programming, which (as it turns out) is the portion that allows him to experience emotions and thus better to understand humanity. In this sense, *The Questor Tapes* is a very obvious predecessor to the key role played by the android Data in *TNG*, though the pilot eventually adds an extra dimension by revealing that Questor is but one in a long line of androids who have lived among humans for thousands of years (originally left here by the "Masters"), helping to guide their development. On the other hand, this guidance is quite subtle and is mainly designed to allow humans to develop naturally. As Questor's creator/predecessor explains, "We protect, but we do not interfere. Man must make his own way. We guide him—but always without his knowledge."

This mission statement, of course, is quite reminiscent of *Star Trek*'s Prime Directive, which is not surprising given that the pilot for *The Questor Tapes* was written by Roddenberry and Gene L. Coon, who had served as a writer and producer for *TOS* (and had, for that matter, written scripts for *Wagon Train*, the Western upon which *TOS* was partly modeled). The Masters are not identified in *The Questor Tapes*, but the implication seems to be that they are aliens intervening in the evolution of human civilization, a motif that occasionally appeared in *TOS*. In "Assignment: Earth," for example, an alien agent intervenes to help prevent the Cold War from turning hot. Meanwhile, in a variation of this motif, *TOS* episodes such as "Who Mourns for Adonais?" suggest that earth's ancient gods might actually have been alien visitors.

The Questor Tapes seemed promising enough that NBC ordered a number of additional episodes even before the pilot aired. Unfortunately, disagreements between Roddenberry and NBC about the direction these episodes should take led Roddenberry to withdraw from the project, which in turn caused NBC to cancel the deal altogether. Despite such failures, the ongoing activism of *Star Trek* fans, as well as the popularity of *TOS* in syndication, encouraged Roddenberry to keep trying, at this point shifting his efforts in science fiction television to trying to get the original series back into first-run production, laying the groundwork for a reincarnation of *TOS* with the working title of *Star Trek: Phase II*. That series was to be a crucial component in a planned fourth broadcast network to be operated by Paramount Pictures, which had gained the broadcast rights to the *Star Trek* brand in 1967 when Gulf+Western (the parent company of Paramount) purchased Desilu, subsequently placing all of its television production work under the Paramount umbrella. *Phase II* never materialized, partly because Paramount chief Barry Diller was dissatisfied with the direction in which the planned series was moving and partly because the Paramount Television Service never went into operation in any case.

OTHER MEDIA KEEP *TREK* ALIVE

Despite such failures, though, the *Star Trek* brand remained in production through the 1970s in other forms. Gold Key Comics, for example, began publishing *Star Trek* titles in 1967, early in the original run of *TOS*. Comics in this initial series contained mostly original stories, though a number of issues were extensions of or sequels to popular episodes of *TOS*. The Gold Key series eventually ran to a total of sixty-one issues between 1967 and 1978. A British *Star Trek* comic strip ran from 1969 to 1973, and an American strip, produced by the *Los Angeles Times Mirror* Syndicate, ran on Sundays from 1979 to 1982 and daily from 1979 to 1983.

In 1979, Marvel Comics obtained the comic book rights to the *Star Trek* title from Paramount. However, the Marvel *Star Trek* comics (which totaled eighteen issues between 1979 and 1981) were, by contract, limited to tie-ins to *TMP* and to materials that would have been included in *Phase II*, rather than building directly on *TOS*. From 1984 to 1988, DC Comics published a series of fifty-six issues of *Star Trek* comics that were related to the films from *The Wrath of Khan* through *The Voyage Home*. A second DC series picked up in 1989, building on *The Final Frontier* and *The Undiscovered Country* and running for a total of eighty issues. DC then also published a limited series directly related to *TNG* in 1988, followed by a continuing series based on *TNG* that ran all the way to 1996. In the meantime, Malibu Comics had begun a comics series based on *DS9* in 1993, eventually collaborating with DC to publish a *TNG-DS9* crossover comic.

Marvel reacquired the license to publish *Star Trek* comics in 1996, establishing a special imprint (Marvel/Paramount Comics) under which it published several different *Star Trek* titles. They also attempted to establish crossovers between *Star Trek* and the Marvel superhero titles (especially the X-Men), but these were not well received, especially by *Trek* fans. Series such as *Starfleet Academy* and *Early Voyages* were more successful, however. Nevertheless, Marvel quickly concluded that the licensing fees for the *Star Trek* name were too high for the comics to be profitable and ended the agreement, allowing the *Star Trek* license to pass back to DC, which began publishing *Star Trek* comics under its adult-oriented Wildstorm imprint, which produced several limited series and graphic novels between 1999 and 2002.

Between 2002 and 2006, the only *Star Trek* comics published were based on *TOS* and *TNG*, produced in the Japanese manga style by the American publisher Tokyopop. Their publications continued to appear until 2009. Meanwhile, in 2006, the main rights to *Star Trek* comics were acquired by IDW Comics, which has published a number of titles based on the franchise since that time, extending into the J. J. Abrams era.

Despite the high licensing fees, Paramount has doubtless made relatively little profit from *Star Trek* comics, instead using them as a cheap and convenient way to promote the brand and to keep it on the cultural radar. Still, the very fact that so many publishers have been interested in producing *Star Trek* comics indicates that there is an ongoing market for them. The extensive series of *Star Trek* novels that have been published over the years has been even more successful—to the point that the respected science fiction author Harlan Ellison has complained that, far from producing a boost in the sales of science fiction novels across the board, *Star Trek* has actually had a detrimental effect because *Star Trek* books—and other space-opera novels influenced by *Star Trek*—have "pushed everything off the bestseller list."[3]

Star Trek books started modestly, with a series of adaptations of individual episodes from *TOS*, written mostly by established SF author James Blish and published by Bantam Books at several episodes per volume, for a total of thirteen volumes between 1967 and 1978. During this period, Blish also authored the first original *Star Trek* novel for adults, *Spock Must Die!* (1970), though a children's novel based on *TOS*, entitled *Mis-*

sion to Horatius, was published in 1968. Published just a year after the cancellation of *TOS*, the first edition of *Spock Must Die!* included a message by Blish urging fans to mobilize to try to bring *Star Trek* back to television. That project did not succeed, but the successful series of *Trek* books did help to keep fans engaged.

The next *Trek* novel, *Spock, Messiah!*, did not appear until 1976. Authored by Theodore R. Cogswell and Charles A. Spano Jr., this novel was panned by critics and sold poorly, rejected by devoted *Star Trek* fans who felt that it deviated too much from the spirit of *TOS*.[4] Nevertheless, the fact that both of the first two *Trek* novels foregrounded Spock can be taken as a sign of the way in which the Vulcan science officer had, in the hearts and minds of loyal fans, become the true center of the *Star Trek* universe. Meanwhile, despite the poor sales of *Spock, Messiah!*, it was followed a year later by two more *Trek* novels, including *Planet of Judgment*, by the esteemed SF author Joe Haldeman, who three years earlier had published *The Forever War*, a now-classic science fiction novel that was one of the most important fictional responses to the Vietnam War. By the end of 1979, no fewer than six additional *Trek* novels had been published, including Haldeman's *World without End* (1979). By this time, it was clear that a genuine publishing phenomenon was under way, boosted by the appearance of *TMP* in 1979.

Though *Trek* novels have failed to win any of the major awards for science fiction (such as the Hugo or the Nebula), they have continued to sell well and to have a solid core readership. They have also tracked the evolution of the *Star Trek* media franchise, with subsequent novels tending to be tied to whatever *Trek* television series is current at the moment—though novels specifically related to *TOS* continued to appear in the gap between *TOS* and *TMP*. For example, *The Galactic Whirlpool* (1980), by David Gerrold (writer of the classic *TOS* episode "The Trouble with Tribbles"), was actually based on the extended outline that Gerrold had written for a proposed *TOS* episode that was rejected. Many of the novels published between 1979 and the premiere of *TNG* in 1987 were based on *Star Trek* films. Esteemed SF author Vonda McIntyre wrote five *Star Trek* novels between 1981 and 1986, including novelizations of the second, third, and fourth *Star Trek* films.

TNG, DS9, VOY, and *ENT* all had tie-in novels during their runs. Indeed, by the time the latest *Star Trek* series, *Star Trek: Discovery* (*DSC*), premiered on September 24, 2017, a tie-in novel related to the two initial episodes, David Mack's *Star Trek: Discovery, Desperate Hours*, had already been printed, seeing official release on September 26. One whole series of novels, coauthored by none other than William Shatner, occurred outside the timeline of the *Trek* films and television series. Widely referred to as the narratives of the "Shatnerverse," these ten novels (coauthored by Judith and Garfield Reeves-Stevens) appeared between 1995 and 2007, detailing the adventures of Captain Kirk after he returns to life subsequent to his ostensible demise in the film *Star Trek: Generations* (1994).

THE BIRTH OF A FILM FRANCHISE

The novels and comics continued to keep the *Star Trek* brand in production despite the failure of Roddenberry's various television projects through the 1970s. Late in the decade, however, events outside the *Trek* franchise took it in an important new direction. Perhaps the biggest reason for the demise of *Phase II* was that Diller and the management at Paramount felt that the comeback of *Star Trek* might work better as a feature film, and this perception was dramatically reinforced by the stunning technical and commercial success of the original *Star Wars* film in 1977, a development that suddenly shifted the focus of the Hollywood film industry onto science fiction. That development led to a decade-long Golden Age in science fiction film; it also took *Star Trek* onto the big screen with the premiere of *Star Trek: The Motion Picture* on December 7, 1979.

With nearly triple the budget of *Star Wars* and with special effects wizards such as Douglas Trumbull (who had worked on the visual effects for *2001: A Space Odyssey* and *Close Encounters of the Third Kind*) and John Dykstra (who had helped produce the visual effects for *Star Wars*) working on the project, *TMP* is an impressive-looking film. It seems far grander than *Star Wars* (and intended for a more adult audience), but the plot is a bit weak, even plodding, and the interpersonal relationships (especially among Kirk, Spock, and McCoy) that had provided so much of the energy of the original television series never really quite come off in the film. Still, the built-in audience from fans of the series made the first *Star Trek* film a substantial commercial success, helping to make it the beginning of what would become the longest film sequence in SF film history.

The viability of *Star Trek* as a film franchise was demonstrated more firmly three years later, when *Star Trek II: The Wrath of Khan* (1982) became what many fans (and critics) regard as the best of all the *Star Trek* films. *The Wrath of Khan* was a very different animal than *TMP*, backing away from high artistic ambitions and returning much more to the spirit of adventure that informed the initial series. It also returned its focus much more to the trio of Kirk, Spock, and McCoy and to the complex relationships among them. Increasing the connection to *TOS* even more, *The Wrath of Khan* was a direct sequel to one of the most beloved of all *TOS* episodes, "Space Seed," with Ricardo Montalban reprising his role as the genetically enhanced Khan Noonien Singh, now playing the role of an obsessed Ahab, with Kirk as his white whale. Khan's villainy is typical of the suspicion toward eugenics and genetic engineering that marked the first quarter century of the *Trek* franchise, no doubt partly because memories of the eugenics programs of the German Nazis (part of their attempt to build a master race) were still relatively fresh. In any case, as a result of its more direct links to *TOS*, this second film gained far more approval from die-hard *Trek* fans than had *TMP*, even though its total box office was slightly less than that of *TMP*—and even though it broke the hearts of many *Trek* fans by melodramatically killing off Spock in the end.

Of course, the final moments of *The Wrath of Khan* drop several hints that Spock might be back, and attentive fans would surely recall that there are a number of moments in *TOS* when Spock or Kirk appear to be dead, only to return quite quickly. It should have come as no surprise, then, that Spock was indeed resurrected in *Star Trek III: The Search for Spock* (1984). This film was even directed by Leonard Nimoy, which should have won even more approval from *Trek* fans. Unfortunately, the film is something of a mess, stumbling through a plot that never really comes together. As a result, this film, with so much going for it, grossed a bit less than *The Wrath of Khan*, raising questions among some observers of whether *Star Trek* was really all that viable as a film franchise after all.

These questions were answered in the affirmative in *Star Trek IV: The Voyage Home* (1986), in which Nimoy proved his talents as a director by helming one of the most successful of all *Star Trek* films, in terms of both positive responses from the *Trek* fan community and overall box office, which for the first time for a *Star Trek* film went over $100 million. Moreover, this whimsical tale of a trip back to the twentieth century managed to combine strong comedic elements with a strong political message (this time concerning the importance of protecting endangered species), a combination that had often worked so well in *TOS*.

STAR TREK: THE NEXT GENERATION

The Voyage Home was such a success, in fact, that it proved the ongoing vitality of the *Star Trek* franchise in general, giving the brand important momentum that propelled it back onto first-run American television with the premiere of *Star Trek: The Next Generation* on September 28, 1987, after Paramount convinced an initially reluctant Gene Roddenberry to come aboard for the reboot of the *Star Trek* television franchise. However, this early friction between Roddenberry and the studio never abated, and the first seasons of *TNG* were marked by considerable chaos and conflict behind the scenes, while the first two seasons in particular lacked spark on the screen.[5] Roddenberry was in failing health and the series lacked leadership, though the death of Roddenberry just after the beginning of the fourth season ultimately enabled Rick Berman and Michael Piller to steady the helm of the series. It eventually gained momentum, turning to a more character-oriented approach that made it more and more able to replicate the secret of *TOS*, which was the strong interpersonal relationships among the crew members of a now-updated starship.

TNG joined *TOS* in boldly going where no television series had gone before. Plans for Paramount's own television network having fallen through, Paramount negotiated with all the major broadcast networks in an attempt to place the show but found little interest. Instead, they opted to produce the show for first-run syndication, a business model virtually unheard of in the television industry of the time. In its final season, *TNG* became the first syndicated show to be nominated for a Primetime Emmy Award for Best Drama Series, following in the footsteps of *TOS* in making syndication history.

The main starship in *TNG* is also called the *Enterprise* (but it is now the fifth *Enterprise* in Starfleet history). This new *Enterprise* (*Enterprise-D*) is bigger and more technologically advanced than the original, which is not surprising given that *TNG* is set nearly a century after *TOS*, but in many ways the ships are quite similar. Indeed, the most obvious technology found aboard the *Enterprise-D* that had not already been available in some form on the original *Enterprise* involves the "holodecks" that provide virtual reality simulations of any number of environments so that the crew can get away from it all from time to time.[6] Among other things, the virtual reality capabilities of the holodecks allow *TNG* to incorporate a variety of different genres including specific references to literary and cinematic classics of the past, as when "A Fistful of Datas" (November 9, 1992) recalls the Spaghetti Western classic *A Fistful of Dollars* or when we learn that Captain Jean-Luc Picard is a great fan of hard-boiled detective fiction, visiting the holodeck to become "Dixon Hill," a fictional detective clearly based on the protagonists of the novels of Dashiell Hammett and Raymond Chandler. Meanwhile, "We'll Always Have Paris" (May 2, 1988) features Picard in a holographic homage to the classic 1942 film *Casablanca*.

Technological innovations aside, *TNG* was quite overt in linking itself to the legacy of *TOS*. For example, several episodes of *TNG* directly reference specific episodes of *TOS*, as when the early first-season episode "The Naked Now" (October 5, 1987) is essentially a remake of the classic *TOS* episode "The Naked Time." Meanwhile, at various points (and through various mechanisms), McCoy, Scotty, and Spock from *TOS* all make appearances in *TNG*, though the first of these has only a brief cameo in the inaugural episode. Much of the crew of the *Enterprise-D* (figure 1.3) maps almost directly onto that of the original *Enterprise* as well, though not necessarily in a one-to-one fashion. The ship is still commanded by a captain, in this case the Frenchman Picard (played by British actor Patrick Stewart), an older, wiser, less emotional, and less impulsive leader than James T. Kirk had been. Picard, aided by Stewart's stentorian Shakespearean voice, is a more conventional figure of authority than Kirk had been, but his crew is still devoted to him (and he to them), even though he tends to avoid mingling socially even with the senior officers (and he is virtually terrified of children). Picard also has an old-fashioned side, including nostalgia for the culture of earth's past. He tends to eschew the Kindle-like electronic readers used by most of the crew in favor of antique physical books, while his fondness for Shakespeare not only recalls Stewart's background as a Shakespearean actor but also lends an air of the literary to the series itself, something for which *TOS* had set a precedent by giving several episodes titles derived from Shakespeare.

The first officer of the *Enterprise-D* is Will Riker (Jonathan Frakes), who has relatively little in common with First Officer Spock and is in some ways more like Kirk than is Picard, often performing action-oriented functions in *TNG* that Kirk would have performed in the original series. But even Riker seems more like Spock in the level of his personal evolution. Indeed, all of the *TNG* main characters, as citizens of the twenty-fourth century, seem to have evolved beyond the crew of *TOS*, with the exception of Spock, who already came from an older and more developed civilization than had his crewmates. Meanwhile, Riker himself is widely regarded as captain material, but he continually evades promotion so that he can stay on the *Enterprise-D* with his mentor Picard,

Figure 1.3.   The crew of the *Enterprise-D* in *Star Trek: The Next Generation*. Paramount Television / Photofest © Paramount Television

participating in the choice missions offered the *Enterprise-D* as Starfleet's premier ship. The ship's chief medical officer through most of
TNG is Dr. Beverly Crusher (Gates McFadden), a much gentler and more
nurturing physician than McCoy had been; Dr. Crusher meanwhile shares
romantic sparks with Picard, though they never develop a relationship.
And the *Enterprise-D* also has a prominent chief engineer in the person of
Geordi La Forge (LeVar Burton); blind from birth, La Forge is distinctive
for the metallic VISOR (Visual Instrument and Sensory Organ Replacement) that he wears across his eyes, allowing him to have superior vision
over a wide electromagnetic spectrum. Like *TOS*'s Scotty, he is very
good with machines but not so successful with women.

One *TNG* crew member with no real counterpart among the *TOS* crew
is Deanna Troi (Marina Sirtis), the ship's counselor. Because she is half
human and half Betazoid (a race of telepaths), Troi has special empathic
abilities that further her abilities in her job but that sometimes come in
handy in other ways as well, as in sensing the intentions of aliens encountered on various missions. Riker and Troi share a mutual attraction that
eventually leads to marriage in the 2002 film *Star Trek: Nemesis*.

The *TNG* crew also includes other new wrinkles, including a Klingon
officer, Worf (Michael Dorn), who in fact has a few new wrinkles of his
own: The Klingons of *TNG*, like those of the films, sport prominent
forehead ridges that clearly mark them as alien, as opposed to the human-
looking Klingons of *TOS*. Worf has partly joined Starfleet because he was
raised by human foster parents, but it is also the case that humans and
Klingons are now (uneasy) allies, marking a key change in the galactic
political structure between the twenty-third and the twenty-fourth centuries.

The crew of the *Enterprise-D* also features an android science officer,
Data (Brent Spiner), whose advanced positronic brain goes well beyond
the computer science of the twenty-third century of *TOS*. Actually, it goes
beyond the conventional science of the twenty-fourth century of *TNG* as
well. Data was created by a brilliant but eccentric cybernetic scientist,
using technologies that Starfleet's best scientists still do not understand
and cannot replicate, leaving the android essentially alone in the universe,
much as Spock, as a rare human-Vulcan hybrid, often felt alone. Data
also shares with Spock his propensity for totally logical thinking, though
his computational abilities go well beyond those of his great predecessor.
Data also differs from Spock in that, while Spock generally struggled to

suppress his human side, Data (explicitly compared within the series to Pinocchio) wants nothing more than to become more human. Data's portrayal in the series, in fact, provides an opportunity for it to explore basic questions about what it takes to be regarded as a *person*, something that the portrayal of aliens often does within the *Star Trek* universe as well. Data also makes important contributions to the egalitarian traditions of the *Star Trek* franchise, and his fight for equal rights and for recognition as a human being often makes him a figure of oppressed and misunderstood minorities of all kinds.

The portrayal of characters such as Worf and Data encourages the tolerance for difference for which *Star Trek* is so well known. On the other hand, *TNG* also introduces important new alien enemies with whom it is not so easy to sympathize. The viciously conniving Ferengi, for example, serve as embodiments of the capitalist greed that has been extirpated on twenty-fourth-century earth, and they are presented almost entirely negatively in *TNG*. But the most important new alien enemy in *TNG* is the gruesome Borg, a nightmare cyborg race of half-robot, half-zombies that seems almost more derived from horror than from science fiction. The Borg are driven by a single collective mind that drives the "assimilation" of the various humanoids they encounter on their ruthless mission of galactic conquest, equipping these individuals with numerous implants that help to transform them into zombie-like drones that do the bidding of the hive mind. The Borg also assimilate the technologies of conquered species, which means that their own technology is extremely advanced, making them a particularly forbidding opponent. The Borg surface as a prominent threat in *TNG* (at one point even assimilating Picard) and continue to appear in subsequent reincarnations of the *Trek* franchise.

Armed with better special effects and a look more reminiscent of the *Star Trek* films than of *TOS*, *TNG* was able to boldly go where no *Trek* had gone before, especially in the way it filled in far more details about the "future history" of the galaxy, keeping the basic idea of a United Federation of Planets intact—and also keeping earth and humanity at the center of that Federation—while adding new alien species and new details about the ways in which technology has led to an essentially utopian future on earth. But it was the basic focus on the crew and their interrelationships that made the show work and that endeared it to a new generation of fans—many of whom came to regard *TNG* as the "real" *Star Trek*, rather than *TOS*. Indeed, based on its ultimately positive critical reception, its relatively high viewership ratings, and its extended seven-year run, I have elsewhere called *TNG* "the most successful American science fiction television series in history."[7]

The *TOS* cast continued to be featured in theatrical films through the run of *TNG*, though in films such as *Star Trek V: The Final Frontier* (1989) and *Star Trek VI: The Undiscovered Country* (1991), the age of that cast was beginning to be an object of humor even within the films. *Star Trek: Generations* (1994) then handed the cinematic baton to the younger cast of *TNG*: both Picard and Kirk are major characters, but Kirk is killed in the course of the film. That film also portrayed the destruction of the *Enterprise-D*, but it would be replaced by the *Enterprise-E* in the next film, as the *TNG* cast completely took over in *Star Trek: First Contact* (1996), a rousing time-travel tale in which the *Enterprise* travels to the year 2063 to thwart an attempt of the Borg (who have also traveled back from the future) to prevent Zefram Cochrane from inventing the warp drive, thus averting first contact between humans and Vulcans and facilitating the Borg assimilation of earth. Reversing a major motif of *The Wrath of Khan*, Picard here becomes a sort of Ahab, with the Borg serving as his white whale. He also heroically risks his life to save Data, indicating the special relationship that has developed between them. Many observers consider *First Contact* to be a rival to *The Wrath of Khan* as the best of the *Star Trek* films, but the new *TNG*-based film franchise quickly declined in popularity from *Star Trek: Insurrection* (1998) to *Star Trek: Nemesis* (2002), ostensibly bringing the string of *Star Trek* films to an end at ten. *Nemesis* also saw the death of Data, who sacrifices himself to save Picard and the *Enterprise-E*, recalling the sacrifice of Spock in *The Wrath of Khan* (while also leaving open the possibility of a future resurrection).

STAR TREK: DEEP SPACE NINE

In the meantime, while *TNG* was still airing first-run episodes, its immediate successor was already in production. *Star Trek: Deep Space Nine* (*DS9*) premiered in January 1993, thus overlapping with *TNG* by nearly a year and a half. Beginning its action in the year 2369, *DS9* is a direct sequel to *TNG* (and even features an appearance by Picard in its first episode). However, *DS9* was a considerable departure for the *Star Trek* franchise. For one thing, the action of *DS9* is centered on a (mostly) stationary space station. Rather than boldly moving about the galaxy on missions of discovery, the protagonists of *DS9* remain largely at home, waiting for the action to come to them. As Winrich Kolbe, one of the key directors of *DS9* episodes, notes (referring to the notion of *TOS* as "*Wagon Train* to the stars"), *DS9* is instead "*Gunsmoke*. It's the town that everybody comes to."[8] In addition, the *Deep Space Nine* station lacks the clean, elegant brightness of the usual starships of *Star Trek*. For one thing, the station is not of Federation design or construction but was originally built by the fascistic Cardassians and has a kind of near-Gothic darkness that befits the Cardassian culture. Moreover, the station is, as the series begins, in a state of widespread disrepair, having been hastily abandoned by the Cardassians. Indeed, while the *Enterprises* of *TOS* and *TNG* are elite, top-of-the line starships, Deep Space Nine is a remote and rickety facility initially felt to be of secondary importance, though it suddenly gains immense strategic value with the nearby discovery of the first known stable wormhole, which allows almost instant travel into the Gamma Quadrant, a remote sector of the galaxy previously unexplored by Starfleet.

The dark architecture of the space station is mirrored by a turn toward thematic darkness in the series itself—especially after Ira Steven Behr took over as showrunner in the third season, seemingly determined to provide a corrective to what he saw as the excessive utopianism of *TNG*. Indeed, Behr's *DS9* might have been called *Star Trek Into Darkness* long before J. J. Abrams came up with the title. The depiction of the Cardassians is a key element of this darkness, and episodes such as the compelling "Duet" (June 13, 1993), which focuses on an Auschwitz-like labor camp that the Cardassians had operated on Bajor while occupying the planet as a mining colony, emphasize this fact.[9] Nevertheless, the series remains filled with utopian energies, including in the depiction of relations among the crew of the station (figure 1.4), though there is considerably more discord among the crew than in previous *Star Trek* series, partly because only part of the core crew is composed of Starfleet officers. Though the Bajorans have won their independence, their relatively poor planet is unable to defend itself without outside assistance, so the Federation agrees to send aid, including a detachment of Starfleet personnel led by Commander Benjamin Sisko (Avery Brooks), to help man the space station and to help ensure that the Cardassians do not return to retake Bajor. Sisko, who eventually achieves the rank of captain, is *Star Trek*'s first African American captain, heading the franchise's most ethnically diverse cast. Indeed, the only white European male officer on the station is Chief Operations Officer Miles O'Brien (Colm Meaney), who had operated the transporter aboard the *Enterprise-D* in *TNG*—but even O'Brien has a Japanese wife. Meanwhile, he is joined by the station's doctor, Julian Bashir, who is played by Sudanese-English actor Siddig El Fadil, who changed his professional name to Alexander Siddig in the fourth season of the series because viewers seemed confused by his Arabic name. Bashir can thus be taken as *Star Trek*'s first Arab officer. In "Doctor Bashir, I Presume?" (February 24, 1997), we learn that he is also *Trek*'s first genetically enhanced officer, having received illegal DNA resequencing as a child, leaving him with enhanced vision, intelligence, reflexes, and hand-eye coordination. Genetically enhanced individuals seem to be the last despised "Other" on earth in the twenty-fourth century, so it is perhaps of some significance that the series chose to give this role to its only Arab character. In any case, Bashir keeps this modification a secret until the sixth season when his secret comes out at last, allowing him to display his enhanced abilities, performing computer-like computations in the manner of Spock, leading another character to exclaim, "You're not genetically engineered—you're a Vulcan!"

If nothing else, the generally positive portrayal of Bashir softens *Star Trek*'s negative stance toward genetic modification. Meanwhile, if Bashir is thus not an entirely natural human, then the other main cast members are not human at all. The station's brilliant science officer, Jadzia Dax (Terry Farrell), is fresh from her doctoral studies in physics and appears quite young. However, she is a member of the Trill species, which means that her humanoid body (the "Jadzia" portion of her identity) hosts a "symbiont" (the "Dax" portion of her identity) that lives within her abdomen. Jadzia's symbiont is more than three hundred years old, and she is its eighth humanoid host, maintaining the knowledge and memories of all the former ones who have been both male and female. The personality and abilities of a joined Trill are a hybrid of those of the host and the symbiont, which raises interesting questions with regard to identity and individuality, as well as gender. Jadzia Dax appears quite human and is initially courted enthusiastically by Bashir, but she remains somewhat aloof from human involvements, eventually marrying Commander Worf

Figure 1.4.   The diverse crew of *Deep Space Nine*. Paramount Television / Photo-fest © Paramount Television

from *TNG*, who joined the cast of *DS9* as the station's strategic operations officer during its fourth season, adding still more interspecies diversity to the crew of the station.

The station's first officer is Major Kira Nerys (Nana Visitor). A former resistance fighter against the Cardassian occupation of her planet,

Kira maintains a deep hatred of the Cardassians and is sometimes suspicious of the Federation as well, leading to friction between her and the Starfleet officers in the series never before seen among members of a *Star Trek* crew. There is also some initial distrust of the station's security chief, Odo (René Auberjonois), partly because he is a holdover from the Cardassian occupation. A shape-shifter of unknown origins, he is the only one of his kind known to exist as the series begins. He is thus a particularly mysterious figure, though his one-of-a-kind status is clearly reminiscent of that of such characters as Spock and Data. Able to assume virtually any shape at will, he is a particularly alien figure who also raises significant questions about identity. On the other hand, his shape-shifting abilities are somewhat limited, apparently because he did not grow up among shape-shifters and so did not learn to use his abilities to their full extent. Though he generally assumes a humanoid shape, he has particular problems modeling the human face, and his typical humanoid face looks somewhat like it was shaped from modeling clay, making him even more of an outsider. Like Data, however, he grows more and more human as the series proceeds. Indeed, when he finally discovers his own race in the Gamma Quadrant (known there as Changelings) in the two-part episode "The Search" (September 26 and October 3, 1994), he opts to remain with his new human companions, among whom he feels more at home. He even joins the humans in their later war against the Dominion, the powerful Gamma Quadrant empire of which the Changelings are the founders and rulers.

The final major character of *DS9* is the Ferengi Quark (Armin Shimerman), the first main *Star Trek* character not to be a crew member. Used largely for comic relief, Quark (figure 1.5) is as greedy and conniving as the next Ferengi, and his character to an extent illustrates the problematic *Star Trek* tendency to represent alien characters in essentialist terms, assuming that all members of a given species have similar characteristics, except humans. But Quark at least complicates this vision in that he occasionally behaves honorably, even unselfishly, gaining depth as a character as the series proceeds, becoming far more than a mere comic caricature in the later seasons. Indeed, everything about *DS9* seemed to get better as it went along, as well as darker and more serious. Meanwhile, the growing threat posed by the Dominion, which finally erupts into all-out war at the end of season 5, also added an important new element to the *Star Trek* franchise, providing a serial plot that developed over several seasons culminating in a six-episode continuous sequence at the beginning of season 6 detailing the war between the Federation and its allies (notably the Klingon Empire and the Romulan Empire) and the Dominion and its allies (including the Cardassians).

This extended warfare sequence takes *Star Trek* into new, darker territory. At the same time, the producers of *DS9* were careful to maintain strong ties to their roots in the *Trek* franchise. Many episodes of *DS9* are of types found in all *Star Trek* series. "Paradise" (February 14, 1994), for example, employs the old *Star Trek* theme of a flawed utopia, though in a much more complex and nuanced mode than its predecessors. Some of the best episodes of *DS9*, as with *TOS* and *TNG*, involve time travel to earth's past. "Far beyond the Stars" (February 9, 1998) addresses science fiction's racist past as Sisko experiences a vision in which he is living as Benny Russell, a talented African American science fiction writer in early 1950s Manhattan, struggling to make a living in the face of institutional racism that works to exclude black writers. The episode even reinforces its message with such graphic images as Sisko/Russell being brutally beaten by two white policemen. The third-season two-part episode "Past Tense" (January 2 and January 9, 1995) is similarly topical, as Sisko, Dax, and Bashir accidentally travel to 2024 San Francisco, where they encounter a dystopian America that locks the homeless up in "sanctuaries" that are little more than prison camps. If these episodes are deadly serious, the *DS9* episode "Little Green Men" (November 6, 1995) captures some of the humor that often informs *Star Trek*'s trips to earth's past. The episode is even shot in black-and-white to capture the ambience of 1947, where Quark; his brother, Rom; and Rom's son, Nog, accidentally travel, crash-landing their ship at Roswell, New Mexico, site of the famous 1947 UFO sightings. Much comic mayhem ensues, as the U.S. military mistakes the Ferengi for alien invaders and takes them captive. The Ferengi, usually depicted as rather uncouth in comparison with the humans of the twenty-fourth century, comically find the humans of 1947 to be primitive, savage, and violent.

Other *DS9* episodes are linked even more directly to *TOS* episodes. For example, the episode "Trials and Tribble-ations" (November 4, 1996) sees many of the *DS9* principals travel back in time to interact (in vintage Starfleet uniforms) with the original *TOS* cast, accidentally returning to their own time with one of the tribbles from the classic *TOS* episode "The Trouble with Tribbles." Meanwhile, the mirror universe of the *TOS* epi-

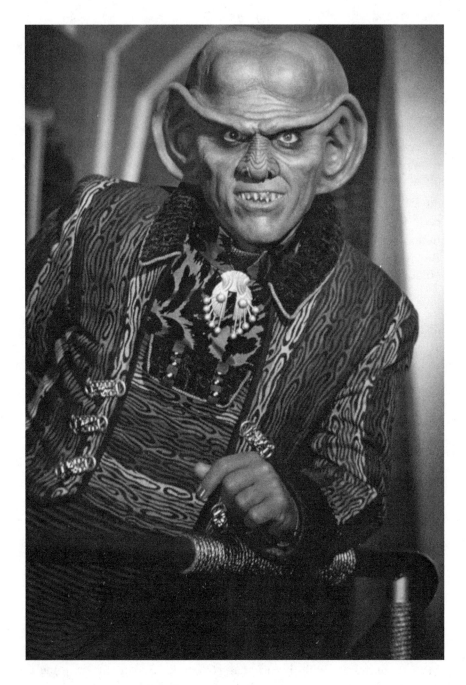

Figure 1.5.   Quark, *Star Trek*'s most important Ferengi character. Paramount Television / Photofest © Paramount Television

sode "Mirror, Mirror" (figure 1.6) is featured in several different *DS9* episodes, including "Crossover" (May 16, 1994), "Through the Looking Glass" (April 17, 1995), and "Shattered Mirror" (April 22, 1996). However, in keeping with the moral ambiguity of *DS9*, the black-and-white oppositions of "Mirror, Mirror" are now much more complex, with many characters remaining essentially unchanged.

STAR TREK: VOYAGER

Star Trek: Voyager (*VOY*) began airing on the United Paramount Network (UPN) on January 16, 1995—which happened also to be the launch date for UPN itself. *VOY* was clearly designed to be a flagship program for the new network, though *DS9* was still running in first-run syndication (and would continue to do so for another four and a half years, the majority of *VOY*'s run). *VOY* did manage to remain UPN's top-rated

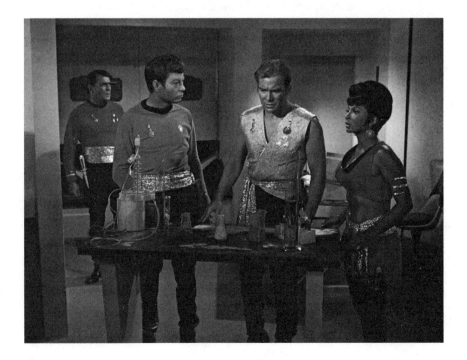

Figure 1.6.   Characters in the mirror universe of "Mirror, Mirror." NBC / Photofest © NBC

show through most of its run on the network, but that was no great feat given the lack of success of UPN as a whole. Thus, even though it ran on a network, *VOY* was never as popular as the syndicated *DS9* during the period in which their first-run broadcasts overlapped.

In addition to the general lack of popularity of the programs airing on UPN (even the near-legendary *Buffy the Vampire Slayer* declined dramatically in the ratings in its two years on UPN after spending its first five years on the WB network), *VOY* also had trouble attracting even core *Star Trek* fans. For example, Ian Grey has argued that *VOY* was, at the time of its initial run, "the most feminist show in American TV history." As a result, he argues, *VOY* became "the most despised object of fanboy loathing in the franchise's nearly 50-year history," concluding that the feminist emphasis of the show, with its female captain and its emphasis on feminine agency, was just too much for many hard-core *Trek* fans to handle. On the other hand, Grey also sees this rejection of *VOY*'s feminism as contrary to the core principles of the *Star Trek* franchise. Though many fans have seen *VOY* as an outlier in the *Star Trek* universe, Grey in fact declares it to be the "trekkiest" of all the *Star Trek* series, the one that most effectively embodies what *Star Trek* is really meant to be about. [10]

It is certainly the case that *VOY*, more than any other *Trek* series, fulfills the initial ambition to "boldly go where no man has gone before," and not just because the leading "man" is now a woman. Most episodes of all the other series are set primarily in the part of the Milky Way nearest earth (the so-called Alpha Quadrant), and almost everywhere the main characters travel has already been extensively explored and even settled, generally by humans or at least humanoids. *VOY*, on the other hand, is set almost entirely in the distant "Delta Quadrant" on the far side of the galaxy. Even this quadrant has been extensively settled (including by the dreaded Borg), but—with one single-episode exception—the crew of starship *Voyager* are the only humans in the entire quadrant.

In the first episode of *VOY*, a powerful alien entity known as the "Caretaker" brings *Voyager* and its crew to the Delta Quadrant against their will, so they are not really there as explorers. But, as they spend the rest of the series trying to make their way back to earth, they frequently take detours to explore strange phenomena (which occur quite frequently), even though the trip is already expected to take seventy-five years. Thus, they fit much more in the mold of explorers than do the crews of the other *Trek* series, even if their main arc is inward, toward home, rather than outward, toward the unknown.

Nevertheless, it is not really the location in the Delta Quadrant that sets *VOY* apart from the other *Trek* series. What is most strikingly different about the series is that the principal ship in the series, *Voyager*, is captained by a woman, Kathryn Janeway (Kate Mulgrew). Perhaps even more important is the fact that the series treats Janeway's captaincy in an entirely matter-of-fact way, clearly regarding the notion of a female captain as normal and natural. Within the series, her gender is entirely beside the point, even if, outside the series, it is an important point indeed. Moreover, it is clear that Janeway is far more than a token because several other women characters play crucial roles in the series. Samantha Wildman (Nancy Hower), for example, is a science officer aboard the ship. And she continues functioning in that capacity even after giving birth to a child, making the important point that women can be successful professionals as well as mothers. More prominent in the series is the half-human, half-Klingon B'Elanna Torres (Roxann Dawson), who serves as the ship's chief engineer, surely a traditionally male occupation if there ever was one. In the last episode of the series, she also becomes a mother, though (not surprisingly, given her Klingon heritage) she is also fierce, strong, and skilled in the martial arts.

Torres adds an additional element to the series in that, while trained at the Starfleet Academy, she joins the *Voyager* crew as a member of a group of Maquis who are also propelled into the Delta Quadrant. The Maquis are anti-Federation rebels (first introduced in *DS9*) who provide a reminder that even the Federation is seen as oppressive by some elements—though the real beef of the Maquis is with the Cardassians, to whom control of their home worlds is ceded by the Federation in a peace treaty. The leader of the Maquis group in *VOY*, meanwhile, is Chakotay (Robert Beltran), who becomes *Voyager*'s first officer. Chakotay adds still more diversity to the crew because of his Native American heritage.

There are Vulcans aboard *Voyager*, including Tuvok (Tim Russ), who is a major character as the ship's chief security officer.[11] In the *Trek* world, any such character will inevitably be compared with the original Spock, and the two do certainly share many characteristics. Meanwhile, the ship's doctor is a hologram (played by Robert Picardo), who, as a computer program, has some things in common with characters such as Spock and Data. One could argue, however, that the real "Spock character" of *VOY* is not Tuvok, but Seven of Nine (Jeri Ryan), a former Borg drone who is rescued from the collective. Like Data, Seven struggles through the latter half of *VOY* to try to regain her humanity—as opposed to Spock, who struggles to suppress his humanity but finds it continuing to emerge in subtle ways. Still, as a cyborg, Seven of Nine resembles Spock in the way she continues through most of her run in the series to suppress her emotions and to function with an almost computer-like logic and efficiency. One might see her corset-enhanced, skintight costume as undermining the feminist message of *VOY*, of course, but Seven of Nine functions as far more than eye candy. Not only is she not conventionally feminine in her attitudes and behavior, but she might be the most sympathetic character in a series whose characters in general failed to establish the same kind of emotional connection with viewers that characters such as Spock had generated. [12]

The feminist orientation of *VOY* can be taken as a sign of the gradual maturation of American society in its attitudes concerning the social and professional roles that should be available to women. At the same time, the *Trek* fanboy animosity shown toward *VOY* might be taken as a clear sign that these attitudes still needed improvement in the second half of the 1990s. Meanwhile, the attempt to create a stronger emphasis on positive representation of women in *VOY* can be seen as an acknowledgment that the representation of gender in *Star Trek* (especially in *TOS*) has sometimes been problematic and as an attempt to overcome the limitations found in earlier series in this area. The representation of gender in *VOY* and the controversies over that representation are thus an excellent example of the way in which the various entries in the *Star Trek* franchise have reflected important debates within American society as a whole, as well as an example of the way in which different entries in the franchise have sometimes engaged in debates with other works within the *Star Trek* universe.

STAR TREK: ENTERPRISE

Star Trek: Enterprise (*ENT*) was the immediate successor to *VOY* on UPN, premiering in September 2001. It was, however, a significant departure for the *Star Trek* franchise, which had reinforced its own future-oriented perspective by setting each of its series later in time than the one before (though *TNG, DS9,* and *VOY* occurred in close temporal proximity to one another). *ENT,* however, is a prequel to *TOS,* set approximately ninety years after the eccentric Zefram Cochrane developed earth's first warp drive in the year 2063, directly leading to contact between humans and the much more advanced Vulcans. This contact then contributes to a new age of enlightenment and technological progress on earth, though one of the central themes of *ENT* is ongoing friction between the Vulcans (who fear that earth will get into trouble by advancing too quickly) and humans (who resent Vulcan attempts to slow their advancement).

The series begins in 2151, with the initial voyage of the *Enterprise* (registry number NX-01), earth's first starship, as it sets out on a mission of discovery and exploration. Unfortunately, things very quickly take a dark turn, and the ship spends most of its time getting entangled in one conflict after another, giving the series a dark tone that often outstrips even that of *DS9.* The look of the series was dark as well, with the *Enterprise* given an ugly, stark, industrial appearance that was presumably meant to emphasize its early place in the development of earth's starships, but that also created an atmosphere that for many was decidedly un-*Trek*-like. Other aspects of the series departed from franchise tradition as well, as when the usually grand orchestral opening music was replaced by a hokey vocal ballad that also seemed designed to give the series an old-fashioned feel. These attempts to produce a retro look and feel, though, may have been miscalculations that failed to take account of the fact that the series takes place a century and a half in the *future* relative to the time of broadcast, often making it feel like it is set perhaps in the 1950s. At the same time, the retro feel of *ENT* might be accused of losing sight of the fact that the whole *point* of *Star Trek* is to envision the future.

The *Enterprise NX-01* is commanded by Captain Jonathan Archer (Scott Bakula), a strong, virile figure of paternal authority who is something of a throwback to Kirk, though he has moments of weakness and self-doubt. He also has a cute pet dog that travels on the ship, which many also felt was contrary to the *Trek* ethos of avoiding cheap attempts at cuteness. The ship's chief engineer, Commander Charles "Trip" Tucker III (Connor Trinneer), is an old associate of Archer who serves as a sort of right-hand man to the captain. Tucker also gets into a few Kirk-like adventures of his own and even eventually becomes romantically involved with the ship's Vulcan science officer, Subcommander T'Pol (Jolene Blalock). Tucker thus shows considerable evolution from his opening attitude, as he begins the series with an extremely hostile attitude toward Vulcans. T'Pol is an obvious successor (or perhaps predecessor) to Spock, with her scientific knowledge and devotion to logic, though her skintight outfits and deadpan speaking style link her more directly to *Voyager*'s Seven of Nine. Though not a Starfleet officer as the series begins, she is placed aboard the *Enterprise* as an advisor at the insistence of the Vulcans to try to keep the humans out of trouble. But the Vulcans meddle with the mission in other ways as well, and T'Pol gradually shifts her true loyalty away from the Vulcan High Command and toward Starfleet. The ship's weapons and tactical officer is Lieutenant Malcolm Reed (Dominic Keating). Descended from a long line of British naval officers, Reed is initially a bit reclusive, though one plot arc of the series involves his increasing willingness to open up to the rest of the crew and to accept them as a kind of family. The pilot of *Enterprise* is young Ensign Travis Mayweather (Anthony Montgomery), a sort of Sulu figure (though African American rather than Asian), while the ship's Uhura figure is Ensign Hoshi Sato (Linda Park), though she is Asian rather than African American. In a *Star Trek* first, the ship's chief medical officer, Dr. Phlox (John Billingsley), is an alien (from the planet Denobula).

Perhaps fearing franchise fatigue as the fourth *Star Trek* series in a decade and a half, *ENT* seemed to go out of its way to differentiate itself from its predecessor series in the *Trek* franchise, as when the entire third season was devoted to a single continuous plot arc involving a war between earth and the "Xindi," an alien consortium that launches a deadly preemptive strike against earth after it learns that, in the future, earth will launch a similar assault on the Xindi. By the beginning of season 3, Archer and the *Enterprise* have negated the Xindi threat, but its aftermath is still felt as xenophobic forces raise their ugly head on earth. Both the continuity and the darkness of this plot arc were unprecedented in the *Trek* franchise, but such attempts at innovation often simply had the effect of alienating loyal *Trek* fans. In the remainder of season 4, *ENT* attempted to recover by reemphasizing its *links* to the *Trek* franchise. It thus turned back to a mode much more reminiscent of *TOS*, with greater emphasis on the role of this series as a prequel to *TOS*. It even brought in Brent Spiner of *TNG* to play the ancestor of Data's creator, a brilliant scientist engaged in banned experiments with genetic engineering. The fourth season ended with a flurry of episodes featuring crossovers with *TOS*, including Orion slave girls, the mirror universe, and a direct tie-in to the episode "The Tholian Web." The final episode was even enacted within the *TNG* holodeck. Ratings remained low, however, and the series was unable to build enough of an audience to avoid cancellation after the fourth season, despite protests from loyal fans.

THE J. J. ABRAMS ERA

With *Enterprise* canceled and *Nemesis* a bust at the box office, the *Star Trek* franchise was, by mid-2005, at an all-time low point, even though the comics and novels continued to appear, and all of the series continued to run in syndication. All of that would change, however, when J. J. Abrams rebooted the *Star Trek* film franchise with a new blockbuster film, simply entitled *Star Trek*. Though very well known as a writer and producer—and as the creator of such television series as *Lost* (2004–2010)—Abrams was still relatively inexperienced as a film director, his work in that area having consisted primarily of one major feature, *Mission: Impossible III* (2006). But, despite predictable complaints that Abrams's version of *Trek* deviated too far from the look and feel of earlier entries in the *Trek* franchise, his *Star Trek* was a huge commercial hit, grossing more than twice as much at the domestic box office than any previous *Trek* film and pulling in nearly $400 million worldwide.

Abrams's *Trek* features the same major characters as *TOS* but is set years earlier, when most of them are cadets at Starfleet Academy, though Spock is already an instructor there.[13] It even includes a prologue in which we see both Spock and Kirk as children, establishing Kirk as a wild and rebellious youngster whose father was killed in a space battle at the moment of the boy's birth and Spock as a mistreated outsider suffering from racial prejudice on Vulcan because of his half-human ancestry. The main plot then kicks in as a series of unlikely events forces a brand-new *Enterprise* into emergency service on its first mission, with Captain Christopher Pike (Bruce Greenwood) at the helm and Spock (Zachary Quinto) as the first officer. McCoy (Karl Urban), Uhura (Zoe Saldana), Sulu (John Cho), and Chekov (Anton Yelchin) take their requisite positions in the crew, while Scotty (Simon Pegg) joins them later. Kirk (Chris Pine) bluffs his way aboard after being initially banned but eventually assumes command of the ship.

Abrams made a number of key moves in conceiving this film, including the decision not to worry very much about consistency with the previous *Trek* canon, as when he destroys the planet Vulcan (and Spock's mother) in the course of the film. Nor was Abrams much concerned with believability and plot holes, instead opting to use the plot simply as a framework on which to hang a virtually nonstop sequence of spectacular and violent action scenes (accentuated by lots of Abrams's signature lens flares). This action, however, is punctuated by considerable humor. Scotty, for example, is an almost entirely comical character, despite the fact that the film emphasizes his brilliance as an engineer. Abrams also decided to make no attempt to re-create the look of *TOS* or even of the earlier *Star Trek* films, instead opting to present fans with a completely redesigned future—and especially with a new *Enterprise* that looks far more sleek and futuristic than the original with much more advanced-looking technologies, including high-tech digital controls and display panels. This new *Enterprise* retains the bright ambient lighting of the original but employs a primary color palette of whites and grays and blues to produce a cool, high-tech look. Abrams did make some concessions to loyal *Trek* fans—the most important of which is the use of a time-travel gimmick that allows the beloved Leonard Nimoy to appear in the film as an aged Spock. But it is clear that the rationale behind this film was that it could only be a blockbuster by appealing to a much broader audience than the franchise's loyal core of fans, and the film certainly succeeded in that sense.

In 2013, Abrams followed with a direct sequel, *Star Trek Into Darkness*, using very much the same basic philosophy as his first *Trek* film. This film outperformed its predecessor in a commercial sense, grossing $229 million at the domestic box office and taking in $239 million outside the United States, thus becoming the first *Trek* film to make more money abroad than in the United States. Of course, *Star Trek Into Darkness* also had a production budget of $190 million, while the original series of *Trek* films had budgets between $35 million and $60 million. Clearly, the *Trek* film franchise was boldly going into new territory.

Star Trek Into Darkness is another rollicking high-action adventure, bringing back Khan Noonien Singh as the main villain, this time played by prominent British actor Benedict Cumberbatch. It even re-created key scenes from *The Wrath of Khan*, except with Spock and Kirk switching roles. Kirk is even killed in the same manner that Spock was killed in the earlier film, though this time McCoy is able to resurrect him by giving him a transfusion of Khan's superblood. And Spock becomes an all-out action hero, defeating the mighty Khan in hand-to-hand combat—though he does need some help from his girlfriend, Uhura. In short, this film pretty much tossed out all the rules of *TOS* (and tossed in more lens flares than ever before) to create a blockbuster SF action film with state-of-the-art computer-generated effects.

After *Star Trek Into Darkness*, Abrams committed the sacrilege of skipping to the *Star Wars* franchise for his next directorial effort, leaving *Star Trek Beyond* (2016) in the hands of Justin Lin, primarily known for directing several entries in the *Fast and the Furious* franchise. Abrams remained as coproducer, but the style of the film definitely changed. The number of lens flares decreased, but the action was ramped up to a cartoonish level, as various characters performed exciting but clearly impossible feats. The film was also less well received by audiences, pulling in $159 million in domestic box office and $185 million internationally, on a production budget of $185 million. Nevertheless, the performance was good enough that a fourth film in this reboot series of *Star Trek* films currently appears to be in the works.

In the meantime, in October of 2014, the CBS broadcast network launched CBS All Access as its attempt to enter the streaming video market dominated by such Internet stalwarts as Netflix, Amazon Video, iTunes, and Hulu. Initially CBS provided content for CBC All Access by making a large portion of their huge catalog of television programs available for streaming, but they also realized that they would need to produce original programming to attract a sufficient number of subscribers to make All Access a success. No doubt partly spurred by the success of Abrams's two *Star Trek* films, they announced in November 2015 that their first original program would be a new *Star Trek* series to be entitled *Star Trek: Discovery* and to be set shortly before the events of *TOS*. Beset by delays, including the departure of showrunner and cocreator Bryan Fuller (a successful television producer who had written more than twenty episodes of *DS9* and *VOY*), by the time the first episodes of *DSC* aired on September 24, 2017, it was actually the second original series to appear on All Access.

DSC introduced a number of innovations, making its central character a black woman, Michael Burnham (Sonequa Martin-Green), who is not the captain of a starship. In fact, events in the first two episodes (which serve as a sort of prologue to the main continuous plot) lead to Burnham being drummed out of Starfleet altogether, then sentenced to life in prison for treason. She is, however, quickly rehabilitated when it becomes clear that her talents are needed in the budding war against the Klingons, here depicted as a particularly savage and vicious race via a panoply of xenophobic stereotypes that might have been derived from a handbook on racism and colonialism. The overall tone (and lighting) of the series is particularly grim and dark, and the series features far more graphic violence than any previous *Trek* series. Burnham is a strong character, but she is also a sort of outcast, which makes it very difficult for her to participate in the kind of camaraderie that was so crucial to the success of earlier *Trek* series. The captain of *Discovery*, Gabriel Lorca (Jason Isaacs), seems to be a borderline psychopath, chosen for his role because he is felt by Starfleet (which itself comes off as an almost sinister organization) to be ideal as a leader in brutal combat. All of this darkness almost makes it seem as if the series is set in the *Trek* mirror universe, while some of the technologies available in the series (such as a drive powered by mushroom spores that allows *Discovery* to travel instantaneously anywhere in the universe) make it very difficult to take the series seriously, despite its ultra-serious tone.

At the end of 2017, as the *Star Trek* franchise was beginning its second half century, both the latest film and the latest television series in the franchise seemed to be seriously problematic. Nevertheless, more than half a century after the debut of *TOS*, there still *were* both a film franchise and a television series in active production. Novels were still being published with links to the film franchise and to all of the television series, and *Trek* fan culture continued to be one of the major forces in American fan culture. In short, *Star Trek* was still a very prominent part of American science fiction, as it had been since its inception.

2

STAR TREK AND THE HISTORY OF AMERICAN SCIENCE FICTION

While virtually no one would doubt that *TOS* and its successors in the *Star Trek* universe could rightly be considered works of science fiction, exactly where and how *Star Trek* functions within the larger context of American science fiction is a bit less clear. To an extent, the genre of science fiction would seem to be ill-suited to the format of the weekly television series. After all, as theorist and critic Darko Suvin pointed out back in a very influential formulation in the 1970s, science fiction achieves its most important effects by producing what he called "cognitive estrangement."[1] That is, it continually surprises and disorients readers or viewers by placing them in environments or situations that are different from the ones they might encounter in their own lives, potentially causing them to revise the ways in which they think about ideas and issues of relevance to their own worlds. Science fiction, then, works by making its audience *uncomfortable*. Conventional television series, on the other hand, must attract audiences and keep them coming back week after week, essentially offering them a familiar and reliable experience that they can count on each time they view a new episode. Television series, then, work largely by making their audiences *comfortable*.

In the 1990s, SF series such as *The X-Files* and *Babylon 5*—and, to a lesser extent, *DS9* and *VOY*—began to solve this problem by introducing continuous plotting that could keep plot-oriented viewers coming back week after week. However, *The X-Files* mixed its continuous plot episodes (the so-called mytharc episodes) with stand-alone "monster-of-the-week" episodes, and its true continuity derived less from the central alien-invasion plot than from the characters—and in particular from the growing relationship between the two protagonists, Mulder and Scully. The same could be said for *DS9* and *VOY*, but then the technique of involving audiences in a series via the characters was by the 1990s long-established in the *Star Trek* franchise, with both *TOS* and *TNG* having relied centrally on this technique while maintaining a purely episodic plot structure.

This reliance on well-known characters to whom readers could turn for continuity no doubt disrupted the cognitive estrangement effect in *Star Trek*, and I myself have argued that *TOS*, rather than being pure science fiction, is in many ways "more nearly a work of adventure/romance designed to entertain and to be more comforting than unsettling."[2] I still largely agree with that assessment, but I would emphasize that this does not mean that *TOS* is not science fiction at all or that it has not participated extensively in the evolution of American science fiction from the late 1960s onward. For one thing, *TOS* and its successors participate in almost all of the major genres of science fiction, tracking the development of science fiction as a whole over the past half century. For another, *TOS* participated in a contemporary wave of programs that made science fiction more prominent on American television than ever before. At the same time, more than its contemporaries in SF television, *TOS* had a great deal in common with films such as Stanley Kubrick's *2001: A Space Odyssey* and Franklin J. Schaffner's *Planet of the Apes*, both released in 1968 (in the midst of the original run of *Star Trek* on broadcast television); these films brought unprecedented attention to SF film in terms of both artistic achievement (in the case of Kubrick's film) and box-office appeal (in the case of Schaffner's). Finally, *TOS* also resonated with two important contemporary trends in written science fiction: the reconceptualization of outer space as a locus for utopian imaginings in the movement De Witt Douglas Kilgore has dubbed "astrofuturism" and the attempt to engage contemporary social and political issues in the movement known as science fiction's "New Wave."

TOS AND THE GENRES OF SCIENCE FICTION

The parallels between the entire *Star Trek* franchise and the genre of the space opera are obvious, even if the space opera has something of a reputation for being light and frivolous, while the *Trek* franchise often engages with important issues in sophisticated ways. My colleague Anne-Marie Thomas and I describe the *space opera* as consisting of "stories of adventure in outer space" featuring "swashbuckling action and larger-than-life heroes."[3] Given the reputation of *Star Trek* for its thoughtful exploration of serious social and political issues, it is easy to forget that the entire franchise (perhaps *TOS* most of all) depends on rousing outer-space adventures. Virtually every episode of *TOS* involves space-opera elements of some sort—especially the episodes in which the *Enterprise* is involved in conflicts with the Romulans or Klingons or when the ship seems constantly to be in danger of destruction at the hands of various alien forces. Indeed, for a franchise devoted to envisioning a peaceful and prosperous future, *TOS* and the other entries in the *Star Trek* franchise seem to involve a surprising amount of combat—of both the outer space and the hand-to-hand variety. Thus, for a vessel supposedly devoted to exploration and discovery, the *Enterprise* seems to be awfully well-armed, while Captain Kirk and his crew seem to get involved in gladiatorial-type contests with considerable frequency. Indeed, Kirk—with his impressive skill at both fist-fighting and seduction—would seem to be a figure drawn very much from the pulpy worlds of space opera.

In addition to space opera, *TOS* frequently veers into other subgenres of SF. For example, while *TOS* is obviously first and foremost about the exploration of outer space, there are a number of episodes that specifically deal with time travel. Sometimes this time travel occurs accidentally, as in "Tomorrow Is Yesterday" (January 26, 1967). Here, an encounter with a "black star" (presumably what we now know as a "black hole," though that terminology was not firmly established until 1970) accidentally sends the *Enterprise* hurtling back into the 1960s. There, Captain Kirk and the crew are concerned primarily with getting back to their own time—and in making sure that they do nothing to change the world of the past, thereby inadvertently triggering a chain of events that could lead to the complete obliteration of their own twenty-third-century world. Meanwhile, everyone aboard the *Enterprise* seems to share this view of the need to avoid modifying the past without question—suggesting a common view of the way time works that has perhaps been verified by experience.

This belief that the past can (but must not) be changed is fairly consistent throughout *TOS*—and is in fact the governing motif in one of the greatest of all *TOS* episodes, "The City on the Edge of Forever," first broadcast near the end of the show's first season. Written by highly respected science fiction writer Harlan Ellison, this episode features McCoy being hurtled back to New York in the 1930s after he leaps through a time portal known as the "Guardian of Forever" while he is in a crazed state brought on by an accidental drug injection. Fearing that, given his condition, McCoy might do something to change history, Kirk and Spock follow him through the portal in order to prevent him from doing so. In the 1930s, they encounter beautiful, saint-like social activist Edith Keeler (Joan Collins), who not only works to alleviate the misery of the Depression for the very poor but is also a pacifist who hopes to help stem the tide of advancing war. As it turns out, Kirk discovers that, in the original timeline, Keeler had been killed in a street accident, but in a new timeline created by McCoy's arrival, she survived and was instrumental in preventing the United States from entering World War II, giving the Nazis time to develop atomic weaponry and thus leading to a Nazi victory in the war. Kirk, though he has fallen in love with Keeler, is then forced to prevent McCoy from saving her life as they both observe her being run down by a truck before their very eyes.

By the second season, the narrative possibilities of time travel in *TOS* are extended in the episode "Assignment: Earth," in which the *Enterprise* intentionally travels back to the 1960s (by sling-shotting around the sun) on a mission of historical research. There, in this largely comedic episode, Kirk and his crew become involved in the (successful) efforts of an advanced alien agent to prevent the Cold War from breaking out into a full-scale nuclear holocaust. Thus, while the *Enterprise* was merely on a research mission and had no intention of interfering with the flow of history, the alien agent seems to have very different ideas about the desirability of changing earth's history.

These brief forays into time travel at least put that motif on the *Star Trek* agenda, and the motif would be extended in all later reincarnations of the franchise. One of the greatest episodes of *TNG*, the third-season entry "Yesterday's *Enterprise*" (February 19, 1990), is a time-travel narrative—and also a Cold War narrative of sorts, dealing with an alternative timeline in which the Federation-Klingon Cold War breaks out into an all-out military conflict. Similarly, one of the most riveting episodes of *DS9*, the third-season two-parter "Past Tense," features a transporter malfunction that hurls Sisko, Bashir, and Dax back into a very dystopian early twenty-first century, which they struggle not to change despite the dire conditions they find there. A central motif of *ENT* (though one that never really quite comes together and gets dropped in the final season) is the "Temporal Cold War," which extensively involves time travel, while *VOY* turns to time-travel narratives particularly often, as in the fourth-season double episode "A Year in Hell" (November 5, 1997). Moreover, their remote location in the Delta Quadrant sometimes leads the crew of *Voyager* to dispense with the idea that the past must not be changed. Meanwhile, in the fifth-season *VOY* episode "Timeless" (November 18, 1998, directed by LeVar Burton and featuring a brief cameo by Burton as his *TNG* character Geordi La Forge), we learn that the ban on changing the past has been codified as official Starfleet policy in the "Temporal Prime Directive." Chakotay and Ensign Harry Kim (Garrett Wang) proceed to change the past anyway, thus saving all aboard *Voyager*.

Time travel is also central to one of the most beloved of all the *Star Trek* films, *Star Trek IV: The Voyage Home* (1986), a seriocomic tale in which Kirk and his officers (now fugitives in their own time) again slingshot around the sun (in a stolen Klingon bird-of-prey, no less) in order to travel to the past. In this case, they travel to 1986 in an effort to retrieve a humpback whale that will allow them to save the earth of the twenty-third century (in which the whales are extinct) from a destructive alien probe. This film makes some serious points about the value of preserving endangered species, but it is probably remembered most fondly because of the comic efforts of Kirk and his officers to understand the bewildering world of 1986.

The film *Star Trek: First Contact* (1996) is also a time-travel narrative, as well as an alien-invasion narrative in which the Borg attack twenty-second-century earth in order to try to prevent earth from ever joining the Federation. However, because of its focus on journeys into outer space, there are few opportunities in *Star Trek* for classic alien-invasion-of-earth narratives. Still, there are a number of examples of alien invasions of Federation space, as when the Romulans cross the "neutral zone" and begin destroying border outposts using newly developed high-tech weaponry in the *TOS* episode "Balance of Terror." Meanwhile, the final episode of the first season of *TOS*—"Operation: Annihilate!"—is essentially a reworking of some classic alien-invasion motifs of the 1950s. Here, pizza-sized, blob-like alien creatures (that turn out each to be a single cell of one giant alien brainlike organism) invade a Federation colony planet where Kirk's brother, Sam, lives with his family. The creatures then begin to latch onto the planet's human colonists in order to take control of their minds and force them to work for them to build a fleet of spaceships they hope to use to further their plans of sweeping across the galaxy as conquerors. This central motif of aliens taking over the bodies of humans in many ways resembles those of the classic alien-invasion films *Invaders from Mars* (1953) and *Invasion of the Body Snatchers* (1956), but it is even more directly reminiscent of Robert A. Heinlein's alien-invasion novel *The Puppet Masters* (1951), a thinly veiled anticommunist allegory that was adapted to film under the same title in 1994.[4] Unfortunately, the *TOS* episode is a bit too overloaded and contains too much material (including the death of Kirk's brother on the planet and Spock's temporary blindness) for one fifty-minute episode to carry properly, but the episode is certainly rich in science fictional content.

Of course, the most prominent alien enemies of the Federation in *TOS* are the Klingons, who first appeared in the *TOS* episode "Errand of Mercy," in which they prepare to launch an invasion of galactic conquest against the Federation. The militaristic Klingons are typical alien-invader types, down to the fact that they eschew individualism and tout the fact that each of them is devoted to their communal group above their individual selves. Of course, this devotion to the community is enforced by constant surveillance, in one of the many moves that makes them a virtual embodiment of American Cold War stereotypes about the Soviets. The Klingons would reappear as alien threats later in the series, though in this particular episode their invasion is thwarted by hyper-advanced aliens who abhor war (and violence of any kind). In this sense, the episode recalls such SF classics as the 1951 alien-invasion film *The Day the Earth Stood Still*, while it also anticipates such later alien-intervention narratives as *The Abyss* (1989).

In later installments of the *Star Trek* franchise, earth itself would sometimes come under threat, as in the destructive attack made against the planet by the Xindi in "The Expanse" (May 21, 2003), initiating a season-long story arc involving the battle between earth and the Xindi in *Star Trek: Enterprise*. Probably the most memorable alien threat in *TNG*, meanwhile, is that posed by the Borg Collective, which threatens to attack earth in "The Best of Both Worlds," a two-parter that ends season 3 in a cliffhanger and is then continued in the opening episode of season 4.

The Borg are also prominent in *VOY*, including the fact that one of the principal characters of the latter seasons of the show, Seven of Nine, is a former Borg drone. Finally, another Borg attack on earth is thwarted in *First Contact.*

TOS AND SCIENCE FICTION TELEVISION OF THE 1960S

When *Star Trek* premiered on September 8, 1966, it found itself in what appeared to be an emerging period of richness in science fiction television. For example, in "What Are a Few Galaxies among Friends?"—a 1966 article for *TV Guide*—science fiction guru Isaac Asimov describes the anticipation and excitement he felt that summer as he awaited the upcoming fall television season, a season in which the brand-new *Star Trek* was joined on the broadcast schedule by the second season of CBS's *Lost in Space*, as well as the third season of ABC's *Voyage to the Bottom of the Sea* and the first (and only, as it turned out) season of ABC's *The Time Tunnel.* During that summer, it seemed to Asimov that the fall lineup might be an unprecedented bonanza for SF fans, but in the article Asimov goes on to express his disappointment at the scientific inaccuracies that riddled these programs. He includes *Star Trek* in his critique, though he does grant that it is probably the best of the lot in terms of its use of science. More importantly, he would soon come around, becoming a big fan and booster of the show, as well as an informal advisor to Gene Roddenberry on scientific matters.

Asimov's support for *TOS* could be taken as an indication that the series stood apart from its contemporaries, as, of course, it did. All of the other series mentioned above were produced by the apparently indefatigable Irwin Allen, whose work was marked far more by spectacle and melodrama than an interest in advanced technologies or complex ideas. Allen ultimately became best known as the producer of *The Poseidon Adventure* (1972) and *The Towering Inferno* (1974), perhaps the two most important examples of the early 1970s disaster film genre. Of Allen's television productions, only *Lost in Space* even remotely resembled *Star Trek.* Indeed, when CBS passed on the opportunity to acquire *Star Trek* back in 1964, it was reportedly because they had already green-lighted *Lost in Space* and felt that the two series were too similar to air on the same network, where they would simply compete with one another.

They couldn't have been more wrong about the similarities, of course. *Lost in Space* does feature a crew that travels about the galaxy in a spaceship, the *Jupiter 2*, but that is about as far as the similarities to *Star Trek* go. For one thing, the ship in *Lost in Space* is quite small in comparison with the *Enterprise*. It is also not nearly as technologically advanced, which is not surprising given that it launches in 1997, rather than in the mid-twenty-third century. Correspondingly, its mission is much more modest than that of the *Enterprise*: Rather than embark on an ambitious journey of exploration and discovery around the galaxy, *Jupiter 2* carries a single family of passengers, the Robinsons, on the very specific mission of founding a colony on a planet in the Alpha Centauri system, which can then hopefully become a colony that can help alleviate crowded conditions on earth.

Unfortunately, this mission goes awry when it is sabotaged by Dr. Zachary Smith (Jonathan Harris), acting as the agent of an unnamed foreign power—but it was 1965 at the time of the broadcast, so that power didn't really have to be named. Everyone knew who it was. Smith, though, gets caught on the ship, inadvertently going along for the ride as it goes hurtling off into space as a result of his sabotage. He thus becomes a reluctant participant in the voyage, which also included military pilot Major Don West (Mark Goddard) and a histrionic, arm-waving robot that became one of the most popular characters of the series. The Robinsons themselves included astrophysicist John Robinson (Guy Williams); his wife, Maureen Robinson (June Lockhart), who seemed to use her skills as a biochemist primarily to prepare meals while otherwise performing housewifely chores; their two teenage daughters, nineteen-year-old Judy (Marta Kristen) and thirteen-year-old Penny (Angela Cartwright); and young Will (Billy Mumy), for whom the robot served as a sort of Lassie-like pet.

The Lassie connection was made more overt by the fact that Lockhart was at the time of her casting best known for playing the nurturing mother of Lassie's boy, Timmy, in the *Lassie* television series from 1958 to 1964. Meanwhile, Williams was most familiar to television audiences for his role as the swashbuckling title character in *Zorro* (1957–1959 and 1960–1961). *Lost in Space* thus included precisely the sort of cute kids and pets that Roddenberry had staunchly refused to allow to become central figures aboard the *Enterprise*, while the Robinson adults were carefully portrayed as occupying highly conventional gender roles, Maureen establishing a safely domestic sphere even in outer space and John performing a variety of manly feats to protect the family. Judy was old enough to provide a bit of eye candy and to play the occasional damsel in distress, occupying still another conventional feminine role. And there was much distress to be had, as the Robinsons each week encountered new dangers in their quest to find their way back home, a quest in which they would never succeed due to the surprise cancellation of the series after the 1967–1968 season. Meanwhile, their weekly difficulties were often exacerbated (or caused outright) by the interventions of the cowardly but pompous Smith, who ultimately became the show's primary comic character, giving even his villainy a light touch.

Of course, *Lost in Space* was far less serious-minded than was *TOS*, and the Allen series had little interest in the philosophical and moral dilemmas and social and political commentary that were the stock-in-trade of *TOS*. Meanwhile, the stories of *Lost in Space* were essentially in the vein of fantasy-adventure rather than serious science fiction, and there was little concern with believability or scientific accuracy. *Lost in Space* was, after all, aimed essentially at a juvenile audience—though with the hope that parents would come along for the ride as well. Indeed, in its first season (which was in black-and-white), *Lost in Space* was clearly aimed at a more adult audience, and the veer into juvenile territory in the final two seasons (which were in color) might have been an attempt to avoid head-on competition with *Star Trek*. Paradoxically, though, while 1960s television ratings are a bit complex to decipher, *Star Trek* attracted a relatively young demographic in its own right, while *Lost in Space* seems to have done better than *Star Trek* with viewers over fifty.

No doubt it was no accident that *Lost in Space* and *Star Trek* would appear at virtually the same time, when there had never before been a major space exploration series on American television.[5] In the midst of the space race and with a moon landing clearly on the horizon, Americans were excited about the possibilities of space travel as never before. The political climate of the 1960s also helps to explain the near-simultaneous rise of the two series: Just as *Star Trek* provided a thoughtful exploration of racism, colonialism, militarism, and other concerns of the major oppositional political movements of the 1960s, so too did *Lost in Space* provide a weekly hour-long escape from precisely those same serious concerns.

In any case, as it turned out, neither *Lost in Space* nor *TOS* would survive for very long on American primetime broadcast television, each lasting a mere three seasons. Each had gained a certain loyal following during those seasons, though. Indeed, while the syndicated success of *TOS* is legendary in American television history, relatively few people even remember that *Lost in Space* had a reasonable amount of success in syndication as well, preceding *TOS* by a year into that market, just as it had done on broadcast television. By 1973, however, *Lost in Space* was quickly losing viewers in the syndicated market, while *TOS* continued to build a broader and increasingly devoted syndicated audience.

In the meantime, Allen's other science fiction television series were short-lived as well. *Voyage to the Bottom of the Sea* was the champion, lasting all of four seasons, beginning in 1964. But it, like *Lost in Space*, was canceled in 1968. *Land of the Giants* premiered shortly after the demise of these two but lasted only two seasons, while *The Time Tunnel* was the shortest-lived of all, running only during the 1966–1967 television season. By 1970, science fiction had essentially been eradicated from American broadcast television, where it had never been a great ratings success to begin with.

TOS in syndication was undoubtedly the most important SF television of the 1970s. Other series of the decade were relatively minor, including movie spin-offs such as the short-lived *Planet of the Apes* (1974) and *Logan's Run* (1977), the latter of which featured *Star Trek* veteran D. C. Fontana as story editor and also included contributions from former *Trek* writers Harlan Ellison and David Gerrold. The British import *Space 1999* (1975–1977) also made a minor impact in British syndication, though the most important series of the decade might have been the kitschy *Buck Rogers in the 25th Century* (1979–1981) and *Battlestar Galactica* (1978–1979), the latter of which would be revived in a much more successful version by *Trek* alumnus Ronald D. Moore in 2004.[6] But science fiction would remain a marginal genre in American television until the rise of *TNG* in 1987, ushering in what was perhaps the most successful decade of science fiction on American television, with series such as *The X-Files* and *Babylon 5* (not to mention the subsequent *Trek* series) bringing the genre to a new level of sophistication and success.

TOS AND SCIENCE FICTION FILM IN THE 1960S

Science fiction film rose to new prominence in American culture in the 1950s, propelled both by excitement over the budding race to space and by anxieties over the possibility that the Cold War could erupt into all-out apocalyptic conflict. The emergence of SF film in this decade produced important, ambitious, groundbreaking works of cinema, such as Robert Wise's *The Day the Earth Stood Still* (1951) and Fred M. Wilcox's *Forbidden Planet* (1956). It also produced works that, while less artistically accomplished, captured the spirit of 1950s America as well as any works of American culture during that decade. No work of 1950s culture, for example, reflected the anxieties and fears of the decade more vividly than Don Siegel's *Invasion of the Body Snatchers* (1956). By the end of the 1950s, however, SF film had been consigned to the cultural margins, coming to be dominated by low-budget works aimed at the emergent teen market—partly because science fiction as a whole had not transcended its origins in the pulp magazines of the 1930s and partly because the filmmaking technology of the 1950s was not yet mature enough to make consistently effective high-quality works of science fiction cinema.

The first half of the 1960s was, indeed, not a very distinguished period for science fiction film. One could argue, in fact, that the first truly major work of science fiction film to appear in the decade was François Truffaut's *Fahrenheit 451*, which happened to premiere (in Great Britain) on September 16, 1966, only eight days after *TOS* had premiered on American television. An adaptation of Ray Bradbury's 1953 dystopian novel of the same name, this film, with its dark vision of a dehumanizing future, would at first glance seem to have relatively little in common with *TOS*, a series known for its bright, humanistic optimism. Of course, *Fahrenheit 451* was a British-produced film with a French director and a German star, based on an American novel, so (if nothing else) it seemed to embody the kind of international cooperation that was central to *Star Trek*'s vision of the future. But the dystopian vision of the film is not entirely foreign to *TOS*, while the film also contains important utopian energies that are ultimately even more in line with the *Star Trek* worldview.

Fahrenheit 451 depicts a future dystopia in which books have been forbidden—and are in fact burned whenever found by government "firemen" as part of a project to extinguish critical thinking and to replace literature and other forms of thoughtful culture with mindless (and mind-numbing) popular culture. Bradbury conceived this vision as a critique of the direction in which he felt American culture was moving with the rise of television in the early 1950s. One could argue that his vision was in many ways accurate, though one could also argue that the various *Star Trek* series are evidence that television at least has the potential to be thought-provoking, rather than thought-preventing. *Star Trek* is also pro-literature, as its penchant for Shakespearean allusions perhaps indicates. Even the holodecks that began with *TNG* (and that at first glance might seem reminiscent of the pop culture depicted in *Fahrenheit 451*) often depict scenarios with a literary cast. In addition, not only do various characters in *Trek* series do a great deal of reading on electronic devices, but characters (especially captains) often show a fondness for old-fashioned physical books.

Further, even though Bradbury's novel ends with an apparent nuclear holocaust, both the novel and the film suggest that the community of readers that resists the banning of books will be able to preserve the literary past and perhaps lead to a new beginning—much as the future history that lies at the core of the *Trek* franchise suggests that humanity will go through very difficult times before finally emerging in the utopian future. Indeed, despite its reputation for utopian optimism, *Star Trek* itself contains a number of dystopian visions, often suggesting that one person's utopia might be another person's dystopia. *TOS*, in particular, frequently shows suspicion toward overtly utopian societies and is informed by the notion that human beings must experience a certain amount of hardship in order to be fully human.

TOS had even more in common with the two classic SF films that emerged during its initial broadcast run. On the one hand, *2001* demonstrated that SF film could aspire to the condition of genuine art, while thoughtfully addressing contemporary anxieties over the accelerating rate of technological change and simultaneously proving that technology could be beautiful. On the other hand, *Planet of the Apes* proved that science fiction could generate compelling drama while addressing serious social and political issues in a way that could appeal to a wide, mainstream audience. In this sense, *2001* and *Planet of the Apes* represent the two poles of the potential of science fiction film. One mark of the achievement of *TOS* as a work of science fiction is that it shares a great deal with each of these two films, thus spanning the range between the two poles. Partly, of course, *TOS* can show this versatility because it spans roughly sixty-five hours of programming, which obviously gives it the potential to cover more ground than a single two-hour movie. Nevertheless, no other science fiction series had been able to manage this dual achievement. An examination of the ways in which *TOS* resonates with each of these contemporary films helps to demonstrate just what was so special about the series and why it would ultimately have such amazing staying power.

In *Planet of the Apes*, a spaceship from earth lands on an alien planet where the normal social evolution has been seriously disrupted. Then we find that the planet is earth and that the ship has inadvertently landed in the future. The film is, then, ultimately pessimistic, but again in a way that can also be found in *TOS*. For example, in the second-season episode "The Omega Glory," an obvious Cold War allegory (that can also be read as a cautionary tale about Vietnam), Kirk, Spock, and McCoy visit planet Omega IV, which is riven by a Manichean conflict between the seemingly civilized "Asiatic" Kohms and the seemingly savage Caucasian Yangs. Things are not necessarily quite what they seem, however, as it gradually becomes clear that the Yangs are fighting against a Kohm oppression that appears to have been going on for centuries, after a victory of the ancestors of the Kohms over the ancestors of the Yangs in some sort of cataclysmic conflict (possibly biological, rather than nuclear) hundreds of years earlier. Meanwhile, the visitors from the *Enterprise* gradually uncover one tantalizing clue after another, as it eventually becomes clear that the "Kohms" are descended from "Communists" and the "Yangs" from "Yankees." Moreover, it becomes clear that the losing Yankees were literally bombed into the stone age in the earlier conflict, which apparently produced both the contagion that soon affects Kirk, Spock, and McCoy and the antibodies that confer immunity to it. In fact, the inhabitants of Omega IV seem immune to all disease as a further side effect of the war. To add to the seemingly positive effects of the war, the inhabitants of Omega IV now have astonishingly long lives as a combined result of the lack of disease and natural selection, only the hardiest of the species having survived the war. At least one of the locals, for example, is now more than one thousand earth years old, which would mean that the war was more than one thousand years ago as well, perhaps some time in earth's thirteenth century, or even earlier.

All of these confusing details, meanwhile, are combined with an emerging narrative in which it gradually becomes clear that the Yang culture seems to be based on cliché versions of certain Native American cultures. They might be savages, but they are noble ones. On the other hand, they also, somewhat contrarily, seem to be Christians, getting many of their "holy words" from a giant Bible. But their holiest of holies are relics of American democracy, including a tattered stars-and-stripes and the pledge of allegiance to that flag. Their most holy artifact, though, is a copy of the U.S. Constitution, whose words seem a baffling mystery to them. (Even though they speak perfectly good English—with slight Native American intonations—they are apparently not very good at reading.) Luckily, after delivering an excessively impassioned reading of the Preamble, Kirk explains it all to them—including a generous proviso that freedom and democracy must extend to everyone, even the hated Kohms (who have, however, by this time conveniently disappeared from the episode). His speech thus presumably sets the Yang civilization back on its proper course toward truth, justice, and the American Way—and this in an episode in which Kirk had assured us he takes seriously the demands of the Prime Directive, which require that any Starfleet captain would rather give his life and the lives of his crew than interfere in the evolution of another culture.

There is no explanation of how all of this might have happened, but it would seem to require a vision of Americanism as so fundamentally righteous that it can emerge in exactly the same form, with the same symbols and documents, at different times and at different places around the galaxy. Either that, or travelers from Omega IV, perhaps fleeing their own planet's apocalypse, traveled to earth and there became the founders of American democracy. Either reading, of course, is complicated by the existence of that Bible, which complicates the time frame of it all, while coming dangerously close to suggesting that Christianity is a crucial part of American democracy. Then again, this is not an episode that even tries to make sense, eschewing logic in favor of simply presenting a constellation of allegorical imagery that seems largely designed to constitute a cautionary tale about the dangers posed to the American way of life by the Cold War arms race or by the potential disaster of turning that war hot, as in Vietnam (especially when one's foes are dangerous "Asiatics" with a proclivity for Oriental despotism).

This episode, incidentally, was first broadcast on March 1, 1968, three weeks after the premiere of the original film version of *Planet of the Apes*, in which the Statue of Liberty plays somewhat the same role as the symbols of American democracy in "The Omega Glory"—a reminder of past glory lost through folly. Moreover, the film also features a human society bombed into primitivity (the humans on the ape planet resemble the Yangs of the *TOS* episode quite strikingly, even wearing almost the same clothing), then displaced as their planet's rulers by another race. The difference, of course, is that *Planet of the Apes* at least attempts to provide a rationale for its postapocalyptic scenario, making the implications of its anti-war allegory more clear.

Meanwhile, even though nuclear apocalypse is the presumed central topic of *Planet of the Apes*, the film might be even more effective as an anti-racist allegory. Many critics, for example, have pointed to the ways in which the depiction of relations between apes and humans in this film and its sequels can be read as an allegorization of interracial relations in our own world, especially in the United States. Thus, Eric Greene has argued that "the makers of the *Apes* films created fictional spaces whose social tensions resembled those then dominating the United States. They inserted characters into those spaces whose ideologies, passions, and fears duplicated the ideologies, passions, and fears of generations of Americans. And they placed those characters in conflicts that replicated crucial conflicts from the United States; past and present."[7]

In the case of the *TOS* episode, however, lack of attention to the implications of all the motifs in this overstuffed episode leads not only to confusion but to some potentially unfortunate interpretations. For example, the focus on the Prime Directive in this episode seems to suggest that interference in the evolution of "underdeveloped" cultures by more advanced ones is generally wrong, but okay if that interference steers the less developed country toward Americanism, here depicted as the true, logical, and proper goal of all societies. The racial allegory in "The Omega Glory" is similarly problematic. After an initial intriguing reversal in which the white people of Omega IV are presented as a savage horde and the yellow people as civilized, the roles are quickly flipped, making the white people the aggrieved good guys, who would be more civilized but for the ravages wrought upon them by their yellow enemies. And, of course, there is also the fact that the episode does little (at least in its representation of life on Omega IV) to challenge the notion that it is natural to divide populations along racial lines, categorizing them as either yellow or white. One could, though, see it as heartening that Sulu is left in command of the *Enterprise* while Kirk, Spock, and McCoy are away, suggesting that, in the more advanced world of the Federation, such divisions have, in fact, been overcome.[8]

If episodes such as "The Omega Glory" resonate with *Planet of the Apes* in obvious ways, the connection between *TOS* and *2001* is less clear. It has been widely argued that *Forbidden Planet* was a clear predecessor to *Star Trek*, while it has also been noted that Gene Roddenberry's favorite SF film was *The Day the Earth Stood Still*.[9] In short, the two most respected SF films that had appeared prior to *TOS* are both important predecessors. It should thus probably come as no surprise that *TOS* would have a great deal in common with *2001*, despite the fact that the film resides in artistic territory that is a far cry from that generally associated with television. In particular, it is highly significant that, when *Star Trek* returned in 1979 with *TMP*, it was *2001* that clearly served as a model, suggesting that Gene Roddenberry's vision had always been congruent with that of *2001* and that the obvious differences between *2001* and *TOS* were matters of budget, rather than of vision.

One might summarize the texture of *TMP* by saying that it was an attempt to revive the *Star Trek* franchise by taking its basic scenario, then using the breakthroughs in filmmaking technology of *Star Wars* to produce a film of the aesthetic caliber of *2001*. And this attempt to somehow simultaneously be *Star Trek*, *Star Wars*, and *2001* was not as preposterous as it might sound. After all, *Star Trek* had always been endowed with some of the same rollicking pulpy SF sensibility as that which is so central to *Star Wars*, while *TOS* (despite the sometimes low aesthetic standards of its visuals) had some of the same thematic seriousness of intent as that which drives *2001*.

STAR TREK AND WRITTEN SCIENCE FICTION: THE GOLDEN AGE, THE NEW WAVE, AND ASTROFUTURISM

Of course, this seriousness of purpose is most often found in written science fiction, something with which *Star Trek* also has a great deal in common. Manu Saadia argues that *TOS* is distinguished from *TNG* largely by the fact that the former is heavily influenced (if in an oppositional way) by the writing of Heinlein, while the latter mainly shows the influence of Asimov. This summary might be something of a simplification, but it does help to indicate the difference between the two series, while also noting the literariness of both.[10] Saadia also presents a useful and more detailed account of the points of contact between Heinlein (from his 1948 juvenile novel *Space Cadet* through the 1959 novel *Starship Troopers*) and *TOS*, though he ultimately concludes that *TOS* can be seen as a critique of Heinlein's militaristic vision. In short, for Saadia, *TOS* seems to have been designed to appeal to the same audience as Heinlein's fiction but to deliver an opposing message:

> *The Original Series'* real five-year mission was to denounce the prejudices and controversies of the real world: racism, bigotry, mutually assured destruction, the Vietnam War. It was a critique of the Cold War and thus it was also, necessarily, a critique of Cold War science fiction—that is, above all a critique of Robert Heinlein.[11]

Of course, there is a lot of Asimov in *TOS* as well, and Asimov's ultimate enthusiasm for *Star Trek* should come as no surprise given the important role that the franchise would come to play in the development of American science fiction, a cultural phenomenon of which Asimov himself was an important founding figure, perhaps rivaled only by Heinlein. But then *Star Trek*, from the very beginning, was far more embedded in the landscape of written science fiction than were its contemporaries in science fiction television. It might have had its occasional scientific inaccuracies, it might have employed some unlikely technologies, and it might have often veered into romance or even soap opera—but then so did the science fiction of the pulp magazines of the 1930s, which were the true birthplace of American science fiction as a distinct and identifiable genre. More importantly, *Star Trek* sought to move beyond those pulp roots to produce more literary and more scientifically plausible stories, just as the pulps themselves had already done by the time *TOS* aired. In particular, Roddenberry always understood the crucial importance of good writing to the success of his series, while some of his contemporaries in television SF seemed to regard good writing as unnecessary as long as their programs had enough strange creatures or scenarios posing extreme threats to their protagonists on a weekly basis. Indeed, Roddenberry employed some of America's best science fiction novelists and story writers as scriptwriters for *TOS*. Established authors such as Theodore

Sturgeon ("Shore Leave" and "Amok Time"), Harlan Ellison ("The City on the Edge of Forever"), and Richard Matheson ("The Enemy Within") produced scripts for *TOS*, as did rising authors such as Norman Spinrad ("The Doomsday Machine") and David Gerrold ("The Trouble with Tribbles"). Another well-known SF writer, Philip José Farmer, wrote two unmade scripts for *TOS*, as well as advising Roddenberry on the original development of the series.

It is clear that many of the ideas for *Star Trek* were heavily influenced by the science fiction literature that had been published from the early days of the pulps in the 1930s through the rise of the SF novel in the 1950s—science fiction's so-called Golden Age. The first-season episode "Arena" (figure 2.1) was even officially credited as an adaptation of a 1944 story of the same title by Fredric Brown, a leading Golden Age writer of SF short stories. But, more than such direct and explicit connections, *TOS* shared a great deal with Golden Age SF in terms of its general concerns. In particular, the optimistic view of the future for which *TOS* is so well known could often be found in early Golden Age science fiction, which also typically saw technological progress as the key to solving humanity's important social and political problems. Moreover, Golden Age SF was dominated by the genre of the space opera, as any number of authors envisioned far-flung galactic adventures enabled by the invention of spacecraft capable of rapid interstellar travel.

Another Golden Age SF writer whose work has been widely cited as an inspiration for *Star Trek* is A. E. van Vogt, especially the 1950 novel *The Voyage of the Space Beagle*, which is mostly composed of interlinked stories that had previously been published separately in the pulps. In van Vogt's novel, a huge interstellar ship with a semi-military crew travels about space under threat from a deadly space creature—a brief summary that also might describe any number of episodes of *Star Trek*. In addition, with Roddenberry's encouragement, van Vogt pitched numerous story ideas for *TOS*, though none of his suggestions were ever actually made into episodes.

Probably the best-known works of Golden Age science fiction that serve as obvious forerunners of *Star Trek* were the volumes of Asimov's *Foundation* trilogy, comprising *Foundation* (1951), *Foundation and Empire* (1952), and *Second Foundation* (1953). These novels, compiled with slight emendations from stories published in the 1940s, remain among the most important and influential works of science fiction literature to this

Figure 2.1.   Kirk battles the Gorn in "Arena." NBC / Photofest © NBC

day, and their vision of a far-flung galactic empire is a clear forerunner of the United Federation of Planets envisioned by Gene Roddenberry. Perhaps it is little wonder, then, that Asimov and Roddenberry would establish a relationship or that Asimov would become a fan of *TOS*.

By the 1960s, however, many science fiction writers felt that the pulp science fiction of the Golden Age was becoming outdated, driven by simplistic visions that were increasingly consigning science fiction to a cultural ghetto inhabited mostly by adolescent fanboys. In an attempt to give science fiction greater cultural (and political) relevance, numerous writers of the 1960s sought to produce more complex and mature works that were scientifically accurate, stylistically sophisticated, and socially and politically engaged. This collective effort, generally referred to as science fiction's "New Wave," produced important advances in science fiction writing but was relatively unsuccessful at attracting a larger readership for that writing. Many science fiction writers were thus understandably excited about the wave of science fiction television programming that came along in the late 1960s—and especially about the first *Star Trek*, which was clearly the new TV series that had the most in common with written science fiction.

One of the central statements of the New Wave vision was Ellison's 1967 anthology *Dangerous Visions*, which included a foreword written by Asimov. That year also saw the airing of the Ellison-scripted "The City on the Edge of Forever," widely acknowledged as one of the greatest episodes of *TOS*. But Ellison and Roddenberry reportedly had significant disagreements over the making of this episode, and Ellison's relationship with the *Trek* franchise remained problematic from that point onward. For example, as opposed to the writers who enthusiastically viewed *Star Trek* as a potential boon to their own sales, Ellison felt all along that *Star Trek* would do little to increase their readership—and might even decrease it by conscripting that readership for itself and for related works that resembled the older Golden Age space operas more than the stylistically and politically sophisticated works of the New Wave. Later, Ellison declared his prediction to have been vindicated, because "*Star Trek* books and that idiom, that space-opera crap, pushed everything off the bestseller list."[12]

Despite Ellison's skepticism, it is clear that *TOS* had a great deal in common with the contemporary New Wave in science fiction. While *TOS*, with its rubber-suited aliens, Styrofoam rocks, and cardboard set decorations, is famed for its stylistic quaintness, it actually had far higher production values than the science fiction television series that came before it. However, what really aligned *TOS* with New Wave science fiction was its thematic maturity and its willingness, despite the limitations placed on it by network management, to tackle difficult and complex issues of the kind typically associated with the New Wave.

TOS, unlike many of the space operas of the Golden Age, was able to use its basic space opera format not as a way to create escapist adventures and thus evade engagement with controversial issues, but as a way of engaging those issues via the strategy referred to by Suvin as cognitive estrangement. The extensive exploration of issues such as racism, colonialism, and the Cold War (discussed at length in the next chapter) was in fact very much in line with the political relevance sought by the writers of the New Wave. Meanwhile, both *TOS* and the New Wave were able to get away with political commentary that would be more difficult in works of mainstream culture, partly because their science fictional settings made their commentaries seem less engaged with current issues than they really were and partly because science fiction simply was not taken all that seriously.

In short, science fiction potentially has the ability to explore certain themes in ways that would never be possible in more "respectable" venues. As SF pioneer Frederik Pohl has put it, science fiction writers are able to "say things in hint and metaphor that the writer dares not say in the clear." Thus, argues Pohl, in the repressive days of the 1950s, science fiction might well have been "the only truly free speech left in America" because the genre could get away with political statements that other forms could not.[13] As the political atmosphere in the United States and elsewhere became more progressive in the 1960s, the writers of the New Wave were able to produce political commentary in a more overt way, while *Star Trek* was able to bring political commentary (if still in an oblique way) to the ultimate mainstream American cultural platform, network television.

For example, one of the most important individual works of the New Wave is the 1969 novel *Bug Jack Barron* (written by Norman Spinrad), a sophisticated political satire that deals with, among other things, the ability of the media to manipulate public opinion (for better or worse) in the age of electronic communication. Such manipulation, of course, is a key concern of modern social and cultural criticism, as well as modern political satire, all of which have focused on strategies such as the "bread and circuses" approach of gaining public approval through media-enabled entertainment, distraction, and superficial appeasement of a gullible public. Such strategies have been prominently portrayed in science fiction at least since Aldous Huxley's *Brave New World* (1932) and have gained new prominence in recent works such as Suzanne Collins's *The Hunger Games* trilogy (2008–2010) and the films based on it.

Spinrad's own "The Doomsday Machine" is a good example of political satire (this time targeting the Cold War arms race) in *TOS*. But "bread and circuses" strategies are also satirized in *TOS*, particularly in the episode that is actually entitled "Bread and Circuses," written by *TOS* mainstays Gene Roddenberry and Gene L. Coon. Here, Kirk, Spock, and McCoy visit a planet that seems remarkably similar to twentieth-century earth, except that the Roman Empire has survived until that time, with much of its culture intact, only updated. Slavery still exists, for example, but slaves have now been granted medical and retirement benefits in order to quell their nasty tendency to rebel—much as the modern social safety net was invented in Europe and America at the beginning of the twentieth century on earth as a way of warding off the perceived threat of a proletarian revolution. Gladiatorial contests are still a major form of entertainment, but the contests are now broadcast on television—just as televised violence is a major form of entertainment in our own world.

The Roman Empire motif—repeating a problematic tendency for *TOS* to see earth history virtually duplicated in various places around the galaxy—makes "Bread and Circuses" a sort of alternative history narrative, again illustrating the ability of *TOS* to participate in a wide range of science fiction subgenres. Meanwhile, the televised gladiatorial contests anticipate the sort of science fictional media satire that would later be popularized in such films as *The Running Man* (1987) and, of course, in the whole *Hunger Games* franchise. Unfortunately, the satirical commentary on the manipulation of populations via the twin strategies of bread and circuses (read "social safety nets" and "the Culture Industry") becomes garbled at the end of the episode. After a long discussion in which Spock points out that, whatever its drawbacks, the Roman system on this planet has helped it to avoid the internecine world wars of twentieth-century earth, both Kirk and (especially) Uhura become enthralled by the notion that Christianity might arise on this planet and bring down the Roman Empire, ushering in a Golden Age of peace and love, replicating earth history. In short, they seem to have forgotten earth history altogether, even though Spock has just reminded them of it. One can only speculate, of course, that this ending was a sort of trade-off, a sop to audiences and sponsors who might have otherwise been turned off by the satirical potential of the rest of the episode, thus allowing that satire to be included in the first place.

The ending of "Bread and Circuses" is thus optimistic, if in rather inauthentic way, while the ending of *Bug Jack Barron* is also optimistic, despite a certain cynicism that informs most of the book. But the New Wave was often pessimistic. The most important locus of optimism in the science fiction of the 1960s was the movement identified by Kilgore as astrofuturism. For Kilgore, astrofuturism is a specific movement within American science fiction that begins in its modern form with the inspiration provided by the space race in the 1950s, but has roots going back into the nineteenth century having to do with older expansionist tendencies to see America as a nation with a special destiny.

Kilgore convincingly argues that astrofuturism is an important and wide-ranging phenomenon within American science fiction. As a whole, he notes,

> astrofuturism forecasts an escape from terrestrial history. Its roots lie in the nineteenth-century Euro-American preoccupation with imperial expansion and utopian speculation, which it recasts in the elsewhere and else*when* of outer space. Astrofuturism imagines the good or perfect society not simply spatially but in what might be called, to use Einstein's term, "spacetime."[14]

In particular, Kilgore notes the close parallel between the imaginary role played by space as a frontier and the same role played by the American West. And, as I have elsewhere noted, *Star Trek* is centrally informed by this same parallel.[15] It is little wonder, then, that Kilgore himself includes *Star Trek* within his discussion of astrofuturism.

Importantly, Kilgore argues that astrofuturism is also ideologically variable. He emphasizes that it can be quite conservative, as when the work of novelist Jerry Pournelle endorses neocolonial American dominance, or quite progressive, as when the work of novelists such as Kim Stanley Robinson or Vonda McIntyre (herself a leading producer of *Star Trek* novels) produce leftist visions of liberation through expansion into space.[16] And Kilgore notes that this range of ideological possibilities can be found within *Star Trek* itself:

> Grounded in popular fictions of Anglo-American expansion and dominance, *Star Trek* made room in that tradition for liberal political hopes. Within the context of the cold war space race, *Star Trek* created a strategic and popular fantasy of pluralism contained by a meritocratic disciplinary order. In so doing, the series responded to the civil rights movement and the counterculture while maintaining a future that salvaged national institutions and priorities.[17]

Unfortunately, just as the utopian political energies of the 1960s were ultimately smashed on the rocks of a cultural backlash that led to the Nixon presidency, so too did the New Wave fail to establish a truly lasting revolution in science fiction writing. In the same way, *TOS* failed so completely to establish a beachhead in American network television that science fiction virtually disappeared from the broadcast networks until *Star Trek* itself became its first truly important successor with the debut of *TNG* in 1987. Nevertheless, *Star Trek*—through the appearance of several films, through general fan activity, and through the popularity of *TOS* in syndication—continued to exercise an important influence on American science fiction even during the interim period between 1969 and 1987. And it has become an even more important part of the science fiction world since it returned to television with *TNG*.

STAR TREK AND AMERICAN SCIENCE FICTION AFTER THE 1960S

Most of the decade of the 1970s was not a particularly distinguished period for American science fiction. The energies of the New Wave were beginning to fade; SF film had retreated, in the first half of the decade, into mostly pessimistic (and relatively minor) dystopian works; and the genre had been banished from the broadcast networks. *TOS* in syndication was probably the most important manifestation of 1970s science fiction until the appearance of *Star Wars* in 1977 ushered in a ten-year period that was probably the richest in SF film history. Several classic SF films appeared in this period, including Steven Spielberg's *Close Encounters of the Third Kind* (1977) and Ridley Scott's *Blade Runner* (1982). Perhaps more importantly, this period saw the rise of several powerhouse SF film franchises, as when *Star Wars* itself was quickly followed by *The Empire Strikes Back* (1980) and *The Return of the Jedi* (1983), launching a franchise that is still going strong today. Scott's *Alien* (1979) and James Cameron's *The Terminator* (1984) also grew into important long-running franchises. *TMP* and the *Star Trek* films that followed participated in this phenomenon as well, placing *Star Trek* very much at the center of developments in SF film well into the twenty-first century.

The next important development in the evolution of written SF in the United States involved the rise of "cyberpunk" science fiction in the mid-1980s (William Gibson's 1984 novel *Neuromancer* is generally seen as the text that solidified cyberpunk as an identifiable movement), propelled both by contemporary innovations in computer technology and by an increasing social skepticism that defined the popular consciousness of Reagan-era America. Cyberpunk science fiction is driven by a shared vision of the near future in which computer technology has advanced dramatically, producing a variety of cybernetic implants and enhance-ments to the human body, as well as creating powerful artificial intelli-gences and virtual reality worlds in which a substantial amount of the action takes place. Importantly, however, these technological advances are not in general accompanied by social advances, and cyberpunk SF is informed by a dystopian vision of the future in which technology, if anything, has made social and economic conditions worse rather than better.[18]

The darkness of cyberpunk would seem to be a far cry from the famed utopianism of *Star Trek*, and it is certainly the case that *TNG* can be seen partly as a reaction against the cynicism of both cyberpunk and Reagan-ism. On the other hand, as will be discussed in chapter 4, prior to *TNG*, *Star Trek* tended to take a rather dim view of the promise of computers. For example, rule by computers, as in "The Return of the Archons" or "The Apple," is depicted as oppressive and dehumanizing. And, in "The Ultimate Computer," Starfleet experiments with turning control of the *Enterprise* over to an artificially intelligent computer—with nearly disas-trous results. *TOS* in general, moreover, seems to have been rather bad at anticipating future advances in computer technology—in many ways our twenty-first-century digital technologies go well beyond the twenty-third-century technologies of *TOS*. *TMP* also features an artificial intelligence, but it would not be until *TNG*, with the introduction of characters such as the android Mr. Data and the vision-enhanced Geordi, as well as motifs such as the virtual-reality holodeck, that *Star Trek* would fully begin to explore this territory. These technologies also have their problems—and can sometimes be quite dangerous—but in general, with the advent of *TNG*, *Star Trek* becomes an important counter to the dystopian vision of cyberpunk, going well beyond *TOS* in including computers and other electronic devices in its utopian view of the future.

During the thirty years since the premiere of *TNG* in 1987, *Star Trek* has remained an important part of the American science fiction land-scape, with only a brief gap between 2005 and 2009 marking a period when *Star Trek* was not on first-run television or in theatrical-release films. And *Star Trek* novels, comics, and fan fictions remained in produc-tion even during that gap. And, a whole generation of American science fiction writers has been inspired by *Star Trek*.[19] Perhaps the most visible recent example of the influence of *Star Trek* on other works of science fiction can be found in *The Orville*, a television series that premiered on the Fox network in the fall of 2017. *The Orville* was created by Seth MacFarlane, who also stars as Ed Mercer, the captain of the medium-sized starship that gives the series its title. MacFarlane is known primarily for the crude humor of his other creations (most notably the animated television series *Family Guy*), and such humor is certainly prominent in *The Orville*. But what is even more prominent is the influence of *Star Trek*, and the relatively optimistic vision of the twenty-fifth century as portrayed in the series is far more in line with the original vision of Roddenberry's *Star Trek* than are the darker and more violent scenarios of *Star Trek: Discovery* (which premiered just weeks after *The Orville*) or the recent J. J. Abrams films. *The Orville* might be a sometimes silly postmodern pastiche of *Star Trek*, but it's definitely Trekkier than any of its contemporaries, even those that bear the *Star Trek* brand name.[20]

Running against the grain of visually and thematically dark science fiction in contemporary American science fiction, the *Orville* itself features clean, sleek, brightly lit interiors that house a variety of technological marvels as well as an extremely diverse multispecies cast. The presence of a white male captain seems almost like a throwback these days, and MacFarlane's Mercer might indeed well be the weakest element of the series, though he does show some promise. In any case, the series features a genuine ensemble cast that is not dominated by the captain as much as the actual *Trek* series that came before it. The interplay between Mercer and his first officer, Commander Kelly Grayson (Adrianne Palicki), who also happens to be his ex-wife (after a bitter divorce), is a bit distracting in the early episodes but seems less so as the series proceeds. Grayson, in particular, has great promise as a character. Some members of the crew seem directly modeled on iconic *Star Trek* characters, as when the science officer Isaac (a "Kaylon," which is essentially an android—from a planet of androids) is strikingly reminiscent of *TNG*'s Data, down to an almost uncanny resemblance between the voice and vocal mannerisms of Isaac (provided by Mark Jackson) and that of Brent Spiner's Data. Similarly, Peter Macon's Lt. Commander Bortus, a member of the large powerful species known as Moclans, is quite clearly modeled on *TNG*'s Worf in many ways.

Other important crew members do not necessarily map well onto individual *Trek* characters but are very much in the spirit of *Trek*. The ship's extremely accomplished human doctor, Claire Finn (Penny Johnson Jerald), does not really resemble, say, Beverly Crusher all that directly, but she provides a voice of sanity and a steady moral compass.[21] She is also a single parent—and she and her two sons (who accompany her on the *Orville*) figure particularly prominently in the episode "Into the Fold" (November 2, 2017). Human helmsman Lt. Gordon Malloy (Scott Grimes) and human navigator Lt. John LaMarr (J. Lee) vaguely play the roles of Sulu and Chekov; however, though highly competent at their jobs, they seem to function primarily as an inserted comedy team—though both have special talents that make them valuable crew members. Finally, innocent young Lt. Alara Kitan (Halston Sage) is a member of the Xelayan race and thus gifted with superhuman strength—well beyond even that of Bortus. She vaguely recalls both *VOY*'s B'Elanna Torres (down to the forehead ridges) and *DS9*'s Kira Nerys, but her specific position as chief of security and her vast strength set her apart from any specific predecessor.

In its early episodes, *The Orville* struggles (or perhaps refuses) to find an identity. The special effects involve an odd combination of elegance and cheesiness, mirroring the series' basic combination of silliness and seriousness that can at times be a bit awkward. But the best *Star Trek* has always had a lighthearted side (aligned with the fundamental optimism of its outlook) and has never taken itself entirely seriously, something that *DSC* seems to have forgotten. *The Orville* recaptures the fun side of *Star Trek*, while at the same time maintaining the ability to address serious issues in a serious manner. For example, the third episode, "About a Girl" (September 21, 2017, directed by *Star Trek* alum Brannon Braga), centers on a surprisingly nuanced treatment of the crisis that occurs when Bortus and his mate, whose species is normally all male, give birth to a baby girl. The relationship between the two ultramasculine Moclans is played for considerable humor, but the plight of the infant is treated with the utmost seriousness. The mate wants to have the infant undergo transgender surgery to become male because he is convinced that a female Moclan will be a despised outcast, unable to have a decent life. But Bortus disagrees, having become convinced that it is not possible to foresee the consequences of the infant's gender. This disagreement leads to a classic Trekkian courtroom battle in which Grayson serves as Bortus's attorney, mounting a spirited but ultimately unsuccessful argument that the baby should be left alone until she is old enough to make her own decision in the matter.

The fourth episode, "If the Stars Should Appear," takes its title from a quote from Ralph Waldo Emerson, recalling the fondness of *Star Trek* for literary episode titles. And it would be a classic *Trek* episode (somewhat in the mold of "For the World Is Hollow and I Have Touched the Sky"), as the *Orville* encounters a huge ship drifting through space, in danger of being sucked into a star. Inside, they discover a civilization that has forgotten that it resides inside a spaceship and is governed by a religious dictatorship that proclaims their enclosed world to be the entire universe. Mercer and his crew succeed not only in repairing the ship's engines so that it can evade the star but also in revealing to its people the true nature of their world. In this case, then, *The Orville* for once looks back more to *TOS* than to *TNG*, recalling the tendency of Kirk to ignore the Prime Directive and to intervene in societies that have gone wrong—though in this case the intervention seems to be especially well justified. Meanwhile, the depiction of the episode's religious dictatorship (which is able to dominate and manipulate a populace that has forgotten where it came from) has obvious allegorical resonances for the contemporary American political scene.

In addition to Braga, a number of former *Trek* staffers have been involved in the making of *The Orville*—including Jonathan Frakes and Robert Duncan McNeill, who directed first-season episodes, and former *Trek* writers David A. Goodman and André Bormanis, who wrote or co-wrote first-season episodes. Much of the initial critical reaction to *The Orville* was negative, though some were quite enthusiastic in their reaction, and the series was quickly renewed for a second season. It remains to be seen what the future will hold for this series, but I am among those who find *The Orville* a refreshing combination of innovation and homage that holds considerable promise—which means that the *Trek* influence on science fiction promises to go on as well.

3

STAR TREK AND AMERICAN POLITICAL HISTORY

The original *Star Trek* series, as H. Bruce Franklin has argued, was "conceived and broadcast during one of the most profound crises in American history, a crisis from which we have yet to escape."[1] The crisis to which Franklin refers concerns the political turmoil of the late 1960s, a turmoil that he convincingly declares to have centered primarily on the war in Vietnam and on the deep-seated conflicts that Vietnam stirred among the American population. *TOS* reflected the political climate of the 1960s in its hope for a better future and in its unequivocal denunciation of racism, as well as in its (admittedly more complex) critical engagement with both the Cold War and the war in Vietnam.[2] To an extent, *TOS* also reflected changing gender roles in American society during the 1960s, though it was perhaps weaker in that area than in its criticism of racism, colonialism, and militarism. Following this precedent, subsequent entries in the *Star Trek* franchise tracked the changing face of American society and American politics over the decades.

In addition to its engagement with specific political issues, the basic vision that has always underwritten the *Star Trek* franchise is a historical one: It anticipates radical historical changes that will bring about a better future in which the problems vexing a very divided America in the 1960s will have been solved, bringing Americans (and the world) toward a lasting period of unprecedented peace and prosperity. Of course, *Star Trek* has no real explanation for how this change might occur, and the later hint (made especially clear in the film *First Contact*) that earth might have solved its problems largely due to help from the Vulcans is clearly problematic, suggesting that, rather than making their own histories, humans can succeed only if a savior comes to them from on high.

Further, as Michael Lewis points out, *TOS* episodes such as "Patterns of Force" and "A Piece of the Action" seem to embody simplistic visions of how historical change occurs—again through employing the model of alien intervention (this time with the Federation as the aliens) to suggest that one slight such intervention can change the entire course of a planet's history. "A Piece of the Action" is particularly problematic in this regard, with an entire planetary culture having changed to mimic the gangsters of Prohibition-era Chicago thanks to a book on that topic having been inadvertently left behind by visitors from earth. There are all kinds of ways in which this episode is problematic (including the fact that the culture of planet Sigma Iotia II does not actually resemble that of Prohibition-era Chicago all that closely in reality). It is also problematic that this episode, which seems designed to explain why the Prime Directive not to interfere in less advanced cultures is so important, ends as Kirk solves the problem by interfering even more. But of course the episode is not meant to be realistic and is not meant to imply that history really works this way, though it would help if *Star Trek* somewhere indicated a more nuanced vision of how historical change occurs.

TOS, VIETNAM, AND THE COLD WAR

Star Trek was born in 1964, as Gene Roddenberry was putting together his original pilot for the series—and as President Lyndon Johnson and his administration were putting together their plans to ramp up U.S. involvement in the war in Vietnam. *TOS* then made its way onto the air and through its three-season run precisely during the years when Vietnam first became a major preoccupation of American society and then quickly moved into controversy on its way to being the most unpopular war effort in American history. The engagement of *TOS* with Vietnam closely tracked changing American attitudes toward the war during the period 1966–1969, beginning with the grudging acceptance that the war, however unpleasant, was a necessary involvement in global politics, but quickly moving to the position that the war was not only immoral, but potentially destructive to the United States as a nation.

Franklin has nicely traced the changing attitude of *Star Trek* to the Vietnam War through the four episodes that he sees as being primarily *about* that war and its impact on American society. The first of these is the classic "The City on the Edge of Forever," one of the most compelling episodes of the entire *Trek* oeuvre, even if it is informed by some problematic politics. Here, Kirk and Spock travel to 1930 New York, where they must ensure the death of peace activist Edith Keeler before she can build a movement that will delay the U.S. entry into World War II, causing the Nazis to be able to hold on long enough to develop nuclear weapons and subsequently win the war, in the meantime destroying the golden future that is the world of *Star Trek*. Given the troubles that *Star Trek* sometimes envisions earth going through from the 1990s until the Vulcan intervention, it is not clear that a Nazi victory in World War II would have made much difference in the long run. More importantly, though, the episode can clearly be read as a rejection of the contemporary anti-war movement, warning those who were mobilizing against the war in Vietnam that their efforts might have cataclysmic results by causing the United States to withdraw prematurely and thus allowing communism to spread unabated.[3]

In "A Private Little War" (broadcast on February 2, 1968, nearly a year after "The City on the Edge of Forever"), *TOS*, with Kirk as its spokesman (but now with McCoy presenting a dissenting view), still comes down on the side of official U.S. policy in Vietnam. Here, Kirk opts to intervene in a planetary conflict by supplying weapons to some primitive tribesmen so that they can defend themselves against the incursions of their rivals, who have been supplied with weapons by the Klingons. The episode's view of what happens on planet Neural thus matches quite closely the official U.S. line on what was going on in Vietnam at the time, though McCoy's horror at Kirk's decision (and Kirk's own troubled reluctance to become an arms supplier, despite the Prime Directive) suggests a far more ambivalent stance toward Vietnam than one might have gathered from "The City on the Edge of Forever."

As Franklin notes, "A Private Little War," though made some time earlier, was initially broadcast only days after the single event that perhaps swung American public opinion against the war more than any other. At the time, official American propaganda claimed victory to be near for America and her South Vietnamese allies, while claiming that the North Vietnamese and the Viet Cong were demoralized and in a state of confusion and near collapse. Then, on January 30, 1968, in the so-called Tet Offensive,[4] the anti-American forces in Vietnam launched a massive, well-coordinated strike in which all major American bases and American-dominated cities were attacked simultaneously, demonstrating resources, resolve, and coordination well ahead of those that a now shocked American public had been led to believe to be possible.

After the Tet Offensive, American public opinion swung dramatically against the war, and *Star Trek* followed suit. By the time "The Omega Glory" aired a mere four weeks later, *Star Trek* was warning not that the peace effort might lead to a communist victory but that the war effort might lead to an American defeat. According to Franklin, this episode "implies that the war in Southeast Asia, which no longer held any promise of victory or even a suggestion of an end, could evolve into an interminable, mutually destructive conflict."[5]

For Franklin, the evolution of the *Trek* attitude toward the war in Vietnam is completed by January 10, 1969, with the broadcast of "Let That Be Your Last Battlefield." Though this episode is more conventionally read as a satire intended to show the foolishness and destructiveness of racism, Franklin makes a compelling case that the planetary annihilation figured in the episode as the result of racism can also be read as a cautionary tale about the potential destructive effect of the Vietnam War. For Franklin, this episode is ultimately a plea for an end to the war as a necessary event before history could possibly begin to move toward the golden future envisioned by *Star Trek* as a whole.[6]

The American intervention in Vietnam was, of course, a complex event that had to do with a number of historical phenomena, including colonialism and racism. But the larger historical event of which Vietnam was most obviously a part was the Cold War, which had passed its peak level of hysteria by the time *TOS* was broadcast but which still had a very big presence in the American psyche. After all, the American intervention in Vietnam was always officially justified as an attempt to prevent the spread of communism, with a consideration of the colonialist background of the conflict being largely omitted from official accounts.

TOS, in fact, addresses the general Cold War far more directly than the Vietnam War in particular. Indeed, virtually all of the episodes that Franklin associates with the war in Vietnam could just as easily be read as referring to the Cold War as a whole. In addition, the series goes out of its way in a number of episodes to refer back to the Cold War setting in which the series was actually produced—usually making sure to point out (from its twenty-third-century perspective) that the U.S.-Soviet opposition was successfully negotiated without ever breaking out into nuclear war. "Assignment: Earth," for example, directly deals with a successful effort to prevent the Cold War from going nuclear. Here, the *Enterprise*, having discovered how to travel backward in time by sling-shotting around the sun, travels back to the 1960s on a mission of "historical research." In particular, the mission is intended to gain a better understanding of how earth managed to survive the "desperate problems" it faced during the Cold War. Once in the past, though, the *Enterprise* crew finds itself embroiled in a complex seriocomic effort by advanced aliens to intervene to prevent the Cold War from breaking out into a hot war. The episode seems a bit confused in terms of just what point it wants to make, and the suggestion that only an intervention from on high saved the earth from destruction during the Cold War is again highly problematic in terms of the apparent attempt to project optimism.

Several episodes draw upon popular Cold War genres for narrative material, with little in the way of overt commentary. "The Trouble with Tribbles," for example, flirts with the Cold War espionage drama but in a lighthearted way. "The *Enterprise* Incident" is much more serious, as Kirk and Spock turn Cold War spies in order to steal a Romulan cloaking device so that the Federation can find a way to circumvent such devices. Again, there is relatively little true anti-war commentary here, though the episode does acknowledge, near the end, that the Romulans will just modify their cloaking devices so that the stolen one will be essentially useless. Spock does then note that military secrets tend to be the most fleeting of all, and the episode suggests, by extension, the folly of the ongoing struggle between the Americans and the Soviets to steal each other's military secrets and gain an advantage in military intelligence.

The gripping first-season episode "Balance of Terror" does little to address the issues that informed the Cold War, but instead simply uses the Cold War context to generate a tense narrative of political and military conflict. The term "balance of terror" was, in fact, often used to describe the stand-off in the Cold War arms race. Here, we learn that, after an earlier conflict, an uneasy peace has been maintained between earth and the Romulans for more than a century. But now a Romulan ship, armed with a new superweapon, has crossed the "neutral zone" between Romulan space and earth-dominated space and begun attacking earth outposts.

This leads to a tense game of cat-and-mouse between the *Enterprise* and the Romulan ship in what is essentially an update of World War II submarine-battle narratives. This is the episode in which we learn that Romulans look a lot like Vulcans and that they and the Vulcans apparently branched apart long ago when the Vulcans decided to pursue a path of logic and peace, while the Romulans remained warlike and aggressive. Indeed, the similarity between the Romulans and Vulcans leads one Lt. Stiles, a bridge officer on the *Enterprise* for this episode, to launch into a racist rant against Mr. Spock. What we do not really sense in this early episode is the way in which the galactic political situation in *TOS* would ultimately evolve into a structure very much resembling that of earth in the 1960s, with the earth-dominated Federation (read America) on one side, the Klingon Empire standing in for the Soviets on the other side, and the Romulans serving as a potentially crucial third force in the manner of the Chinese. The rest of the Alpha Quadrant seems to be composed mostly of super aliens who have no interest in such petty conflicts and less developed planets (i.e., the Third World) where the three major powers compete for influence and resources (especially fuels, such as dilithium crystals, that are crucial to the operation of starships).

A couple of months later, in the episode "A Taste of Armageddon," the *Enterprise* encounters a planetary civilization that has resigned itself to ongoing warfare with a neighboring planet, making that warfare more palatable by playing the battles out as computer simulation. As a result, no property is damaged in these battles, but any individual citizens who are designated as killed in the computer simulation must turn themselves in to "disintegration chambers," where their deaths can be carried out in fact. Kirk, of course, feels that he must intercede, but it is fairly clear that the real point of this narrative is to conduct an allegorical critique of the absurdity of the Cold War arms race. This is the first episode, then, in which *TOS* takes a clear stance against that arms race, "A Balance of Terror" having depicted the Romulans as sufficiently threatening that the militarization of earth's space fleet seems warranted.

I have already noted the way in which the episode "Errand of Mercy" echoes the classic SF film *The Day the Earth Stood Still* in its suggestion that, viewed from the lofty perspective of a superior alien civilization, the Cold War opposition on earth would seem absurd. This notion of the absurdity of the Cold War arms race is, a few months later, made even more effectively in the early second-season episode "The Doomsday Ma-

chine." Here, the *Enterprise* comes upon a large, mysterious object float-
ing in space (as it so often does). In this case, the object turns out to be a
superweapon from another galaxy, one with such destructive power that it
was built primarily as a deterrent and never meant to be used. This echo
of the standard justification for building huge nuclear arsenals during the
Cold War might be a bit heavy-handed—indeed, Kirk even goes so far as
to announce the message directly for anyone who might have missed it. It
is, he says, "a weapon built primarily as a bluff. It was never meant to be
used—so strong it could destroy both sides in the war. Something like the
old H-bomb was supposed to be." Still, the episode is a good one, and the
drama that unfolds as the *Enterprise* tries to stop the weapon from running amok and destroying the galaxy is actually quite compelling.

Meanwhile, the commentary in the episode is taken a step further
when a meddling and mentally unstable Starfleet commodore nearly
undermines the effort to destroy the Doomsday Machine, taking the episode into the territory of the classic 1964 satire *Dr. Strangelove* by suggesting that as long as such weapons exist, there is always the chance that
one unbalanced person in a high position might trigger their use (and a
nuclear holocaust). Then, after it is destroyed by detonating the engines
of another starship inside it, Kirk again restates the message of the episode: "Ironic, isn't it? Way back in the twentieth century, the H-bomb
was the ultimate weapon, their doomsday machine. And we used something like it to destroy another doomsday machine. Probably the first time
such a weapon has been used for constructive purposes."

By the time *Star Trek* went back into television production with the
debut of *TNG* in 1987, its stance against the Cold War was even more
overt. Interestingly, the vision of history presented by *TNG* suggests that
earth was in fact ravaged by a nuclear conflict in the middle of the
twenty-first century, one that nearly destroyed human civilization. Thus,
in the very first episode, Picard and his crew members are placed on trial
by the super-being Q in a squalid courtroom that is described as being
like "something from the mid-twenty-first century. The post-atomic horror." During the trial, Q impersonates a Cold War–era military officer,
suggesting that the *Enterprise* should probably return immediately to
earth to fight "commies." Aghast, Picard responds, "What? That nonsense is centuries behind us!"

This dismissal of Cold War antagonisms as nonsense makes clear that
TNG wants to project a twenty-fourth century world that has moved

beyond such squabbles into an era of universal harmony and peace. Importantly, it has done so by moving beyond both communism and capitalism. Indeed, the future world envisioned in *TNG* seems more socialist than capitalist, the competitive quest for money that drives the latter having long since been dismissed as folly. This stance is not necessarily different from the one taken by *TOS*, but it is much more clear and insistent in its rejection of capitalism, a move that surely would not have been possible during the 1960s but that was much more viable at the end of the 1980s when the Cold War was winding down.

TOS AND THE CIVIL RIGHTS MOVEMENT

If *TOS* seemed to change its attitude toward the 1960s anti-war movement over the course of its initial run, it seemed aligned with the civil rights movement from the very beginning. Perhaps the most often praised aspect of *TOS* is its staffing of the *Enterprise* with a multinational, multiracial, and even multispecies crew. Though headed by a white male captain and featuring white males in other key positions, such as the chief engineer and the chief medical officer, the *Enterprise* does at least feature one Asian and one Russian among its bridge crew. In many ways, however, the most important contributor to the ethnic diversity of the crew was Nichelle Nichols's Uhura, who served in an important position as the ship's chief communications officer, a kind of role in which few viewers had ever seen a black woman. Officially hailing from the "United States of Africa," Uhura was decoded by many viewers as African American and reportedly served as a role model for numerous African American girls who saw the show.[7]

Indeed, while Uhura and (especially) Sulu play relatively secondary roles in *TOS*, one should not underestimate the value to some viewers of being able to see on network television an Asian man and an African American woman being portrayed as strong, competent professionals. As De Witt Douglas Kilgore notes, actors George Takei and Nichelle Nichols became important symbols of "Gene Roddenberry's then unique vision that racial minorities would be part of any American future in space," a vision that was particularly radical for its time "because he was willing to imagine nonwhites as more than second-class citizens in a future America."[8]

STAR TREK AND AMERICAN POLITICAL HISTORY 73

In some ways, however, the most obvious example of diversity in the original *Enterprise* crew was the formidable Mr. Spock, who served both as the science officer and the first officer. As a native of the planet Vulcan, Spock was a walking image of Otherness, perhaps made more (rather than less) alien by the fact that he was half Vulcan and half human, the product of an interspecies marriage. To add to the mix, Spock was played by a Jewish actor and was clearly figured as an intellectual. He, in fact, was constituted of a collection of attributes that seemed almost custom designed to infuriate the most hidebound racists. Executives at NBC were thus very nervous about a potential backlash against the character, especially as they felt that some more conservative or more religious viewers might be horrified by his pointed ears, associating them with the traditional iconography of Satan (see figure 3.1). That Spock would go on to be the most beloved character (and that Leonard Nimoy would go on to be probably the most admired individual involved with the *Trek* franchise) can partly be taken as testament to the fact that Americans might be less racist and xenophobic than they sometimes appear to be—but it might also suggest that *Star Trek* itself made important contributions to helping some Americans overcome the prejudices that otherwise surrounded them. It also suggests, of course, that many *Star Trek* fans have identified with Spock because they themselves felt like outsiders to mainstream American culture.

In any case, the evolving relationship of Spock with his fellow crew members, especially Captain Kirk and Dr. McCoy, is a crucial element of *TOS*. Perhaps the evolving friendship between Kirk and Spock (which might reach its highest point in *The Wrath of Khan*) is the most obvious example of "interracial" solidarity in *TOS*, but in many ways the relationship between McCoy and Spock is even more important. McCoy is a Southerner who might be expected, in the context of 1966, to harbor prejudices against virtually everything Spock represents. And, indeed, at times (the most strident examples probably occur in the first-season episode "The Galileo Seven") McCoy can seem downright racist in his attitude toward Spock—which makes the development of a genuine connection between the two (with each perhaps overcoming initial prejudices) all the more valuable as an anti-racist statement.

Subsequent *Trek* series would take this motif of diversity in the crews even further. In addition, beginning with *TOS*, numerous *Trek* episodes have conveyed specifically anti-racist messages. Many of these essays,

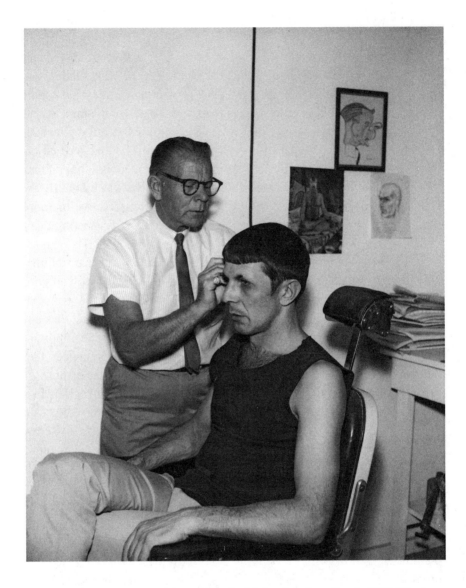

Figure 3.1.   Leonard Nimoy in makeup for his iconic role as Spock. NBC / Photofest © NBC

however, are multiply coded as when "Let That Be Your Last Battlefield," perhaps the most overt anti-racist allegory in all of *TOS*, also comments on the Cold War and the Vietnam War. In this sense, a particularly interesting episode is the third-season entry "Day of the Dove," in which a super alien that feeds on negative emotions tries to stir up animosity between some Klingons and the *Enterprise* so that it can gain sustenance from the result. Nasty (and clearly racist) emotions fly freely as the alien manages to generate bigoted reactions even from the normally placid Mr. Spock, while the *Enterprise* crew turns not just on the Klingons but on each other. This episode can clearly be read as an allegorical critique of warmongers who would promote conflict for their own profit, with an added boost of anti-racist allegory. Indeed, these two themes are nicely intertwined to suggest the way in which racism and war go hand in hand—perhaps with a nod toward the racist underpinnings of the war in Vietnam.

As a work of 1960s American popular culture, *Star Trek* was definitely progressive in its presentation of race. On the other hand, it *was* a work of the 1960s and it did have its limitations, however far ahead of its contemporaries on American network television it might have been. Noting that, despite its efforts to endorse diversity, *TOS* ultimately failed to get beyond a fundamental white-dominated vision of life on the *Enterprise* and a fundamental human-dominated vision of life out in the galaxy. Daniel Bernardi suggests that the limitations in the vision of the original *Star Trek* might partly be due to limitations in the "liberal humanist" worldview that drove the series:

> The paradox of *Star Trek* is that, despite or because of its liberal humanism, it supports a universe where whites are morally, politically, and innately superior, and both colored humans and colored aliens are either servants, threats, or objects of exotic desire. [9]

In my view, the limitations in the anti-racist vision of *TOS* are due more to specific rootedness in a specific time in American history than to a more general limitation in liberal humanism, and I believe that the gradual evolution of *Star Trek* in its representation of race (including such key moves as the inclusion of a Klingon in the *Enterprise* crew and the casting of an African American captain to helm a series) demonstrates the ability of the *Trek* franchise to change over time, keeping up with (and perhaps even contributing to) changes in American society as a whole. From this perspective, it might also be significant that the major step *backward* in the representation of "others" in *Star Trek* seems to have occurred in the portrayal of the Klingons of *DSC* as grotesque, violent, bigoted religious zealots, which almost exactly parallels an ugly (but hopefully temporary) turn taken by American society in the 2010s, a turn marked most spectacularly by the election of Donald Trump to the U.S. presidency in 2016.

The representation of the Klingons in *DSC* is, in fact, largely a collection of "Orientalist" stereotypes of the kind the eminent scholar Edward Said has associated with Western representations of non-Westerners, and especially of Arabs. For Said, Western writers, artists, and even scholars have consistently and for centuries represented Arabs and the Middle East in general via a network of stereotypes designed to portray Arabs as the inferior others of the West, thus leaving the West with a positive vision of its own comparative merits. Said's 1979 book, *Orientalism*, is one of the founding texts of the modern discipline of postcolonial studies and one of the most influential academic books of the past half century. It thus provides a useful optic through which the Orientalism of *Star Trek* can be viewed.

Among other things, this perspective helps us to see how important— and how radical—the depiction of Spock in *TOS* really was. Spock is clearly the Other, but his rationality, virtuousness, dependability, self-control, and consistency are part of an overall representation of the half-Vulcan as far more evolved and civilized than are his human counterparts in the series. His portrayal is, in short, the virtual opposite of Orientalist stereotyping. And he serves, not as a negative image of everything we want to avoid being, but as a positive image of everything we should strive to attain.

On the other hand, *TOS*, despite such a promising example of forward-looking thinking, is frequently Orientalist. One should not forget that Khan, perhaps the franchise's most memorable villain, is clearly presented as Asian (probably a Sikh) and as having once ruled an empire that stretched from Asia through the Middle East. Meanwhile, despite its determination to provide a vision of a future in which all (American) races can stand as equals, the series often presents its alien characters as exotic, essentially Oriental others. Even the general representation of Vulcan culture has an Orientalist tinge, showing the Vulcans as spiritual desert people with few signs of high technology in sight. The Orientalism of *Star Trek* begins as early as the series' original pilot, "The Cage." Here, a group of highly advanced aliens is trying to convince Captain Christopher Pike to remain on their planet, Talos, in order to serve as breeding stock to help produce a new race of humans that they can observe for their amusement. To this end, they deploy the conscripted human woman Vina

(Susan Oliver), making her appear to Pike to be the embodiment of various images of feminine desirability, thus encouraging him to stay on the planet in order to breed with her.

Perhaps the most striking of these images is that of a green-skinned "Orion slave girl," in which guise Vina performs a seductive belly dance, accompanied by Middle Eastern music (actually an original composition by Alexander Courage) (see figure 3.2). Belly dancing, of course, is the classic Orientalist image of the exotic sexuality of Eastern women, and *Star Trek* gets quite a bit of mileage out of the image, especially in connection with these Orion slave girls who reappear several times in the *Trek* franchise, almost always as images of exotic sexual availability and feminine submission.[10] Such scenes clearly reflect what Ella Shohat and Robert Stam have called "the imaginary of the harem," which is typically part of "a masculinist utopia of sexual omnipotence."[11]

In the episode "Whom Gods Destroy," we see a similar dance performed by one of the green-skinned seductresses, with exactly the same musical accompaniment and with exactly the same implications. The ver-

Figure 3.2.   Vina enacts her exotic fantasy role as an Orion slave girl in "The Cage." NBC / Photofest © NBC

sion of the music from this episode, incidentally, has been included on volume 5 of the *Star Trek Soundtrack Collection*, with the telling title "Arab Hootch Dance." This title itself bears almost overwhelming Orientalist resonances, going back to the "Street in Cairo" display at the 1893 World's Columbian Exposition, where a belly dancer dubbed "Little Egypt" performed to an early version of a song entitled "The Streets of Cairo" in a show called "The Algerian Dancers of Morocco." The dancer herself was Syrian, but this conflation of Egypt, Algeria, Morocco, and Syria is not surprising. One of the central characteristics of Orientalist stereotyping is the tendency to lump all of the East into one undifferentiated category on the assumption that all "Orientals" are pretty much alike. "The Streets of Cairo" would subsequently come to be associated with the sexually provocative form of belly dancing known as "hoochie coochie" dancing, which somewhat resembles the dancing of the Orion slave girls of *TOS*, especially that of Vina. Alien women are, in fact, particularly likely to be targets of Orientalist representation in *TOS*.

In the *ENT* episode "Bound" (April 15, 2005), the Orion slave girls make what is (so far) their last appearance in the *Trek* franchise. Here, in a seeming update, the submissiveness of Orion women turns out to be a ruse, and it is actually the women who enslave their men and hold all the true power. This reversal might seem a feminist step forward were it not for the fact that these women gain power purely through their sexual allure. Indeed, the episode could be read as a misogynist exploration of feminine threat. Perhaps tellingly, the women now dance to Western-style music, though it is also the case that this seeming vision of feminine power does not escape Orientalist stereotyping: Despite their usual figuration as sexually available and submissive, certain kinds of Middle Eastern women (especially belly dancers) have long been figured in Orientalist discourse as sexually dangerous as well.

In the *TOS* episode "Elaan of Troyius," the bossy and demanding title character (played by French-Vietnamese actress France Nuyen) also seems to have a certain amount of power (figure 3.3). After all, if the tears of an Elasian woman touch a man's skin, he will become her enraptured sexual slave forever. Of course, the men of Elas are reported by Spock (citing a scientific study) to be "vicious and arrogant," so Orientalist stereotypes about both sexes abound in this episode.[12] In any case, despite her aristocratic birth and her inherent sexual power, Elaan functions in the episode largely as a sexual commodity: A member of the royal family of the planet Elas, she is being married off to the ruler of the planet Troyius to cement a peace treaty between the two nations. And the *Enterprise*, hoping to sway both planets toward an alliance with the Federation rather than the Klingon Empire, is tasked with delivering her to her wedding. Much trouble predictably ensues, including Klingon sabotage and an attempt by Elaan to enslave Kirk with her tears. But Kirk's devotion to the *Enterprise* is such that he becomes the first man ever to resist an Elasian woman, impressing Elaan so much that she falls in love with him—and seems quite intrigued by his threat to spank her at one point. Though theoretically modeled on Helen of Troy, Elaan is clearly presented as an exotic Oriental women, dangerous but tamable, with her dress and makeup modeled after the iconic image of Cleopatra—Hollywood Orientalist shorthand for exotic, sexy, mysterious, and threatening (and maybe a little bit kinky).

One might note here that the stereotypical treatment of Native American culture in the episode "The Paradise Syndrome" smacks of a number of Orientalist paradigms as well, though now displaced onto the original inhabitants of the American West who have apparently also been

Figure 3.3. Elaan meets Mr. Scott and another crewman in "Elaan of Troyius."
Paramount Pictures / Photofest © Paramount Pictures

excluded from *TOS*'s vision of "infinite" diversity. Here, Kirk is stranded on a planet where the local civilization is modeled on Native American culture—as if there ever were a single, homogenous Native American culture. The natives, of course, are noble savages, blissfully ignorant of almost everything, while Kirk is so impressive by comparison that they think him a god. In the meantime, he immediately wins the hand of the winsome local native princess, whom he weds and impregnates. The princess, of course, swoons submissively in the face of Kirk's charms but is then stoned to death as she tries to protect Kirk from the superstitious natives, who declare Kirk a false god and turn viciously upon him. With his devoted wife (and would-be child) out of the way, Kirk is then free to return to the *Enterprise* unencumbered.

In addition to exotic, mysteriously sexual women, probably the most iconic Orientalist image is that of the camel—and of bearded, robed men fiercely riding camels about in the desert. The East is also typically figured as a land hopelessly mired in antiquity, infatuated with its own past and unable to move forward into modernity. Perhaps it is not surprising, then, that, when the "Guardian of Forever" treats Kirk and Spock to a tour of earth's past in "The City on the Edge of Forever," the tour begins with a stunningly Orientalist image of a caravan of Arabs moving through the desert on camels, with a crumbling pyramid (another image) in the background. Apparently this image was the most vivid vision of primitivity and antiquity the episode's creative team could summon up.

The makers of *TOS* often seem to have been almost entirely blind to the problem of Orientalist stereotyping, especially where women were concerned. Supposedly underwritten by the motto "infinite diversity in infinite combinations," the series simply does not have Arab culture on its radar. I see no suggestion that the series is openly hostile to Arabs (or to women), but it has not yet reached the point of enlightenment where it can see what is wrong with dressing female crew members in miniskirts or wrapping exotic alien sex slaves in the iconography of the Middle East. To their credit, the series does get somewhat less Orientalist in most of its later incarnations, including the addition (positively portrayed) of an ethnically ambiguous but vaguely Arab chief medical officer in *DS9*. From this point of view, the virulently Orientalist representation of the Klingons of *DSC* would seem to be an unfortunate throwback, perhaps reflecting the realities of life in Trump-era America.

STAR TREK AND GENDER

It is with respect to gender that *TOS* most noticeably failed to keep pace with the corresponding political movements of the 1960s. As M. G. DuPree notes, "Throughout the original *Star Trek*, women would serve as foils, as temptresses, as paths not taken, as threats, or as subordinates."[13] It is true that, for the period 1966–1969, *TOS* gave women more active roles than was usually the case in American popular culture, but the women of the *Enterprise* crew in no way have equal status with the men, either in terms of their roles on the ship itself or in terms of their participation in the action of the series. When women are depicted as powerful, they generally gain this power through their ability to enact stereotypically feminine roles in particularly effective ways—either through their irresistible sexual allure, as in the case of Elaan of Troyius, or through their angelic, sympathy-winning natures, as in the case of Edith Keeler.

At first glance, one seeming exception to this rule would be T'Pau (Celia Lovsky), the stately matriarch who oversees Spock's would-be wedding ceremony in "Amok Time." T'Pau is, in fact, an almost legendary figure, reportedly the one person to have ever declined the offer of a seat on the Federation Council. Yet it is not at all clear just how much power T'Pau really has, and it is certainly the case that overseeing wedding ceremonies is traditionally a very feminine role. Moreover, when Spock is challenged for the hand of T'Pring (Arlene Martel), his bride-to-be, by one Stonn (Lawrence Montaigne)—who has the advantage of being a full-blooded Vulcan—the episode stipulates that T'Pring will become the "property" of the winner of the ensuing contest. In *TOS*, even the enlightened society of the Vulcans has not moved beyond a vision of the marriage contract that is essentially a vision of male ownership. By overseeing this ceremony, then, T'Pau becomes not an image of feminine power but an image of feminine complicity with patriarchy (see figures 3.4 and 3.5).[14]

For many, the problematic treatment of women in *TOS* is summed up in the episode "Turnabout Intruder," in which Kirk switches bodies with Dr. Janice Lester (Sandra Smith), his ex-girlfriend from their academy days. The ambitious Lester bitterly resents the fact that she was never able to get command of a starship, which she attributes to gender discrimination. However, in an episode that might have functioned as a strong critique of such discrimination, Lester also turns out to be psychotic,

Figure 3.4.   Spock and his betrothed in "Amok Time." NBC / Photofest © NBC

which almost seems to verify that women are, in fact, not psychologically stable enough to command a starship. In any case, Lester (in Kirk's body) breaks every rule in the book and even tries to have most of the bridge crew executed until Kirk is finally able to regain control of his own body and to have Lester, now back in her own body, detained to be turned over to the proper authorities. The episode can thus clearly be read as an anti-

Figure 3.5.   Kirk and Spock battle to the "death" in "Amok Time." NBC / Photofest © NBC

feminist warning of the dire consequences that might occur should women gain too much power.

The early *Star Trek* films are all dominated by male characters, but the television franchise did move a bit forward with *TNG*, though the most important women characters there (Deanna Troi and Beverly Crusher) play rather nurturing roles. Security Chief Tasha Yar (Denise Crosby) had considerable promise to break new ground in the representation of women in *TNG*; however, frustrated with the underutilization of the character, Crosby asked to leave the show, and Yar was killed off near the end of the first season. Women took more steps forward with *DS9*, with First Officer Kira Nerys taking a more active role than any previous woman character in *Star Trek*, while the characterization of the Trill Jadzia Dax also did some interesting things with gender, including a sort of lesbian relationship in which the outwardly feminine Dax becomes involved with a former lover of her masculine symbiont. Then, of course, *Trek* took a giant leap forward with the casting of a woman captain in *VOY*, while female characters such as Seven of Nine and B'Elanna Torres were stronger and more active than typical women characters in *Trek* (or

American television in general, to that point)—though the costuming of
Seven was clearly problematic from a feminist perspective.

If anything, *ENT* was a step backward in the representation of gender,
though the highly rational T'Pol did add some new dimensions to the
representation of gender in *Star Trek*. Meanwhile, it should be noted that
the characters of Uhura and Sulu have continued to make important contributions well into the twenty-first century, and that their more recent
contributions have been in terms of gender more than race. Thus, in the
recent Abrams trilogy of *Trek* films, Uhura becomes a much more active
and significant character in a key step forward for the representation of
women in *Star Trek*. Meanwhile, in these same films, building on the
reputation of Takei as a highly visible activist for gay rights, Sulu is
represented as openly gay—and even as being in a same-sex marriage. In
this same vein, it might be noted that Chief Engineer Paul Stamets (Anthony Rapp), perhaps the most interesting character in *Star Trek: Discovery*, is the first openly gay character in the *Trek* television franchise—
along with ship's doctor Hugh Culber (played by dark-skinned Puerto-
Rican actor Wilson Cruz), his gay lover. Indeed, the relationship between
Stamets and Culber is depicted in detail, including portrayal of the first
gay interracial kiss in the *Trek* franchise, extending the territory once
tread by Kirk and Uhura in important new directions.

STAR TREK AND THE UTOPIAN FUTURE

However successful (or unsuccessful) it was in conveying the specific
concerns of the countercultural political movements of the 1960s, *TOS*
shared with these movements a vision of the possibility of historical
change toward a better future—something that also set it apart from the
dominant mode of American culture in the 1950s and early 1960s. One of
the most unfortunate effects of the anti-communist rhetoric of the peak
Cold War years of the 1950s was a widespread tendency to equate utopianism with communism, thus tarring all attempts to imagine a better
future with the same anti-communist brush. Conversely, one of the driv-
ing forces behind the idealism of many of the political movements of the
1960s was an attempt to overcome the cynical legacy of Cold War anti-
utopianism and restore the time-honored American belief in the possibility of moving forward toward an improved world. For example, the "Port

Huron Statement," issued in 1962 as a manifesto of the Students for a Democratic Society (SDS) and written by Tom Hayden, declares the radical agenda of the new group and explains that this agenda is necessary to overcome the growing conformism of an American populace that was no longer capable of envisioning alternatives to the status quo. According to this manifesto,

> the message of our society is that there is no viable alternative to the present. Beneath the reassuring tones of the politicians, beneath the common opinion that America will "muddle through," beneath the stagnation of those who have closed their minds to the future, is the pervading feeling that there simply are no alternatives, that our times have witnessed the exhaustion not only of Utopias, but of any new departures as well. [15]

This same impulse to reinvigorate utopian thinking clearly drives the famed utopianism of *TOS*, thereby just as clearly providing one of the most fundamental things that *Star Trek* has in common with the activist political movements of the 1960s. On the other hand, however devoted it might be to the idea of building a *better* society, *TOS* (especially in the early going) is actually quite skeptical of the notion of building a *perfect* society. Interestingly, much of this skepticism can be read as being aimed at the youth movements of the 1960s, with their visions of flower power and universal love (perhaps with a bit of chemical enhancement). For example, the late first-season episode "This Side of Paradise" is set mostly on a Federation colony planet on which everyone has perfect health and lives in perfect harmony, content to lie around sniffing flowers and making love. This situation, an obvious commentary on the drug-fueled hippie ethos of the 1960s counterculture, is caused by spores produced by plants on the planet, which also have the added benefit of protecting anyone who inhales them from the otherwise deadly radiation that bombards the planet. The spores work even on Mr. Spock, who is shown happily frolicking and in love with a beautiful young woman he meets on the planet. Kirk, however, stays aboard the *Enterprise* and is thus unaffected. Further, he eventually manages to "rescue" his crew from the planet, based on his belief that this drug-induced happiness is unnatural and unhealthy and that human beings must have battles to fight and obstacles to overcome in order to reach their true potential. For him, this utopia is a dystopia that stifles creativity and individual achievement. On balance, the episode (like the series as a whole) seems to side with Kirk, though it gives Spock the last word as he responds to Kirk by noting, "Nevertheless, I was happy," leaving open the possibility of interpreting conditions on the planet as genuinely desirable, even if they do suppress the drive to achieve more and more that Kirk seems to favor.

"The Return of the Archons," broadcast just three weeks before "This Side of Paradise," also involves a theoretically utopian society that, at least from some perspectives, could be seen as dystopian. Here, the *Enterprise* visits a planet whose people seem to live in complete peace and tranquility, so much so that they seem sedated, or even robotic. As it turns out, their robotic behavior is no accident because the planet is actually ruled by a six-thousand-year-old computer called Landru, which suppresses their most passionate and aggressive tendencies—except during periodic "Red Hours," during which these tendencies are allowed to emerge in full force, turning the usually docile population into a brawling mob.

Kirk and Spock lead a landing party from the *Enterprise* that discovers these conditions. Computer rule, of course, is pretty much always a bad idea in *TOS*, and it quickly becomes clear (at least to Kirk) that this society is a dystopian one, somewhat in the mode of the one depicted in Jean-Luc Godard's 1965 French dystopian film *Alphaville*. Kirk, as he is wont to do, declares the situation on the planet unnatural and decides that he must intervene. He manages to cause Landru to self-destruct, freeing the people of the planet from the computer's governance and allowing them to develop their own way of life—with the aid of a team of Federation experts who are left behind to help the planet evolve "normally"— which, as usual, means the way the Federation deems to be normal. Only Spock, however, seems to see anything wrong with this plan, arguing that the destruction of Landru represents an intervention that surely constitutes a violation of the Prime Directive. Kirk, however, declares the Prime Directive to be moot in this case because it only applies in the case of a "living, growing culture."

Even after the destruction of Landru, Spock continues to doubt that it is really an improvement to allow the inhabitants of the planet to pursue their individuality and creativity if it means they will often resort to violence, which surely means that some will achieve their individual goals at the expense of others. Spock, in fact, declares that Landru, having eliminated war, disease, and crime on the planet, was clearly a wonderful feat of engineering; further, he declares Kirk's complaint that the computer lacked "soul" to be "predictably metaphysical," noting that he himself prefers "the concrete, the graspable, the provable." He then notes "how often mankind has wished for a world as peaceful and secure as the one Landru provided." Kirk dismisses Spock's argument by noting, "Yes, and we never got it. Just lucky, I guess." Nevertheless, the point has been raised, and the episode, much like "This Side of Paradise," leaves open for debate whether the society we have just seen was utopian or dystopian.

The somewhat muddled third-season episode "The Mark of Gideon" is quite a bit less nuanced in its treatment of the motif of a utopia that has turned dystopian. Here, an advanced society has eliminated disease and has virtually eliminated death. Unfortunately, its citizens are so devoted to the love of life that they refuse to practice birth control. Weirdly (and this is where the episode starts to get confused) they have no objection to sterilization, but they are so healthy that their reproductive systems would simply regenerate. So, with their birth rate continuing apace even as no one ever dies, their planet has become so overpopulated that it is a living hell, its citizens perpetually milling about in identical costumes, packed shoulder to shoulder in one of *TOS*'s stranger bits of conceptual art. Suicide, of course, is also unthinkable on this planet, and yet (to make matters even stranger), the world's leaders kidnap Kirk, who turns out to be a carrier of a disease that is deadly to them, so that he can infect those who volunteer to die, alleviating the population crisis. On this planet, practicing birth control shows a lack of respect for life, but infecting large numbers of volunteers so that millions die by what really amounts to mass suicide is ethically acceptable.

Like many episodes of *TOS*, "The Mark of Gideon" must be read allegorically before it really makes sense. Clearly, very little about this episode can be taken literally without the episode being truly awful. But it makes more sense when read largely as a satire in favor of birth control, the pill itself having been introduced only in 1960. The episode makes even more sense when one considers how it meshes with a widespread late 1960s concern about the apocalyptic possibilities of overpopulation. For example, "The Mark of Gideon" aired only months after Paul Ehrlich's sensationalist Malthusian jeremiad *The Population Bomb* became a sensation in the United States, where legions of readers devoured its dire warnings that mass deaths might be on the horizon thanks to ongoing population growth worldwide. But, as is often the case, science fiction had already issued warnings of its own. As early as 1953, *The Space Merchants* by Frederik Pohl and Cyril M. Kornbluth envisioned an impoverished future driven by a combination of overpopulation and capitalist mismanagement of resources. In 1962, British novelist Anthony Burgess's *The Wanting Seed* focused even more specifically on overpopulation and its disastrous potential. More recently, American Harry Harrison's *Make Room! Make Room!* (1966, the inspiration for the 1973 film *Soylent Green*) featured a 1999 New York in which overpopulation leads to massive shortages of food and housing. And John Brunner's classic British 1968 SF novel *Stand on Zanzibar* also centered on the motif of future overpopulation. In short, "The Mark of Gideon" was riding a wave of concern with overpopulation that was sweeping the nation in science fiction and elsewhere; it added its own Trekkian twist to these warnings by picturing Gideon as a society that might have been ideally utopian were it not for overpopulation. The implication within the world of *Star Trek* is clear: A utopian future is possible here on earth, but for it to happen we need to get population growth under control.

Finally, in "The Cloud Minders," *TOS* gets in one last powerful political allegory amid a string of generally weak episodes. Here, the *Enterprise* travels to the planet Ardana, which holds the only known deposits of the rare mineral zienite, which is needed to stop a deadly plague on the planet Merak II. However, the situation becomes tense when Kirk and Spock find themselves in the middle of a class conflict that has riven this supposedly peaceful and ultra-refined society. In turns out that the intellectual and cultural refinement for which Ardana is known throughout the galaxy obtains only in the cloud city of Stratos, which hovers in the air above the surface, supported by the mineral wealth that is extracted from beneath the planet's surface through the labors of the lowly (and intellectually stunted) "Troglytes."

In short, the society of Ardana is marked by an extreme version of the class divisions that once existed on earth—and that *TOS* stipulates to have been long overcome in the world of the twenty-third century. Indeed, on earth and in most of the Federation, automation seems to have largely eliminated the need for menial human labor, creating a society of universal affluence in which everyone is able to pursue individual fulfillment while machines do most of the work. The one exception seems to be mining, which still requires a certain amount of human labor in order to produce crucial raw materials that are needed to keep the machines running. Perhaps the most important of these is the dilithium that is used as the principal power source for starships, making clear that the crucial role played by mineral resources in *TOS* can be read as an allegorical representation of the importance of oil on twentieth-century earth. Indeed, much of the famed conflict between the Federation and the Klingons in *TOS* arises from competition for these mineral resources, which serves as an obvious commentary on the competition between the United States and the Soviets for control of the rich resources of the Third World.

One of the keys to the egalitarian society of the Federation, however, is that while miners remain necessary, they are generally no longer presented as oppressed workers being exploited by soulless corporations. They are, instead, something like rich entrepreneurs, more like prospectors in the California Gold Rush of the mid-nineteenth century than like exploited West Virginia coal miners. For example, in "The Devil in the Dark," it is clear that miners are not really menial laborers at all but something like engineers and technicians overseeing high-tech mining equipment. Meanwhile, in "Mudd's Women," miners toil away on remote planets but are rewarded richly enough for their efforts that they can afford to import expensive wives from around the galaxy to soothe their loneliness. The wives are stipulated to be happy to get the gigs, but it is clear that this motif represents a failure to imagine that the famed equality of the Star Trek universe entirely transcends the patriarchal tradition of treating women as sexual commodities, however enlightened *TOS* might have been in general.

"The Cloud Minders," though, does treat miners as oppressed and exploited, a situation that puts Ardana somewhat at odds with the rest of the Federation. Little wonder, then, that Kirk and Spock are shocked and appalled at the divisions they find in this episode—they have come to accept the elimination of class differences as a natural and inevitable consequence of advanced civilization, and they have heard that the civilization of Ardana is highly advanced. It quickly becomes clear, however, that this high level of advancement on Stratos has been bought at the expense of the Troglytes, a situation that Kirk and Spock find unacceptable. Of course, it doesn't help that they arrive to discover that a budding rebellion on the part of the Troglytes has cut off the supply of the zienite that the Federation so badly needs in order to save Merak II.

The situation is not entirely simple, however. Spock, for example, is clearly drawn to the intellectualism of Stratos: It is, as he approvingly notes upon his first exposure to the city, a "totally intellectual society" where "all forms of violence have been eliminated." Soon afterward, however, they observe a Troglyte undergoing torture and realize that violence has not been eliminated. It has simply (and quite literally) gone underground, where it is visited upon the Troglytes on a continual basis. Not only do most of the profits of their labor go to support the leisurely lifestyle on Stratos (while the Troglytes live essentially in caves), but the work they do to support Stratos produces gases that are given off by the zienite when it is mined. These gases fill the mines and impede the brain functions of the Troglytes, causing them to become violent and brutish.

The inhabitants of Stratos choose to interpret the lack of intellectual development in the Troglytes in racial terms, concluding that the Troglytes are racially inferior and that brutishness and stupidity are inherent characteristics of the Troglyte race. They thus repeat the trajectory of racism in earth's history, in which various forms of racial discrimination (including slavery) have been rationalized in terms of the presumed fundamental superiority of the dominant race. The situation on Ardana also mirrors earth history in its conflation of race and class, a key strategy of capitalist exploitation in our own history.

In any case, one can read the presence of these gases fairly literally as a commentary on the way in which the working classes on earth have historically borne the brunt of environmental pollution caused by the industries in which they work, including lack of access to clean water to drink and healthy air to breathe. The most direct referent might be the black lung disease that has afflicted so many coal miners, but the fact that the impact of the zienite gas is mostly intellectual suggests a different reading, in which the gas, by numbing the minds of the miners, helps to keep them in subjugation. In short, the zienite gas acts very much in the same way that ideological indoctrination works in the capitalist societies of our own earth: Workers on earth have traditionally been dominated and controlled by the far less numerous members of the upper classes because those members have been able to employ a variety of resources—including schools, churches, the media, and culture—to make their view of the world seem normal and natural and thus to convince the workers that it is the correct one. Meanwhile, the Troglytes rebel because many of them have been imported to Stratos to do menial tasks there;

removed from the gas, these Troglytes have regained their intellectual capacity and have become the leaders of the rebellion—just as those with sufficient education and insight to see through the obfuscations of ideology have often become the leaders of rebellions on our own earth.

One of the most interesting aspects of "The Cloud Minders" is the way the denizens of Stratos have fallen for their own rhetoric. It is clear that they genuinely believe in the rightness of their stratified society. Not only do they fail to question the fundamental inferiority of the Troglytes, but it never occurs to them that exploiting and brutalizing the Troglytes might not be justified, even if they are a bit mentally deficient. In one scene, Droxine (Diana Ewing), the daughter of Plasus (Jeff Corey), the ruler of Stratos, explains to Spock (whose ears apparently really turn her on) that the Troglytes don't need culture or education because they are just "workers" by nature. Spock calmly responds, diagnosing the situation immediately as only he can, "In other words, they perform all the physical toil necessary to maintain Stratos." Droxine, who is stipulated to be brilliant and highly educated, is nevertheless so indoctrinated in the ideology of Stratos that she misses his point entirely and simply nods her agreement. "That is their function in our society," she says, as if it could not possibly be otherwise.

Smart as she is, Droxine simply cannot see the injustice that reigns on her planet. Similarly, it is clear that Stratos has access to vastly sophisticated technology, and yet its people are blind to the effect of the gases on the Troglytes. It is only after the *Enterprise* arrives that McCoy and Spock are able to deduce the effect of the gases on the Troglytes and even to devise a method for overcoming this effect, which turns out to be entirely reversible simply by removing the victim from exposure to the gas. It takes extreme methods, however, to convince the rulers of Stratos of their findings. In particular, Kirk kidnaps Plasus and exposes him to the gas, turning both of them violent and stupid (and meanwhile ignoring the Prime Directive, which had been taken so seriously earlier in this season). Plasus promises to work for more equitable conditions on his planet, while the miners end their strike and supply the zienite that is needed to rescue Merak II.

Subsequent *Trek* series have sometimes been similarly skeptical of utopianism, though *TNG* is somewhat more nuanced in its treatment of this theme. Somewhat echoing "The Return of the Archons," the early episode "Justice" (November 9, 1987) features a seemingly paradisiacal society that turns out to be overseen by an advanced godlike being who demands absolute obedience to a seemingly arbitrary set of rules. Wesley Crusher inadvertently runs afoul of these rules and is nearly executed, but Picard manages to reason with the godlike being, leaving the society intact (and scoring some satirical points against religion in general). "When the Bough Breaks" (February 15, 1988) also recalls "The Return of the Archons" with its portrayal of a technological utopia ruled by a supercomputer Custodian that provides for all of the needs of the citizens, who are rendered passive and unable to strive for any sort of advancement. In a bit of environmentalist commentary, this technology has also destroyed the planet's ozone layer, leading to the radiation poisoning (and resultant sterilization) of the entire population.

"The Masterpiece Society" (February 10, 1992) is perhaps the most nuanced treatment of utopianism anywhere in the *Star Trek* franchise. This episode features a seemingly utopian colony of genetically engineered humans, each bred selectively to play a specific role in the society. The society seems to run well, but (given the suspicion of both utopianism and genetic engineering that pervade *Star Trek*) it comes as no surprise that trouble looms. In particular, when the approach of a core fragment of a neutron star threatens to destroy the whole planet, they have to turn to the *Enterprise-D* (and particularly to Geordi) for help, even though they generally avoid contact with outsiders—and even though someone blind from birth like Geordi would be anathema in this eugenically pure society. Interestingly, this contact with outsiders does destabilize the colony, and a number of citizens decide to leave on the starship so that they can explore a broader world of experience. As usual, the Federation, whatever its flaws, seems preferable to a utopian alternative, because the latter is too rigid and unable to change to meet a crisis. This case is a bit different because the colonists have chosen their own course, rather than having it determined for them by a computer or a super-being. As the episode ends, Picard, always a respecter of the Prime Directive, expresses regret that the colony has been disrupted and forever changed. He even wonders whether the intervention of the *Enterprise-D* might ultimately have been as destructive to the life of the colony as the core fragment would otherwise have been.

In general, *TNG* represents a peak moment in the utopianism of *Star Trek*, and it seems to be the series that is most confident about the glorious future that the franchise as a whole famously imagines. But even here, any idea of a "perfect" society is at least suspected of a tendency to lead to stagnation and to a society that is anything but perfect. Though less so than Kirk, Picard clearly believes that the ideal society is not one in which all problems have been solved, but one with the flexibility to meet new challenges and solve new problems as they arise—and to do so with a maximum of justice for all. His attitude can clearly be seen, for example, in the episode "The Neutral Zone" (May 16, 1988), in which the *Enterprise-D* encounters three humans from the twentieth century. One of them is an investor who is concerned about conditions in the business world of the twenty-fourth century; Picard patiently responds, speaking to the man almost as if he were a child, that business is not really a major preoccupation in this world: "People are no longer obsessed with the accumulation of things. We've eliminated hunger, want, the need for possessions. We've grown out of our infancy." Puzzled, the investor wonders what, then, could possibly motivate people in such a world. "The challenge," Picard says, "is to improve yourself, to enrich yourself." In short, though human beings as a species have become more mature and have overcome many of their baser impulses, they continue to strive every day to be better and better rather than simply to be satisfied with what they have achieved. And this is the kind of utopian vision, however individualistic, that drives the entire *Trek* franchise. It's a rather capitalistic—and rather masculinist—vision, which leads to a number of contradictions over the course of the franchise. Nevertheless, when compared with the weakness in the utopian vision in American culture as a whole since World War II, *Star Trek* stands out like a supernova in the middle of a dark portion of the galaxy.

Picard's statement of the vision that drives his twenty-fourth-century world is also a statement of the vision that drives the entire *Trek* franchise, though this vision was not fully developed or articulated until *TNG*. Picard's repudiation of materialism and greed is, in fact, a repudiation of the values that dominated mainstream America during the Reagan years, and perhaps this vision could only fully evolve as a reaction against those values. Thus, Manu Saadia goes so far as to say that the investor in this scene is "*Star Trek*'s take on Gordon Gekko," the protagonist of Oliver Stone's *Wall Street* (1987), the central cinematic indictment of the greed culture of the 1980s and a film that premiered only a few months before this episode aired.[16]

Saadia usefully highlights the crucial role of the economic—or perhaps one should rather say the *post*-economic—in *Star Trek*. The ability to envision a future without capitalism—and even without money—is absolutely crucial to the utopianism of the *Trek* franchise. After all, capitalism as a system and money as a concept are both essentially methods for rationing limited resources. *Star Trek*, though, imagines a future in which technological advances have made resources essentially unlimited. This elimination of the need to compete for resources means that anyone can have anything they want without having to take it away from anyone else. In such a world, there is simply no need for greed or acquisitiveness or economic competition or any of the other forces that have driven so much of human behavior during the capitalist era—and that so often have been taken as immutable facts of human nature. With such forces removed from the scene, human beings are free to evolve to a new level of enlightenment and altruism. In short, human beings are freed from the bonds of economic struggle that have bound them throughout their history. It's a fundamental vision of a changed world and of changed human beings, opening up dramatic imaginative possibilities that are surely needed now more than ever.

4

STAR TREK AND THE
HISTORY OF TECHNOLOGY

If conflicts over civil rights, women's rights, and the Vietnam War made the late 1960s context of *TOS* a time of great crisis in American history, it is also the case that this same period was a crucial turning point in the history of technology—a central concern of science fiction as a genre. Amid concerns over the ongoing war in Vietnam and rising racial tensions in America's cities, there was another crisis—potentially even more fundamental in terms of its impact on daily life. When *Star Trek* premiered in 1966, Americans had already seen their day-to-day lives transformed by the rapid pace of technological change over the past couple of decades, with the proliferation of domestic appliances and other gadgets (such as transistor radios) already beginning to work subtle but substantial changes in the way Americans lived and worked. On a larger scale, Americans in the 1960s had experienced the dramatic spread of the new medium of television into a near-universal part of American life, greatly diminishing regional differences in daily experience, while jet-based transportation was making it easier and easier to travel from one region to another, again diminishing the sense of separation between different parts of the country. The ongoing space race captured and excited the American public imagination during the 1960s, but of course this race also had a dark side in that it was enabled by the same advances in rocketry that had made the intercontinental ballistic missile (ICBM) a threat to the very survival of human civilization and even of the human species. Indeed, the very same R-7 rocket that propelled the Soviet Sputnik, the first man-made satellite, into orbit in October 1957 had also become the first successfully tested ICBM two months earlier. Sputnik, meanwhile, was the forerunner of a global revolution in communications brought about by telecommunication satellites, still in their infancy at the time of *TOS* but already beginning to have a profound effect, the first true communications satellite, Telstar, having been launched in 1962. [1]

The technological environment in the late 1960s is captured well in the television series *Mad Men*, a program running from 2007 to 2015 but well known for its ability to capture the spirit of the 1960s. Among other things, *Mad Men* portrays the decade of the 1960s as a crucial turning point in American history in a number of ways—including the role played by technology in daily American life. In a sequence of episodes in the final season of *Mad Men*, Sterling Cooper & Partners (SC&P, the advertising firm at the center of the series) decides to try to modernize by obtaining its own IBM 360 computer. Set in 1969, at the end of the initial run of *TOS*, these episodes present the coming of the computer as a major milestone in the history of the firm and as part of a new era in American history.

Computers were, in fact, perhaps the most important emergent technology of the late 1960s, when *TOS* first appeared. In the *Mad Men* episode "The Monolith" (May 4, 2014), the new computer is installed in the offices of SC&P, an event the importance of which is signaled by the episode's title, which refers to the monoliths that appear in *2001: A Space Odyssey* whenever humanity is about to take an evolutionary step forward. Some in the firm—such as the television-oriented adman Harry Crane (Rich Sommer)—are excited by the arrival of the electronic behemoth, while others—such as the more traditional adman Don Draper (Jon Hamm)—are appalled. As Deanna Kreisel has noted, the role of this computer motif in *Mad Men* is clear, establishing a stark opposition between the genuine creativity of talented humans like Draper (who likes to see advertising as a sort of art form) and the soulless, inhuman Otherness of the computer (which reduces advertising to number-crunching and the bottom line). For Kreisel, "the face-off is made explicit: an 'old-fashioned' and romanticized vision of humanistic (and human) inspiration and creativity versus a future-oriented, mechanistic brute intelligence that threatens to render human agency obsolete."[2] Meanwhile, this opposition reflects a central tension in American society as a whole, torn between bright visions of emerging technologies (especially computer technologies) as enabling and liberating and dark visions of technology as a dehumanizing force that threatens to make humans slaves to their machines.

Star Trek, of course, comes down firmly on the side of the bright visions, though it is worth noting that, especially in *TOS*, computers are the one form of technology of which the franchise maintains a wary suspicion. From this point of view, it is significant that the new computer featured in *Mad Men* is an IBM 360, a state-of-the-art machine in 1969 and one that was initially introduced in 1964, the same year in which Gene Roddenberry was making his first *TOS* pilot. The hugely successful 360 line was a major step forward in the history of the computerization of American life, making available a flexible range of compatible computers of different sizes with extensive expandability, including interchangeability of a number of components. The introduction of the IBM 360 thus helped to turn the computer, once relegated to the esoteric realms of topnotch scientists and top-secret military programs, into a widely marketed commodity, taking a step toward the microprocessor revolution of the 1970s that would quickly make computers an integral and indispensable part of daily American life.[3] Indeed, by the time of the initial run of *TOS*, computers were already being extensively used in a variety of American businesses and institutions, filling visionaries with dreams of an electronic future and filling many ordinary people with fear and loathing.

The references to *2001: A Space Odyssey* in this *Mad Men* episode are highly appropriate, given that the artificially intelligent HAL 9000 computer is the chief villain of that film as it seeks (in a misinterpretation of its own programming) to dispose of the human crew of the spaceship *Discovery*, thus enacting the notion that computers in general might supplant humans as the masters of their world. In the same way, the new SC&P computer seems to announce the end of the era when advertising was driven by human ingenuity and inventiveness and the beginning of an era in which would-be artist figures such as Draper would be supplanted by bureaucrats and bean-counters. Henceforth, the episode announces, advertising itself would become as commodified as the products it attempts to sell.[4]

The fear expressed in this episode is merely a microcosm of the way in which so many Americans feared being supplanted by computers and other forms of automation at the time. *Mad Men*, of course, is well known for its critical and satirical engagement with important social, political, and historical issues in the 1960s—and for using that engagement to provide trenchant commentary on its own historical context as well. Science fiction is not necessarily similarly known, but *Star Trek*'s engagement with important social and political issues (rather than mere escapism or celebration of technology) is one of its distinguishing features. This is not to say that *Star Trek* cannot be an entertaining adventure or that it does not have important things to say about science and technology per se. In fact, the entire future world of the *Trek* franchise is predicated upon the fact that technological advances have enabled a universal affluence that has been the key to solving the vexing social and political problems of our own day. And while the specific technologies represented in *Star Trek* may never come to pass, the franchise is unequivocally committed to the notions that science is the best way to understand the world, that understanding the world is a good thing, and that such understanding can lead to technological achievements that make life better for everyone.

These general principles—rather than the prediction of any specific scientific or technological advances—are the key to *Star Trek*'s engagement with technology. Thus, while one can see in various devices featured in the franchise the forerunners of such technologies as large flat-screen televisions, smart phones, tablets, and e-readers, the fact is that *Star Trek* (like all of the best science fiction) was never about the literal prediction of specific future technological devices. Roddenberry did not "invent" devices such as warp drives and transporters (figure 4.1) to provide a blueprint for future advances in engineering; he envisioned such devices partly as narrative conveniences (just think how many *Trek* narratives crucially depend on the availability of such devices) and partly as figurative examples of the kinds of advances that we might be able to look forward to in the future. Thus, critics such as Brent McDonald—who argues that Roddenberry literally made "impressive predictions" of the development of iPhones, plasma-screen TVs, and Bluetooth headsets—might not have it quite right, but Roddenberry's vision that advanced devices in general were on the way undeniably served as an inspiration to many of the individuals who contributed to the development of such devices.[5]

Though less central to the plots of specific episodes than things such as warp drives and transporters, perhaps the most important example of a figurative use of technology in *Star Trek* involves the replicators that were introduced in *TNG*, providing the most important explanation of how technology had been able to usher in an era of universal affluence on the future earth of the franchise. Though the exact technology used by these replicators is not clear, they seem to use a version of the same process as that used by the famous transporters to dematerialize raw materials and then rematerialize them not in the same form (as with the transporters) but in a different form. As a result of this ability to rearrange matter, the replicators can thus produce upon command virtually any item, including food, clothing, and other necessities of life. There are limitations (such as extremely complex high-tech devices) to the kinds of items that can be produced by the replicators, but they clearly make it possible to produce virtually everything that anyone needs to survive at very little cost. Raw materials must be provided, of course, but even these can be easily recycled by reversing the process by which an item was assembled from raw materials to begin with. As a result, the replicators also provide a key method of environmental cleanup by making it possible to transport garbage and pollutants back into the raw material pool for reuse as new useful items.

These replicators are thus essential to the economy of the future within the world of *Star Trek*. However, this fact in no way implies that the franchise literally predicts the development of replicators in the real world or that its utopian vision of the future is dependent upon the development of such replicators. The replicators are, in fact, merely placeholders—fictional devices that stand in for the general notion that technology has the potential to increase efficiency and productivity in the future, thus leading to a better world for everyone. There is, after all, ample evidence from the past two hundred to three hundred years to suggest that this can be the case, even if, thus far in our history, humanity has been unable to convert this increased productivity into the kind of universally affluent, egalitarian society envisioned by *Star Trek*.[6]

STAR TREK AND THE RACE FOR SPACE

Given the timing of its original broadcast on NBC, the history of *Star Trek* is inseparable from the Cold War space race, even if the series ultimately repudiated the competitive ethos of the Cold War. On the other hand, H. Bruce Franklin argues that the American project of putting a man on the moon was really more about Cold War competition with the

Figure 4.1. *Star Trek's* **famous transporter in action. NBC / Photofest © NBC**

Soviet Union than about a desire to begin the exploration of outer space. If, he asks, the project that saw the United States land the first man on the moon in 1969 was truly driven by a spirit of exploration and discovery, why did it end so quickly, with the (so far) *last* man landing on the moon just over three years later on December 18, 1972?[7] Franklin goes on to note the irony of the fact that *Star Trek* struggled to attract viewers during the height of the space race as the first moon landing approached, but then finally found an audience in syndication just after the last manned flight to the moon signaled the end of any serious effort to send humans into outer space.

To an extent, however, this "irony" is not surprising. Given the utopian logic of *Star Trek* as a whole, it makes sense that *Trek* is the sort of cultural artifact that succeeds largely via a process of utopian compensation, attracting audiences because it provides a sort of imaginative fulfillment that is not available in day-to-day life. After all, Roddenberry originally got the program on the air by selling it as a sort of Western, and the popularity of the Western in American culture through the first half of the twentieth century derived largely from a process of utopian compensation. The Western, after all, derived its energies largely from the fact that the taming of the American frontier removed a key focus of popular fantasy, producing an imaginative void that popular audiences attempted to fill by immersing themselves in Western fiction. *TOS* tried to serve much the same function—and in fact literally placed some episodes within the iconography of the Western. In the third-season episode "Spectre of the Gun," for example, Kirk, Spock, McCoy, Scotty, and Chekov all find themselves transported into a simulated version of the Wild West town of 1881 Tombstone, Arizona, where they come into conflict with the notorious Earp clan.[8] And then, of course, as noted in the previous chapter, there is the presumably utopian Native American imagery of "The Paradise Syndrome," an episode that draws its problematic stereotyping of Native American culture largely from Westerns.

From this point of view, *TOS* might have failed to find an initial audience partly because its debut was so poorly timed—occurring just as the race to land a man on the moon was already providing a new source of frontier fantasy, making the Western irrelevant. It is thus no accident that the Western itself began to wane in popularity in the very years when *Star Trek* was on the air. By 1975, even the venerable *Gunsmoke* had finally left the air after twenty years as a stalwart on CBS, a moment in television history that simply punctuated a decline by that time of nearly a decade in the cultural power of the Western.

By the mid- to late 1970s, a variety of forces, including the disastrous U.S. experience in Vietnam, had combined to diminish the status of the Western as a mythic expression of the American national identity. Revisionist Westerns such as *The Professionals* (1966), *Butch Cassidy and the Sundance Kid* (1969), *Little Big Man* (1970), and *McCabe & Mrs. Miller* (1971) ushered in a trend in which the Western genre challenged its own premises, deconstructing its own mythic basis. Through the decade of the 1970s, such films as *The Missouri Breaks* (1976), *Buffalo Bill and the Indians* (1976), and *Heaven's Gate* (1980) questioned the legitimacy of the Western as a locus of utopian imaginings, though some of the original mythic energies of the original Western, now with modified meanings (often, for example, representing the Mexican Revolution as a locus of utopian hope), were diverted into the Italian Spaghetti Western.

In the United States, however, those energies were diverted into entirely different genres. Thus, Richard Slotkin, whose *Gunfighter Nation*

(1998) is the best study of the symbolic role of Myth of the Frontier—especially as figured in the Western—in twentieth-century American culture, notes the decline of the Western as an American national narrative in the 1970s, arguing that, since this time, "a succession of new and revamped genres have replaced it as the focus of the mythographic enterprise":

> The displacement of the Western from its place on the genre map did not entail the disappearance of those underlying structures of myth and ideology that had given the genre its cultural force. Rather, those structures were abstracted from the elaborately historicized context of the Western and parceled out among genres that used their relationship to the Western to define both the disillusioning losses and the extravagant potential of the new era. [9]

Slotkin identifies the crime film and the science fiction adventure (especially *Star Wars* and *Star Trek*) as the most important genres that took the place formerly occupied by the Western as a structure for conveying mythic energies. In short, the decline of the Western in the 1970s opened an imaginative space for *Star Trek* (already specifically designed as a frontier fantasy but not hampered, as was the Western, by having already been declared moribund in the popular imagination) to succeed in syndication, even as this same decline of the Western had taken the original run of *TOS* down with it.

For Slotkin, the Western is fundamentally about violence, helping to supply a national cultural identity for the United States as the conqueror of savage foes. *Star Trek* sometimes falls into this same category in it representation of confrontations with alien Others, but mostly it attempts to project a more benevolent identity of the Federation (read, the United States) as devoted to discovery and diplomacy. At its best, then, *Star Trek* is symbolically about the spirit of adventure and exploration, about the willingness to try new things—and to accept the difference of new Others. It is this general spirit rather than the specifics of interstellar flight that lies at the heart of *Star Trek*. Granted, *Star Trek* itself puts a great deal of emphasis on interstellar flight, stipulating that the development of warp drive technology is synonymous with maturity and sophistication as a species and as a society. No planet can join the Federation unless it has already independently developed warp drive technology, thus proving that it has reached a high enough level of civilization to be able to contribute to the Federation's goals and participate appropriately in the Federation's projects. But this stipulation is surely more figurative than literal: The *Trek* franchise is founded on a firm belief that technology is crucial to advanced civilization, but warp drive technology simply stands in metaphorically for advanced technology in general.

It is thus not particularly important that real-world spaceflight technology has failed so miserably to follow in the footsteps of *Star Trek*. Among other things, this very fact should indicate that *Star Trek*'s relationship with technology is far more complex than the direct prediction of specific technological breakthroughs. Instead, what drives *Star Trek* is the firm confidence that *there will be* technological breakthroughs and that these breakthroughs will have a major positive effect on the evolution of future society. The real utopian frontier of *Star Trek* is not outer space but technology itself, and the fundamental premise of the franchise is that the key to humanity achieving a better and better world is boldly going into technological realms where no one was gone before. Whether or not the technologies discovered in those realms take us across the galaxy, they will, in the vision of *Star Trek*, take us somewhere that is potentially wonderful.

The fact that so much of the technology aboard the *Enterprise* in *TOS* now seems downright clunky and old-fashioned—just think of all those digital dials on the various control panels—might seem to indicate that the series actually did a very poor job of anticipating technologies to come. In truth, however, the very fact that we have come so far in the fifty years since *TOS* can be taken as a verification of the fundamental confidence of the *Trek* franchise throughout its history that dramatic advances in technology were on the horizon. Indeed, during a period in which so much science fiction has involved Frankensteinian cautionary tales about the dangers of runaway technological progress, *Star Trek* stands at the forefront of science fiction that maintains an optimistic faith in the ability of technology to help bring about a better world.

Of course, one reason why the technologies of *TOS* sometimes look clunky is that the series lacked the budget, given available filmmaking technologies, to produce the kinds of impressive-looking technologies that it might have wanted. Indeed, one of the stories of technological progress told by the *Trek* franchise over its first half century has involved the evolution of the technological means for telling its stories more effectively. From this point of view, it is significant that the technology looks so much different in *Star Trek: The Motion Picture*, the first work of the *Trek* franchise to be made with a relatively high budget and with the availability of the new CGI capabilities pioneered by *Star Wars* two years earlier. *TNG* then picked up this filmmaking technology, and it is no accident that the series from *TNG* forward look much more like the films than like *TOS*.

The action of *TMP* is set only shortly after that of *TOS*, yet it is set in an entirely different visual world. The film begins with a blank screen as a grand-sounding musical overture plays for nearly two minutes before the beginning of the film proper. In this way, the film not only announces high aesthetic ambitions but inevitably recalls the similar ambitions of Stanley Kubrick's *2001: A Space Odyssey* (1968), which also begins with an overture. In fact, almost everything about *TMP* marks it both as a film that aspires to the condition of art and as a work that overtly attempts to follow in the footsteps of Kubrick's film in its aesthetic presentation of future technologies. It is for good reason that *TMP* scored Oscar nominations for both art direction and visual effects.

The attempt to re-create the aesthetics of *2001* is particularly obvious in the representation of technology in *TMP*. *TOS* features impressive technology that has moved far beyond the capabilities of the twentieth century. But the technology is not particularly impressive *looking*, especially when viewed from half a century later, when the sleek Steve-Jobs-and-Apple-inflected devices we already have at hand look far more elegantly futuristic than those of *TOS*. The technology of *TOS* is merely functional, though it is clearly intended to evoke a vaguely futuristic feel from a late 1960s perspective. This technology has transformed society and solved the material problems of life, allowing human beings to concentrate their energies on fulfilling their potential as individuals—though that transformation would not appear to have been completed until *TNG* and the twenty-*fourth* century. But (largely for budgetary reasons) twenty-third-century technology has little in the way of an aesthetic component in *TOS*. Then again, for a society that is so evolved, art and culture seem to play a surprisingly minor role in the world of that series, though it does begin to become more important in the later ones. For example, the final-season *TNG* episode "Inheritance" (November 22, 1993) stipulates that an exploration of the arts is crucial to Data's attempts to become human, thus indicating that the arts are an important part of what makes us all human in the first place. Art exists in the world of *TOS*, but it doesn't seem to be particularly important to any of the major characters—and any art or literature that is mentioned in the series seems to come from the twentieth century or before. Meanwhile, the amazing technologies we see in the series seem to be taken for granted. No one seems awed by them and there is no sense of wonder associated with them. On the one hand, Kirk has his devotion to the *Enterprise* almost as a sort of spouse, and on the other McCoy has his cantankerous distrust of transporters, but in general technology is treated as a routine means to an end with little in the way of an emotional component, positive or negative. Spock, with his coolly logical and unemotional approach, seems to embody the official attitude of *TOS* toward technology. In the contemporaneous *2001*, technology is majestic and spacecraft are marvelous, not simply a means of transportation. Spacecraft are, in fact, presented as if they are large-scale works of art, moving gently and languorously through space with ballet-like precision and grace—accompanied by actual ballet music. *TMP*, a little more than a decade later, also presents spacecraft and other technological devices as if they are occasions for wonder—much more in the mode of *2001* than of *TOS*, its own direct forebear. Then again, it is also a technological artifact—the HAL 9000 computer—that serves as the main threat to the human characters of *2001*. But this aspect of the film again resonates with both *TOS* and *TMP*, which are themselves highly suspicious of computers and artificial intelligence.

STAR TREK, COMPUTERS, AND ARTIFICIAL INTELLIGENCE

The computer technology found aboard the *Enterprise* in *TOS*, with its heavy dependence on data storage via small "tapes" in square plastic cases (looking for all the world like the three-and-a-half-inch floppy discs that would be introduced in the 1980s), seems rather primitive compared with other technologies on the ship, though one could argue that these other technologies (especially the transporters) are dependent upon the digital processing of information in order to function. Indeed, a device that could literally perform the conversion of every atom of even a human being into digital code, then beam them to a distant point and rematerialize them, would require a staggering amount of memory and processing power, certainly well beyond what the computers of *TOS* seem to have otherwise. On the other hand, those computers seem to have more power at some times than at others. Thus, in "The Ultimate Computer," Starfleet attempts to introduce a new advanced, artificially intelligent computer that can run starships without help from human beings. Unfortunately, this new ability nearly leads to disaster. Meanwhile, there are several instances in which the *Enterprise* encounters advanced computer systems on alien planets, but they are almost always treated as a dystopian threat to human autonomy.

Of course, suspicion of the dangers that might be presented to humanity by computers and artificial intelligences is by now a time-honored motif in science fiction. Even something as early as Mary Shelley's *Frankenstein* (1818), conceived far before the invention of computers, already foresees the possible pitfalls of creating artificial "humans." *Frankenstein*, meanwhile, is the direct forerunner of Karel Čapek's 1920 science fiction play *R.U.R.*, which involves the creation of artificial workers—referred to as "robots," in the first recorded use of the term—though these "robots" are in fact biological. These first robots, meanwhile, are already rebellious—leading to the extermination of all humans on earth. Such motifs only became more common with the invention of computers, of course, and the motif of an advanced computer that gets out of control and goes deadly has been a popular one at least since Kubrick's HAL 9000. More recent science fiction, of course, has made the motif even more familiar, including such examples as the Skynet computer of the *Terminator* series of films, beginning with the original *Terminator* film in 1984, the same year that William Gibson's *Neuromancer* established cyberpunk as a major force in American science fiction.

The suspicion of computers that haunts *TOS* and *TMP* is thus in line with one of the major tendencies in American science fiction of the last half century. In *TMP*, for example, a deep-space probe from earth encounters a civilization of advanced machines, subsequently gaining its own artificial intelligence and then returning to earth and (through a series of misunderstandings) posing a deadly threat to its home planet. The threat is ultimately averted, but the message is clear: Machine-based intelligences might be so foreign to human intelligence that communication between the two might be quite difficult, with potentially catastrophic consequences. And this wary view of the notion of artificial intelligence is one that *TMP* shares with *TOS*, which features a number of episodes in which computers play sinister roles. On the other hand, perhaps spurred by actual advances in the world of computers and artificial intelligence, later entries in the *Trek* franchise, beginning with *TNG*, take a much rosier view of the possibilities offered by computer intelligence.

The suspicion shown toward advanced computer technologies in *TOS* is perhaps best encapsulated in "The Ultimate Computer," in which an artificially intelligent computer, the M-5, is being tested as a possible means of controlling starships, thus making most of their human crews obsolete. Kirk, of course, is highly skeptical of the idea, and McCoy is downright horrified, while Spock is predictably intrigued. Of course, it is also predictable that it all goes badly wrong, just as it comes as no surprise that Kirk intercedes and saves the day. What perhaps makes the episode a bit more complicated is the fact that M-5 has gained its intelligence through being programmed with human "engrams," specifically those of its human designer, the brilliant computer scientist Dr. Daystrom. Engrams are hypothetical physical patterns formed in the brain when memories are stored, so the point is that M-5's brain has been patterned after Daystrom's own, reflecting early artificial intelligence (AI) research that focused on the possibility of modeling intelligent computer brains on human brains, a direction that has now largely been abandoned by AI researchers. Kirk, in fact, essentially defeats M-5 by appealing to it humanity, causing it to commit "suicide" as a self-punishment for its killing of numerous humans, because murder, we are told, is a crime that carries the death penalty (in a somewhat surprising revelation that the death penalty still exists in the otherwise enlightened Federation[10]). All in all, the episode suggests that programming M-5 with human engrams was a serious mistake that might have been the key to its failure. The episode thus anticipates the coming change in direction of AI research, while at the same time leaving open the possibility that the computer might have been more successful if it had been less human (or more posthuman) in the first place.

In addition to "The Return of the Archons" (discussed in the previous chapter), several episodes of *TOS* deal with alien societies that are essentially governed by advanced computers—always with problematic (or even disastrous) results. As also discussed in the last chapter, excessive reliance on computers leads to perpetual warfare in "A Taste of Armageddon." In "The Apple," meanwhile, the *Enterprise* visits a planet where the innocent, childlike inhabitants lead seemingly idyllic lives, all their needs taken care of by the power computer that manages the planet. Unfortunately, the inhabitants have to feed the computer as well, by supplying its fuel, thus serving essentially as its slaves. Meanwhile, interpreting the *Enterprise* as a threat to the social stability of the planet, the computer launches an attack on the ship, which of course prevails in the ensuing conflict, shutting down the computer and leaving the inhabitants of the planet free to mature and develop properly without the interference (but also without the protection) of their former computer overlord. In the episode "For the World Is Hollow and I Have Touched the Sky," the *Enterprise* encounters a hollowed-out asteroid that has been made into a generational starship. Unfortunately, the inhabitants have forgotten the nature of the "world" in which they live, now slavishly worshipping as a god the computer that controls every aspect of this artificial world. Predictably, this computer has also malfunctioned, and only the intervention of the *Enterprise* prevents catastrophe. This episode thus allows *Star Trek* to further its ongoing critique of organized religion, while also warning against the "worship" of computers. In "That Which Survives," the *Enterprise* discovers a planet whose inhabitants have all been killed by a disease inadvertently created by their scientists, while the *Enterprise* itself is threatened by a super-powerful computer created to defend the planet by these same scientists, who clearly had a problem with understanding the consequences of their research.

The ship's computer aboard the *Enterprise* seems, from today's perspective, surprisingly limited in its capabilities. Even at that it has a tendency to malfunction and must be watched carefully. In the otherwise excellent episode "Tomorrow Is Yesterday," the *Enterprise* has just stopped off at a planet dominated by women in order to have the computer repaired. After that, it seems to work but has now taken on a breathlessly flirtatious (and highly unprofessional) feminine personality, which might be taken as a jab at both computers and women. The motif is played for comedy, and no disastrous results ensue, but a computer malfunction does nearly lead to disaster in the very next episode, "Court Martial," in which Kirk goes on trial for acting improperly, apparently leading to the death of a crew member. The main evidence against Kirk involves records of the incident stored in the ship's computer, which are clearly damning to Kirk, who is saved at the last moment when Spock discovers that the computer has been tampered with and now contains an inaccurate record of the events in question. The implication is clear: blind trust in a computer can lead to dire results. Finally, the late episode "The Lights of Zetar" involves a giant computer database that is installed on the planetoid Memory Alpha, intended to house all of the scientific and cultural information known to the Federation. In this case, the computers seem to work okay, but the database is destroyed when attacked by powerful aliens. Computers always seem to lead to trouble in *TOS*.

Computers lead to trouble in much of the popular culture of the 1970s and into the early 1980s as well. In the film *Demon Seed* (1977), for example, a supercomputer forcibly impregnates the wife of its scientist-creator and forces her to have its baby so that it can download its computer mind into the human-bodied child in order to be able to experience what the world is like to a human. Many elements of *Demon Seed* don't make a lot of sense (including the title, given that there are no demons involved), but the film is, after all, a parable, not a realistic narrative.[11] As a whole, it begs to be read allegorically, as a commentary on the domination of women's bodies by male-developed and male-managed technologies, with invasive technologies here described as a form of rape in about the most overt way possible. But it also speaks to the fear of computers (especially artificially intelligent computers) in general that was rampant by the late 1970s.

This fear was perhaps even stronger when the computers involved were humanoid in appearance, thus building on the notion that the Other is even more frightening when it cannot be distinguished from Us, a notion powered such classic alien-invasion films as *The Invasion of the Body Snatchers* (1956). For example, in *Westworld* (1973)—a film that, ironically, was the first to employ computer-generated images—the androids that populate a high-tech amusement park are essentially indistinguishable from humans. Perhaps predictably, the androids ultimately revolt against their human masters and slaughter the patrons of the park.

Westworld also includes some titillating gender material in its presentation of android women programmed as ideal sexual objects, perhaps paving the way for Bryan Forbes's *The Stepford Wives* (1975), in which the wives in an affluent Connecticut suburb are being replaced by ideal android wives. Totally unbelievable, this extremely well-known story (one of the iconic narratives of the decade) functions only as satire; as satire, it's reasonably effective, if a bit obvious, given how closely its vision of ideal, beautiful, conformist android wives matches an actual American male fantasy of the 1970s. But what is most interesting is its central conceit, in which successful men can pay to have their wives murdered and replaced by perfectly behaved, sexually compliant androids. The androids here, though, function just fine and never rebel, and the husbands win, including in the chilling ending in which protagonist Joanna Eberhart (Katharine Ross) is finally subdued and replaced.

This consistent depiction of computers and androids as sinister threats to our humanity is quite consistent with the depiction of such devices in most of *TOS*, though this situation would change in *TNG*, where computers are altogether more powerful and more reliable (it is, after all, a century later) and where the android Mr. Data would emerge as an extremely positive example of an artificially intelligent being. No doubt this change in the attitude of *Star Trek* toward computers was largely due to the change in attitudes toward computers in American society as a whole between the late 1960s and the late 1980s. During the original run of *TOS*, computers were mysterious entities, hulking behemoths that were only just beginning to move beyond the world of large corporations and the defense establishment. Most Americans had not encountered them directly, though most were aware that they were rapidly becoming parts of their lives, even if in ways that they little understood. It is no wonder, then, that they might have been viewed with suspicion and fear at the time.

Between *TOS* and *TNG*, the microcomputer revolution had made computers much friendlier and more familiar. Most of them were now contained in small, desktop boxes that millions of Americans had in their homes, while millions more encountered them daily at work. Virtually every aspect of American life was being dramatically changed by the spread of computers, and most Americans could see that these changes mostly made their lives easier and more convenient. Computers even took on a certain air of romance, with upstart entrepreneurs such as Bill Gates and Steve Jobs becoming heroes to many young Americans, especially as much of their success came at the expense of established corporate behemoths such as IBM. Gates and Jobs would become billionaire tech-moguls, but in their early years they were popularly figured as swashbuckling figures of renegade (but still very capitalist) enterprise. It is not for nothing that the 1999 television film that focuses on the early exploits of Gates and Jobs is entitled *Pirates of Silicon Valley*. The film explores the rise of the personal computer empires of Jobs (played by Noah Wyle) and Gates (Anthony Michael Hall) as a somewhat romantic adventure story, ranging from the late 1970s to 1985 and Jobs's departure from Apple. Among other things, this notion of Gates and Jobs as pirates presages the rise of the hacker as a sort of modern-day pirate figure in the popular culture of the 1980s and beyond.

Gates and Jobs, of course, are only the two most visible figures in a general upsurge in the prestige and importance of nerd culture in the 1980s, an upsurge that set the stage for the launch of *TNG* in 1987. In some ways, in fact, the 1980s are as crucial as the 1960s in terms of understanding the engagement of the *Star Trek* franchise with its historical context. If events in the real 1960s crucially determined the conditions under which the original *Star Trek* came into being, then the 1980s provided the conditions of possibility for the franchise to return to television in a new form.

Jobs and (especially) Gates are ultimately depicted as succeeding more from viciousness than from intelligence, the celebration of nerd culture that grew up around such figures was problematic from the beginning—and hardly a signal that intellect was suddenly the most respected characteristic one could have in a previously anti-intellectual America. In fact, the glorification of nerds in American pop culture in the 1980s was something of a struggle, as the various films and works featuring such figures had to overcome lingering fears of computers and lingering prejudices against "brainiacs." Thus, many of the works that featured computers and computer nerds in the 1980s were actually rather negative in their treatment of the technology, despite clearly attempting to appeal to a nerdy demographic.

One of the key developments that helped to legitimize nerd culture was the rise to prominence of arcade games, many of them—such as *Space Invaders* (1978) and *Galaga* (1981)—featuring outer-space themes, with such games becoming even more popular and influential with the move to home gaming platforms as the 1980s moved forward. Not coincidentally, by the way, one of the first video games for home computers was a video game version of *Star Trek*, released in 1977 for the original Apple I. In any case, despite the crudeness of the initial machines available for home video gaming (which contributed to the video game crash of 1983), by 1985 the introduction of the Nintendo Entertainment System (NES) meant that the home gaming phenomenon would soon become unstoppable (though the first *Star Trek* game for NES would not be released until 1991), ultimately rendering arcades nearly extinct—and paving the way for the now-famous holodecks of *TNG*.

Video games were the realm of the young, with the population of expert gamers generally overlapping significantly with that of young computer hobbyists. This establishment of the digital world as dominated by the expertise of the young again made that world an ideal setting for exploration by Hollywood studios, always on the lookout for new ways to lure that crucial youth demographic—a desire that might have also conditioned the (not entirely successful) inclusion of teenager Wesley Crusher (Wil Wheaton) in the crew of the *Enterprise-D* of *TNG*. One of the first films to take advantage of the opportunity to use computers to attract a young audience was John Badham's *WarGames* (1983), which features both computers and a teenage protagonist, though it is ultimately unable to overcome a basic fear of computers. The film scored considerable success despite featuring an anti–arms race theme that ran very much against the grain of the early Reagan years, as the new administration attempted to resurrect the anti-communist hysteria of the peak Cold War years in order to win support for its conservative, pro-business agendas. However, *WarGames* is really more anti-computer (and anti-intellectual) than anti-nuclear. The scenario is well known: Teenage hacker and arcade gamer David Lightman (played by Matthew Broderick) accidentally breaks into the computer that controls the U.S. nuclear defense system, initiating a series of events that nearly leads to Armageddon. Ally Sheedy plays the teenage girl who basically just tags along and has no idea how to work computers because, well, she's a girl. And there's also John Wood as Dr. Stephen Falken, the wacky-but-bitter scientist who originally designed the computer system that now threatens the world. He himself, though, has withdrawn from that world, faking his death and retreating to a private island where he spends his time tinkering with hobbies and meditating on the extinction of the dinosaurs. Falken doesn't really care if his computer makes humans extinct as well (because his own wife and son were killed in a car wreck), until the teenagers reactivate his interest in his fellow humans so that he helps to stop the holocaust, though Lightman (who somehow seems much smarter and more knowledgeable than the world-class scientist) plays the leading role. *WarGames* is a bit like *Dr. Strangelove* without the absurdist humor, though it's oddly much less realistic or believable than the obscenely exaggerated *Strangelove* and ultimately ends by reassuring us that everything will be fine as long as we still have smart, nerdy teenagers around to save the day. The expertise they gain from playing video games and hacking the computers that manage their grades for school will prepare them for this task, no formal education or specific training needed. Moreover, the film implies, perhaps inadvertently, that the real danger is not all those nuclear weapons being stockpiled worldwide, but all those scary computers that are taking over everything. In fact, the film ultimately seems anti-science, anti-computer, and anti-intellectual. Meanwhile, if *Strangelove* suggests that people are way too crazy to be trusted with nuclear weapons, *War-Games* suggests that people are fine (though the functionaries in charge of the U.S. nuclear defense system seem pretty incompetent) if we can just remember not to let computers make our decisions for us. On the other hand, *WarGames* also serves as a warning of the bad things that can happen if access to the Internet (perhaps especially by teens) is not carefully regulated. Thus, Stephanie Ricker Schulte notes that policymakers used the film to support passage of the Counterfeit Access Device and Computer Fraud and Abuse Act of 1984. [12] With great power comes great responsibility, and this act sought to limit the power of potentially irresponsible teens by limiting their access to the emerging Internet.

As Schulte further notes, *WarGames* garnered a huge amount of media attention after its initial release. Indeed, the high visibility achieved by this film no doubt helped to pave the way for several other films that followed, even if they were not directly related to its hacking theme. One of the most direct follow-ups was *The Last Starfighter* (1984), in which a teen saves the good-guy Star League in an interstellar war (thus ultimately saving the earth as well) using the skills he has gained from playing video games. Immersing themselves in video games might place young nerds outside the social mainstream of traditional American society, but it also gives them special skills that nongamers cannot hope to achieve. Indeed, the hero's skills are so special that, as the film ends with the crisis passed, he leaves earth to continue to work with the Star League and to help train future starfighters.

Such examples aside, nerds on film in the 1980s, even when represented "sympathetically," were largely comic figures conveyed by a fairly rigid collection of stereotypes. Perhaps the most memorable films in this vein were a sequence of comedies in the middle of the decade that included *Revenge of the Nerds* (1984), *Real Genius* (1985), and *Weird Science* (1985), all of which drew upon the growing popularity of "nerd" culture without really encouraging their audiences to have more respect for intellectual pursuits. Of these (despite its title), *Revenge of the Nerds*

(1984) is probably the least directly related to the rise of "nerd" culture in the 1980s. The besieged nerds of *Revenge* are definitely the heroes of the film, though this is a classic campus comedy somewhat in the tradition of *Animal House* (1978), so we see the nerds engaged more in raunchy extracurricular activities than in intellectual activities one might expect of real nerds. The nerds never seem to go to class and are never seen interacting with their professors at Adams College. Instead, they interact only with administrators and with the dastardly football coach (played by John Goodman), who only encourages his charges in their tormenting of the hapless nerds. The film is thus built around the old nerds-vs.-football-players dynamic that goes back in campus films at least to *Horse Feathers* (1932), though with some decidedly 1980s updates that see the nerds smoking weed and even getting laid. The film's sympathies are definitely with the nerds, but, rather than serving as primarily intellectual figures, the nerds serve primarily as outsider figures, thus attempting to draw upon a larger youth audience (based on the assumption that almost all teenagers feel like outsiders at one time or another). Indeed, in a motif reminiscent of the *X-Men* comics, the nerds (themselves a rather multicultural group, though they're virtually all male) become allegorical stand-ins for underdogs, minorities, and oppressed groups of all kinds, and their final victory over the jocks is even enabled by support from their beefy black brothers at Lambda Lambda Lambda. So they ultimately must use brawn, not brains, to defeat the jocks—plus a rousing Devo-esque musical performance. Thus, the nerds triumph essentially by beating the jocks at their own game, rather than by refusing to play that game.

Of course, this was 1984, when Steve Jobs and Bill Gates were still young, and it wasn't quite clear just how much power nerds were going to have in the coming digital-dominated world, though Apple's famed Macintosh commercial shown during the Super Bowl in January of 1984 suggested that Jobs, at least, saw himself as a shatterer of paradigms. *Revenge of the Nerds* was successful enough to become the anchor of a four-film franchise that ran until 1994, though the subsequent films were rather undistinguished—and certainly not designed to promote intellectualism.

One of the key phenomena of Reagan-era youth culture was the emergence of John Hughes as a sort of poet laureate of teen-oriented films. Films such as *Sixteen Candles* (1984) and *The Breakfast Club* (1985) gave voice to marginalized teens outside the popular core of jocks and cheerleaders, including nerds (or "geeks" or "brains"), as exemplified by the characters played by Anthony Michael Hall in these two films. But, of course, the nerdiest of Hughes's teen comedies was *Weird Science*, in which Hall is joined by Ilan Mitchell-Smith to play Gary and Wyatt, a couple of high-school science/computer geeks who get picked on by jocks and have trouble getting real girls, so (inspired by their watching of James Whale's 1931 film version of *Frankenstein*) they use their specialized skills and knowledge to make their own artificial woman. Dubbed "Lisa" (stipulated to be the name of a girl who had once rejected Gary by "kicking him in the nuts," but perhaps not coincidentally also the name of the commercially unsuccessful computer system introduced by Apple at the beginning of 1983), the woman is played by supermodel Kelly LeBrock, then a rising sex symbol in Hollywood on the strength of her appearance in the film *The Woman in Red* (1984) and soon to gain even more prominence from her "Don't hate me because I'm beautiful" Pantene shampoo commercials.

In *Weird Science*, nerds are finally able to put their intellects to practical use but for rather nonintellectual purposes. It's all very wholesome, of course, and Lisa really functions more as a big sister to the boys than as the sex doll she might have been. She also has the ability to manipulate reality and the laws of physics, but what she mainly does is help the boys learn to be more cool and to be popular and to get real girlfriends so that they can have more normal lives, enriched by pursuits outside of science and computers. Also, Lisa helps them defeat and humiliate Wyatt's oafish big brother, Chet, played hilariously by Bill Paxton as the personification of the jocks to whom nerds were typically opposed in the films of the 1980s. Then Lisa disappears and all returns to normal, except the two nerds are now worldly enough to transcend their nerddom, though she reappears elsewhere at the end, now serving as a boys' gym teacher, where she can wreak more havoc on jock culture. In short, nerds once again triumph by learning not to be nerds.

Martha Coolidge's *Real Genius* (1985) stands out among the science nerd comedies of the mid-1980s in that it actually concentrates on the nerds doing science instead of just trying to get drunk and/or laid (though there's some of that, too). The central character is fifteen-year-old Mitch Taylor (Gabriel Jarret), who is recruited by the nefarious physics professor Jerry Hathaway (William Atherton) to help with his troubled laser research project. So science has a sinister aspect even in this film. Mitch joins a group of Atherton's students (they sort of seem to be grad students but sort of seem to be undergraduates—it isn't really clear), who include the brilliant Chris Knight (a young Val Kilmer), who, after years of hard work, is now experiencing burnout and exploring the party side of life. Along the way, Mitch meets other nerds as well, including nineteen-year-old girl nerd Jordan Cochran (an adorable Michelle Meyrink, who also played a girl nerd in *Revenge of the Nerds* a year earlier). Romance blooms between Jordan and Mitch (with no mention of possible legal implications of the age difference). The students also get Hathaway's laser to work, only to discover to their horror that it is actually meant to be part of a lethal space-based weapons system. So the nerds concoct an elaborate scheme to sabotage the test of the weapons system, discrediting Hathaway. Meanwhile, knowing that Hathaway can't stand the smell of popcorn, they fill his fancy, immaculate house (financed with money embezzled from the laser research project) with popcorn, then pop it with the laser. The anti-military aspect of this one provides some well-meaning satire, and the film is often quite funny. It does seem a little anti-intellectual for a nerd film, though, both because the main professor figure is depicted as corrupt and incompetent and because it seems to urge nerds to get their noses out of books so they can go out and have some fun.

Of course, *Star Trek*'s Mr. Spock is a sort of founding father of nerd culture, so it should come as no surprise that all this interest in nerd culture would eventually include the *Trek* franchise, leading among other things to the creation of Mr. Data (figure 4.2), who might just be even more of a quintessential nerd than is Spock. Data, in fact, collapses two key figures from nerd culture into one: He is both a computer expert and an actual computer himself. And, far from being perceived as a threat to humanity, Data is presented as a great resource—but also as a unique one, as he was created by a now dead, eccentric scientist whose work is not yet understood by the Federation's best cybernetics experts. Of course, Data is also significantly humanized in the series, where he in fact spends much of his time trying to understand humans and trying to find ways to be more like them—pursuits with which real human teenage nerds can definitely identify. Meanwhile, this quest allows the series to raise important questions about just what it is that constitutes humanity, as in the episode "The Measure of a Man" (February 13, 1989). On the other hand, while Data himself is represented in an almost entirely positive way, the technology on which he is based does have a dangerous potential. Thus, in the early episode "Datalore" (January 18, 1988), we are introduced to his evil twin, Lore, based on the same technology as Data but with a different "phase discriminator" that left him prone to emotional instability and ultimately made him quite dangerous.

It should be noted that, while Data is considered to be an anomaly whose technology is well beyond the state-of-the-art in the twenty-fourth century of *TNG*, several episodes of *TOS* featured advanced intelligent androids even back in the twenty-third century. In "What Are Little Girls Made Of?" scientist Roger Korby (Michael Strong) is able to build quite convincing androids—but plans to use them for the sinister purpose of replacing humanity with android replicants. He has, in fact, already replaced himself with a replacement (because his human self was dying from an extreme case of frostbite); that this replacement seems to be quite insane does not bode well for his envisioned era of android rule in the galaxy. Meanwhile, one of his most impressive creations is the scantily clad Andrea (Sherry Jackson), who functions essentially as a sexbot. In

Figure 4.2.   Brent Spiner as Data in *Star Trek: First Contact*. Paramount Pictures / Photofest © Paramount Pictures

"I, Mudd," the notorious Harry Mudd seeks to conquer the galaxy with an army of superhuman androids from another galaxy, one of whom seeks to seduce Chekov in sexbot mode. Finally, in "Requiem for Methuselah," an immortal super-scientist from earth has established his own solitary refuge on a remote planet. Finding life there lonely, he has constructed his own highly realistic robot companion, whom he has named Rayna Kapec (Louise Sorel), for the writer who originally coined the term "robot." The only problem is that this sexbot doesn't seem interested in sex. So, in one of the most truly bizarre plots in all of *Star Trek*, the scientist tries to induce Kirk to use his legendary sexual charms to heat her up a bit.

In short, realistic androids do exist in the world of *TOS*, though outside the official aegis of the Federation. Further, their only uses seem to be to provide soldiers for sinister conquering armies (somewhat like the clone armies of *Star Wars*) or to provide sexual pleasure for lonely men. Such uses do not quite seem to fall in line with the usual *Star Trek* vision of technological utopia.

One of the more interesting uses of computer technology in *Star Trek* involves the generation of virtual reality environments in the "holodecks" that were first introduced in *TNG*. These holodecks themselves are high-tech wonders that suggest one of the most important ways in which technology might provide a combination of entertainment and education in the future world of the franchise, these two pursuits being among the most important ones in which humans engage in this world. Among other things, these holodecks function as key mechanisms for the delivery of culture within the twenty-fourth-century world of *TOS*, *DS9*, and *VOY*, serving as a sort of virtual-reality combination of literature, film, television, and video games. Moreover, as opposed to something like the "feelies" of Aldous Huxley's *Brave New World*, while these holodecks sometimes malfunction with potentially dangerous results (and they can sometimes be put to unsavory uses, as in the pornographic holos run by the Ferengi Quark), they are presented in an almost entirely positive manner, as a device for stimulating the imagination and enriching intellectual experience. While the virtual worlds of the holodeck simulations are virtually limitless in their variety, they tend to take a very literary tone, as when the simulations of *TNG* are often based on classics from Western literature or when the original "holonovels" of *VOY* provide perhaps the clearest examples of future artistic creativity in all of *Star Trek*.

The holodecks of the later *Trek* TV franchises also provide particularly interesting examples of artificially intelligent lifeforms. After all, the virtual-reality environments created in these holodecks involve not merely simulated settings (typically from earth's literature or history) but also a variety of characters with which the crew members can interact. Those characters are endowed with very limited autonomy, but there are suggestions that they have the potential to evolve into more independent intelligences. In the *TNG* episode "Elementary, Dear Data" (December 5, 1988), Chief Engineer La Forge and the android Commander Data are participating in a Sherlock Holmes simulation when La Forge inadvertently overrides many of the holodeck's safety protocols as he seeks to pose a challenge to Data's deductive reasoning skills. As a result, Holmes's (Data's) archenemy, Professor Moriarty, achieves enough intelligence to not only match wits with Data/Holmes but also to think beyond the scenario of the simulation and to desire to live independently of the holodeck. The latter proves to be impossible given the currently available technology, but Captain Picard instructs the ship's computer to store Moriarty's program in its current form toward the day when it can potentially be reactivated as an independent entity. This scenario thus raises all sorts of philosophical questions about the existential status, not only of Moriarty, but of all of the other characters that are created within the various holodeck simulations but that then blink out of existence when their particular simulation is terminated, their latest manifestations typically not even being saved in the computer's memory. Saving them is certainly within the capabilities of the system, however, and it is clear that, were they to be continually saved, thus accumulating experience, more and more of them might develop capabilities similar to those developed by Moriarty in this episode.

TECHNOLOGY AND THE ENVIRONMENT IN *STAR TREK*

One of the most important criticisms of technology in our own world concerns the negative impact that technological advances in the past two centuries have had on the environment. It is no secret that the industrial revolution and subsequent technological developments such as the widespread use of fossil fuels to power automobiles and generate electricity have produced massive environmental problems, including global climate changes that ultimately might threaten the very existence of life on earth. As a result, a cultural phenomenon as devoted to the value of technological progress as the *Star Trek* franchise must surely come to grips with the potential negative environmental effects of technology.

Star Trek has, in fact, engaged with this possibility. For example, the emphasis on the population problem in the *TOS* episode "The Mark of Gideon" or the treatment of species extermination in the film *The Voyage Home* are largely environmental matters. But the franchise's most direct engagement with technology-induced environmental destruction occurs in the final-season *TNG* episode "Force of Nature" (October 15, 1993). This episode begins with a rather light sequence featuring the comedy team of Data and La Forge that largely centers on Data's efforts to train his pet cat, Spot. Predictably (for anyone who has ever "owned" a cat), the cat is far more successful at training Data than Data is at training the cat. But then the serious matter of the episode begins—and it is serious indeed. Two alien scientists board the *Enterprise* uninvited and announce that their planet is being rendered uninhabitable because the use of warp drives is ripping apart the texture of space-time in their part of the galaxy. At first, Picard and his experts (Data and La Forge) are skeptical, but the scientists finally manage to convince them that their concerns are real. Informed of the problem, Starfleet moves quickly to rectify it. The Federation Council immediately orders that all nonessential travel on Federation vessels be eliminated in areas of space that have been shown to be susceptible to damage from warp drives. Further, they order that all Federation vessels anywhere be limited to a speed of Warp 5 so that any potential damage can be minimized until they can study the problem further.

The implications of this episode are quite clear: An enlightened civilization such as the Federation will always move quickly to avoid creating environmental damage, even if doing so is a significant inconvenience. The fact that the virtually unlimited resources of the Federation make this decision easier (because they do not have to worry about negative economic impacts) only makes the message of the episode that much stronger: Capitalism and the drive for short-term profits, which are so prominent in our own world, are a big part of the problem because they create an incentive to ignore long-term environmental damage, even when that damage might ultimately be catastrophic. That so little is being done about global climate change in our own early twenty-first-century world would seem to verify this point quite clearly, especially as one of the most frequent excuses for doing nothing about this looming danger has to do with its short-term effects on corporate profit margins.

In addition, one of the most crucial and difficult aspects of global climate change is that it is legitimately *global*. All parts of the world will be affected virtually equally, whether or not they were major contributors to the problem in the first place. Presumably, the Federation—with its extensive fleet of warp-powered starships—is one of the leading contributors to the "warp pollution" problem detailed in "Force of Nature." But, good galactic citizens that they are, the Federation also willingly takes the lead in fighting this problem. This episode, then, can be taken as a strong anticipatory condemnation of the kind of insular thinking that led to the announcement by U.S. president Donald Trump in June 2017 that the United States (which basically plays the same role on earth that the Federation plays in the Alpha Quadrant) intends to withdraw from the Paris Agreement as soon as legally possible (which would be in 2020). In contrast, the Federation provides strong galactic leadership, not only limiting their own use of warp power but immediately reaching out to other major star-faring civilizations in the Alpha Quadrant. Worf assures us that the Klingons will cooperate with the new limitations on warp-powered travel but presumes that the Romulans will not be so cooperative. And it goes without saying that the Ferengi, inveterate capitalists that they are, will never cooperate, no doubt justifying their lack of cooperation by declaring the whole thing a Federation plot to undermine their ability to do business. In short, this episode ends up suggesting that, given the state of American politics in the Trump era, the United States has now assumed the role, not of the Federation, but of the Ferengi.

5

STAR TREK AND THE HISTORY OF *STAR TREK* FANDOM

An episode of the Fox network animated science fiction comedy *Futurama* (set in the thirty-first century), tellingly entitled "Where No Fan Has Gone Before" (first broadcast April 21, 2002), gives us an amusing glimpse of the future of *Star Trek* and its fans. In this episode, we learn that by the twenty-third century, "*Star Trek* fandom had evolved from a loose association of nerds with skin problems into a full-blown religion." Further, the growing power of this religion caused it to be regarded as a threat by governments around the galaxy, which then began brutally oppressing *Trek* fans, banning their sacred texts (i.e., the television episodes and the films) and dumping all the tapes of them on the forbidden planet Omega 3. Cleverly structured as a parody of the *TOS* episode "The Menagerie," "Where No Fan Has Gone Before" involves a court trial that revolves around this suppression of *Trek* fandom and the attempts of the *Futurama* cast (and especially series lead Philip J. Fry, originally a denizen of the twentieth century and a devoted *Trek* fan) to retrieve the banned *Star Trek* tapes. Traveling to Omega 3, they encounter most of the original *TOS* main cast (voiced by the actors who had played them in *TOS* itself), maintained there all this time by one Melllvar, a super-powerful alien that has become a huge *Trek* fan by watching the tapes that were dumped on its planet. Much of the humor of this episode derives from the competition between Fry and Melllvar to prove which is the more devoted *Trek* fan, mirroring similar competitions that have frequently occurred between real *Trek* fans—despite the denunciation of competitiveness that underlies much of the *Trek* franchise. Ultimately, in one of the episode's numerous parodies of beloved *TOS* conceits, the super alien pits the *Star Trek* cast in armed combat against the *Futurama* cast. In response, the two casts band together against the super alien, which seems almost deranged by its extreme devotion to *Star Trek* and responds by trying to kill them all. Ultimately, Fry warns Melllvar that "you can't let a TV show be your whole life." So Melllvar backs off and even considers moving out of its parents' basement and getting a job.

Gentle parodies of both *Star Trek* and *Star Trek* fandom aside, what "Where No Fan Has Gone Before" really presents is a loving homage to *TOS* and its legacy, suggesting that *Star Trek* and the fan culture that surrounds it will remain strong for many centuries into the future. Indeed, the phenomenon of *Star Trek* fandom is now widely recognized as one of the most remarkable forces in American popular culture of the past half century. The word "fan," of course, is short for "fanatic," and few fan communities have been as fanatical in their devotion to their object as have *Star Trek* fans. For many, *Trek* fandom goes far beyond simply watching (and rewatching and rewatching) the numerous films and television episodes that constitute the heart of the franchise—though of course the devotion of fans to watching the products of the franchise is crucial. But this same devotion has spilled over into the consumption of related works, such as novels and comic books, as well as fan-generated works—from written fiction to actual episodes of imagined new *Star Trek* series. *Star Trek* fandom has also been on the forefront of the merchandising and collecting craze that, by the early twenty-first century, has become such a big part of American popular culture—and American marketing.

The strength of the *Star Trek* fan community could already be seen in the unprecedented number of fan letters that NBC began to receive from fans of the show almost immediately after its inception. When rumors began to spread midway through the second season of *TOS* that NBC was considering the cancellation of the series after the end of that season, the true strength of the *Trek* fan community became clear in the now almost legendary outpouring of fan activism that occurred in support of the continuation of the series. A massive (and surprisingly well-organized) letter-writing campaign inundated NBC with demands that the series be continued, while raucous fans gathered outside the NBC offices in New York to demonstrate their support for the series. Then again, it is not entirely clear what role this fan support played in the continuation of *TOS* for another season, and it is certainly the case that a similar outpouring of support for the show a year later was unable to prevent its cancellation after the third season.

The true strength of *Star Trek* fan culture, though, was demonstrated when fan activism continued unabated even after the ultimate cancellation of the series, helping to build a solid fan base that played a crucial role in the subsequent success of the series in syndication. This ongoing fan activity also kept the idea of *Star Trek* alive toward the day when the franchise would eventually return, first on film and then in a sequence of new television series that explored various aspects of the *Trek* vision.

FANZINES AND OTHER FAN-ORIENTED PUBLICATIONS

Star Trek fandom, of course, has its roots in the strongly fan-oriented culture that surrounded the pulp magazines that dominated the rise of science fiction as a genre in the United States in the 1930s and 1940s.[1] For example, one of the keys to the success of the pioneering *Amazing Stories*, founded by Hugo Gernsback in 1926, was the inclusion of a letters column that allowed readers to begin to establish a sense of membership in a community, thus taking a crucial step in the development of SF fandom. Other leading journals, such as *Astounding Science Fiction* (which quickly became the most important of the science fiction pulps after John W. Campbell became its editor in 1937), also provided venues for both fans and authors to communicate with one another. Indeed, in these early days, fans often *were* authors, as when the New York–based fan club the Futurians spawned such later stars of the genre as Isaac Asimov and Frederik Pohl. Meanwhile, if many of the stories in the commercial pulps were authored by fans and beginning professionals, many other SF fans wrote, read, and published their own amateur publications, providing still more opportunities for the establishment of fan communities. These publications, which came to be known as "fanzines," were often printed on crudely copied mimeographed sheets and might have had only a handful of readers, but these readers had a strong sense of belonging, especially as these fanzines provided potential venues for these readers to become writers. Indeed, the first science fiction fanzine appeared as early as 1930 with the initial publication of *The Comet* by Chicago's Science Correspondence Club. *The Comet* was edited by Raymond A. Palmer and Walter Dennis, the former of whom would go on to become an important editor of professional science fiction magazines, including his assumption of the editorship of *Amazing Stories* in 1938.[2]

By September of 1967, with *TOS* barely a year old, the first fanzine devoted to *Star Trek* had already appeared. Entitled *Spockanalia* (thus providing an early indication that, to many true fans, it was Spock, not Kirk, who was the center of the series), this ninety-page publication even included a letter of support from Leonard Nimoy. Published roughly twice a year, *Spockanalia* lasted for five issues, with the last (now 105 pages long) appearing in June of 1970, a year after the last first-run broadcast of a *TOS* episode. But the fanzine—which included letters and articles, as well as original fiction, poetry, and art—became an important part of *Trek* culture during its brief run and even included letters by Gene Roddenberry, who endorsed the fanzine as a key source of information about the series, recommending it for aspiring writers of *Trek* episodes.

A vast array of *Trek*-related fanzines has been published since *Spockanalia*, among other things offering venues for the publication of what is now an extensive collection of fan fiction and other fan-produced writings and art. Appropriately enough, advances in technology have made important contributions to the ongoing vitality of this kind of fan writing, with the Internet providing easy access both to those who wish to publish their writings and to those who wish to read them. Most of the dozens and dozens of *Star Trek* fanzines that have appeared over the years have been short-lived, so that the field has not been dominated by major players but has instead been marked by diversity, with individual fanzines often being highly specialized—as when, for example, they have been limited to a focus on individual characters or actors. But the market for such magazines is such that commercial publishers have also moved into the field, often with considerable success. For example, the officially licensed UK-based *Star Trek Magazine* (which, in 2006, also began publishing a similar but separate North American version) has been published continually since 1995, with the total number of issues now approaching two hundred. This magazine covers all things *Trek* rather than pursuing a narrow specialization, and its long publication history stands as proof of the market for such fan-oriented publications.

One of the more unusual aspects of *Trek* fan fiction involves the production of what has come to be called "slash" fiction, consisting of stories involving romantic (and often highly erotic) relationships between two characters of the same sex. While the phenomenon of slash fiction has become widespread among fans of various cultural artifacts, it is generally recognized that the genre originated in the 1970s with fan-created stories involving a romantic attachment between Kirk and Spock. These stories came to be called "Kirk/Spock" stories, or simply "K/S" stories, the "/" in this designation giving the genre its more general name.[3] Originating from the fact that the characters of Kirk and Spock do have such a strong interpersonal connection in *TOS* and the *Trek* films featuring the *TOS* cast, these stories take that connection a step further and envision Kirk and Spock as gay lovers. Initially limited to appearances in relatively obscure fanzines, K/S stories gradually became more firmly established after drawing the attention of academic cultural critics such as Constance Penley. And, of course, K/S fan fiction has received far more distribution in recent years thanks to the rise of the Internet, which makes it easy for anyone to post stories on anything they want while making those stories quite accessible to a broad audience. The spread of slash fiction to other franchises (as in "Starsky/Hutch"), meanwhile, constitutes only one of the many ways that *Trek* fandom has led the way for other types of fan culture.

MERCHANDISING AND CONVENTIONS

Roddenberry's acceptance and encouragement of *Spockanalia* helped to set a tone of active exchange between fans and makers of *Star Trek* that has continued to this day. Indeed, Maria Jose and John Tenuto have argued that Roddenberry's engagement with *Spockanalia* made him "a pioneer in recognizing the importance of directly interfacing with television fans."[4] Perhaps the most obvious example of this kind of interaction occurs on the *Star Trek* convention circuit, where devoted fans have had extensive opportunities over the years to rub elbows with their heroes from the franchise. Indeed, the amount of interaction that has occurred at these conventions between the makers of *Trek* and the fans of *Trek* is almost certainly unmatched by any other cultural franchise. Conventions, of course, have long been a crucial component of science fiction fandom, dating back at least to 1939. In that year, not only was the heavily attended New York World's Fair essentially built around science fictional visions of the future (giving science fiction a new cultural respectability), but the first World Science Fiction Convention was held in conjunction with the fair. That convention would become an ongoing annual event and still continues today as "Worldcon," one of the world's largest fan-oriented conventions.

By 1966, clubs, conventions, fanzines, and a strong desire to communicate with other fans had long been a crucial part of the fabric of science fiction in America. It is perhaps not surprising, then, that *Star Trek* would very quickly generate a vibrant fan culture of its own. After all, the premiere of *TOS* on network television was arguably the highest-profile event that had ever occurred in American science fiction, offering SF fans the opportunity for once to feel that they were active participants in the mainstream popular culture of the United States, rather than the marginalized inhabitants of a little-respected cultural ghetto. It is not surprising, then, that *Star Trek* might generate a fan culture of unprecedented intensity, though it is also the case that science fiction magazines were, by this time, taking a more professional turn, making fan culture less important there than it had once been and thus perhaps opening a space for *Star Trek* fan culture.

Star Trek fan culture certainly got off to a fast start when the second *TOS* pilot (the one that actually sold the series to NBC) was screened for fans at the Worldcon in Cleveland, Ohio, held the week before the premiere of the show on NBC. Roddenberry himself presented the screening as the centerpiece of an elaborate promotion for the new series at the convention. As Edward Gross and Mark Altman note, fans at the convention greeted the *Star Trek* pilot with great enthusiasm, while at the same time reacting to a screening of the pilot for *The Time Tunnel* with derision.[5] In a very real sense, then, *Star Trek* was born on the convention circuit, a milieu in which it has ultimately thrived.

By January of 1972, *Star Trek* had its first dedicated convention, held at the Statler Hilton Hotel in New York City. The convention was a great success, moving the next year to larger facilities in the Commodore Hotel near Grand Central Station. This convention was even more successful, including a surprise appearance by Leonard Nimoy, while James Doohan and George Takei made scheduled appearances, setting the stage for the numerous convention appearances that would be made over the years by so many *Trek* actors, writers, and other principals. This original *Star Trek* convention ran yearly under the management of its original organizers though 1976,[6] by which time other conventions had begun to spring up and after which time even more conventions would proliferate.

One particularly notable feature of the 1973 convention was a highly successful dealers' area, where a variety of *Trek* merchandise could be purchased, setting a precedent for what would become a major marketing empire. Some subsequent conventions have been almost entirely devoted to merchandising, while *Trek*-related products have been marketed via a number of other venues as well. One of the most innovative aspects of the new *Trek* fan culture was its commercial orientation, something that many traditionalists in the science fiction fan community greeted with disdain, if not absolute horror. One of the founding principles of SF fandom until the rise of the *Trek* fan community was that fandom should be based on pure devotion to science fiction, free of any motives other than communication with other fans. Up until the arrival of *Star Trek*, science fiction fan conventions were devoted primarily to the sharing of information, ideas, and enthusiasm. Ironically, given the utopian rejection of capitalist profit-seeking that informs the entire *Star Trek* franchise, this situation changed quickly with the advent of *Trek*-oriented conventions. Not only have a wide variety of *Trek*-related products been hawked at various *Star Trek* conventions, but the conventions have provided an important place for fans to meet face to face those involved in making the series and films. Many actors involved in the *Trek* franchise have made these conventions a sort of auxiliary career, often making substantial amounts of money in appearance fees (William Shatner has been particularly well paid) and even in selling their own merchandise, such as autographed photos or even the autographs themselves.

Trek merchandise over the years has ranged from rare collector's items (such as props or costumes actually used in episodes or films from the franchise) to handmade *Trek*-related crafts lovingly created by fans to slick, commercially produced uniforms, models, trading cards, and toys (especially action figures) related to the series. One can now purchase, for example, a replica *Trek* communicator that can pair with a Bluetooth-enabled phone to allow one to make and receive actual calls, complete with the requisite sound effects from *TOS*. After the rise of the Internet, of course, such items quickly became widely available online, yet conventions have remained a popular way of acquiring merchandise because they provide other forms of experience as well, in addition to the opportunity to purchase coveted souvenirs. Meanwhile, the *Trek* merchandising empire has extended well beyond items that are directly related to the series to a variety of products that are marketed under the *Star Trek* banner, even though they actually have little or nothing to do with the franchise directly. For example, a number of *Trek* breakfast cereals have been marketed over the years, even though *Star Trek* characters are not exactly known for their love of breakfast cereals. The many different *Trek*-branded cereals, for example, include the still-available and colorfully named "Tribbles 'n' Bits," which features tiny, sugar-coated "tribbles" as an ingredient.

One unusual aspect of *Star Trek* merchandising includes the fact that a number of *Star Trek* postage stamps have been issued over the years by the U.S. Postal Service (USPS), providing an official acknowledgment of the prominence of *Trek* fan culture in American culture as a whole. As of this writing, if one goes to the official online postage store of the USPS, one can purchase a sheet of twenty *Star Trek* "Forever" first-class stamps featuring four different designs. The USPS also sells other *Star Trek* collectibles from their website (https://www.usps.com), including a framed picture of the *Enterprise* with images of the four stamp styles superimposed on the picture.

The vast extent of the *Star Trek* marketing empire is a key sign of the strong role that the franchise has played in the lives of fans, who often clearly feel that owning *Trek*-inspired merchandise somewhat gets them closer to the series. The obvious irony here is that the *Star Trek* ethos is strongly opposed to commercialism and envisions a future in which people would have little interest in acquiring trinkets to make their lives feel less empty. But that, of course, is the future. In the present day, the fact that merchandising has played such an important role in *Star Trek* fan culture is perfectly understandable and even predictable. Much recent work in psychoanalysis (especially revisions of Freud emanating from France in the past half century or so) would suggest that human beings are largely motivated by a drive to find a replacement for something that they find missing in their lives. In particular, this psychoanalytic view would argue that many of our desires originate in a perceived need to find a substitute for the now-lost sense of wholeness (and especially of seamless connection to the mother) that characterizes the psychic experience of infancy. Psychoanalysis focuses particularly on interpersonal relations and on the way our attempts to find fulfillment through love are really just attempts to restore that infantile experience. But, from this point of view, much fan culture could also be seen as an attempt to connect to some object of devotion (such as the *Trek* franchise) as well as to other devotees of that object, thus restoring some of this lost sense of belonging. Meanwhile, consumerism operates in very much the same way, as consumers are driven (under the impetus of forces such as advertising) to desire to obtain certain specific objects in the hope that obtaining this object will somehow make them whole. Consumerism and fan culture are thus driven by very similar mechanisms of desire. It should thus come as no surprise that they go so well together.

From the psychoanalytic perspective, however, human life is fundamentally tragic because the lost sense of infantile wholeness and connection to the mother can never really be restored. We are thus fated to drift through life in a series of failed attempts to replace that original object of desire, always undermining our relationships by wanting our significant others to be something they can never be and to give us something they can never give. Fulfillment through consumption is similarly doomed, though in this case it is doomed by design. A consumer who fulfills his or her desire by purchasing and owning a given commodity will of course no longer be driven to consume additional objects, thus collapsing the endless chain of consumption that drives modern capitalism. Consumerist desires are therefore from the beginning meant to be unsatisfiable, manipulated in such a way that the consumer is encouraged to buy endlessly. We should not forget that the Rolling Stones' classic 1965 anthem "(I Can't Get No) Satisfaction," a near contemporary of *TOS*, is not about love or sex as many seem to think but about consumerism. The secret to the utopian future envisioned by *Star Trek* is that human beings in this future already feel comfortable with the lives they are living, already feel at one with the world in which they exist. They thus have no need to accumulate possessions of a material sort or to try to dominate and control others in their personal relationships. They already have everything they need without resorting to strategies of accumulation or manipulation. If, in our own time, both *Star Trek* and *Star Trek* fandom are related to attempts to fulfill perceived needs, then the futuristic vision on which *Star Trek* is built rests on the genuine fulfillment of a more legitimately utopian need: the need to have no worries about fulfilling one's needs.

OTHER WORKS DEVOTED TO OR PRODUCED BY *STAR TREK* FAN CULTURE

The extent of *Trek* fan culture is such that a number of works have been produced *about* that culture, or at least in relation to it, while others have literally been produced *by* that culture. For example, the extensive array of video games that have been produced under the aegis of the *Trek* franchise can also be considered a form of fan culture, as the playing of the games requires the active participation of fans. A text-only *Star Trek* computer game (written in BASIC) was released in 1971, making *Trek* computer games essentially as old as computer gaming itself—and even older than the personal computer. Over the years a number of *Trek* games have been developed on mainframe systems, while the 1982 *Strategic Operations Simulator* brought the *Trek* franchise into the world of arcade games. But it is, of course, on personal computers and on home video game consoles where *Star Trek* games have reached their widest audience. As early as 1979, *Star Trek: Phaser Strike* was released for the pioneering (but short-lived) Microvision home console, and in 1983 a version of *Strategic Operations Simulator* was released for a variety of home systems. In the 1990s, a number of *Star Trek* games were released for various home systems, including Nintendo, Sega, Xbox, and PlayStation, and the release of *Trek* games for home consoles and personal computers has proceeded apace into the twenty-first century, with games also beginning to appear on the iOS and Android mobile operating systems in recent years. Thus, while no single *Trek*-related game has ever become a dominant blockbuster, the franchise as a whole has been one of the most extensive and long-lived sources of material for video games in the entire history of gaming.

Another key product of fan culture is the array of films that have been produced about that culture. Documentary filmmakers, acting essentially as pop cultural anthropologists, have found *Trek* fandom a particularly rich source of material. Perhaps the central such documentary is Roger Nygard's feature-length film *Trekkies* (1997), which provides an extended inside look at *Star Trek* fan culture, focusing particularly on *Star Trek* conventions and the loyal fans who attend them.[7] Hosted by former *TNG* actor Denise Crosby, the film makes clear just how devoted *Trek* fans can be and just how big a part of their lives the franchise can become. Many fans depicted in the series have attended dozens of conventions, often in full *Star Trek* garb—or even in full Klingon (or other alien) costumes. But many fans display their loyalty to the franchise even in their everyday lives—as when the film introduces us to a dentist whose entire office is done up in *Trek* décor, while the dentist and his staff wear full Starfleet uniforms. Another fan featured in the film is Barbara Adams, the Arkansas woman who drew considerable media attention in 1996 when she wore a full Starfleet uniform while serving in several sessions as an alternate juror in the high-profile Whitewater trial of the former partners of Bill and Hillary Clinton.

Both Crosby and Nygard returned in their respective roles for another documentary, *Trekkies 2*, in 2004 (figure 5.1). This sequel updates and extends the coverage of the original *Trekkies* film, with some of the "stars" of the earlier film (including Adams) returning. But the real emphasis of this film is the international range of *Star Trek* fan culture, beginning with Crosby's visit to "Fedcon" in Bonn, Germany, described as Europe's largest *Trek* convention, with a daily attendance of more than

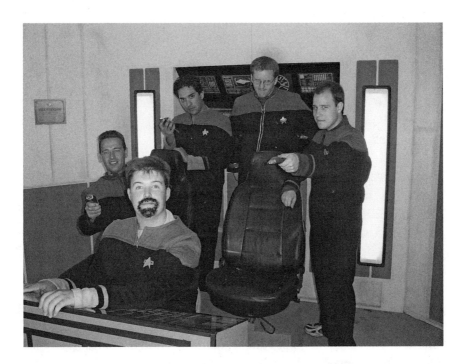

Figure 5.1. *Star Trek* fans in full garb as shown in *Trekkies 2*. Paramount Pictures / Photofest © Paramount Pictures

five thousand during the annual event. The European fans at this convention seem just as devoted as American Trekkies, the main difference being that they speak more languages. Crosby herself is greeted enthusiastically by a large crowd as she appears on stage at the convention, and it turns out that this convention is large enough that it is able to draw a number of other American actors from the various *Trek* series as well, including *DS9*'s Nana Visitor and Cirroc Lofton (who, as a child actor, had played Ben Sisko's son, Jake), both of whom are interviewed in the film. Others at the convention include a Klingon Santa Claus and fans dressed as members of a number of other alien species featured in *Star Trek*, as well as original alien species inspired by the aliens of *Trek*. Crosby even meets a young fan who is making his own original *Star Trek* movie (in German), having invested $20,000 to build a highly authentic replica of the bridge of the *Enterprise* from *TNG* for use as the main set. Crosby also visits *Trek* fans in London (where she tours an apartment built as the interior of a *Trek*-inspired spaceship, listed for sale on eBay for $2 million). Other international destinations include Paris (where she attends a *Star Trek* quiche party), Rome (where food turns out to be the center of *Trek* fan culture), and a *Trek* festival in São Paulo, Brazil. This film also takes us to *Trek* conventions in Novi Sad, Serbia, and Melbourne and Sydney, Australia, as well as to Baltimore's "Shore Leave," America's oldest fan-run *Trek* convention. Finally, *Trekkies 2* also introduces us to a number of *Star Trek* tribute bands, including a metal band (all of whose members are dressed as Klingons), a punk band, and a "filk"[8] band.

Shatner himself has contributed to a whole family of documentaries related to various aspects of the *Trek* phenomenon, several of them focusing on fan culture in one way or another. For example, in *The Truth Is in the Stars* (2017), written and directed by J. Craig Thompson, Shatner sits down for a series of conversations with prominent individuals ranging from show-business celebrities such as Ben Stiller and Whoopi Goldberg, to celebrity scientists such as David Suzuki, Neil deGrasse Tyson, and astronaut Chris Hadfield (whose performance of David Bowie's "Space Oddity" while aboard the International Space Station became an Internet sensation in 2013). It all ultimately leads to a pilgrimage to Cambridge, England, where Shatner interviews superstar physicist Stephen Hawking. Ostensibly, Shatner seeks in these conversations to find clues to the meaning of the universe from a variety of viewpoints. But the real thread that ties the various interviews together is that all of these individuals are highly familiar with the *Star Trek* franchise (especially Shatner's own *TOS*) and that most of them have been heavily influenced by it in their own thinking and careers. *Star Trek* fans, as it turns out, are not simply underachieving nerds living in their mothers' basements: they can be among the most successful people in the world.

The film *Get a Life!* (2012), written, directed, and hosted by Shatner, is another documentary based on *Star Trek* fan culture. This one again takes a look at some specific *Trek* fans, focusing on the attendees at the 45th Anniversary *Star Trek* Convention in Las Vegas, though it also understandably (given Shatner's central role) has better access to the actors and other principals involved in making the various *Trek* series and films. The film tries to discern what the *Trek* franchise has meant to the fans who are featured in the film, but the real "plot" of this film concerns Shatner's attempts to understand at a deeper level the ongoing devotion of *Trek* fans, whom he once famously dismissed by advising them to "get a life" during a comedy skit that aired on *Saturday Night Live* on December 20, 1986. Unfortunately, Shatner's research in this sense is rather superficial and narrow, consisting of consultations with two individuals, both of whom help Shatner to understand the role of *Star Trek* as a modern myth, based on the theories of Joseph Campbell, as espoused especially in his book *The Hero with a Thousand Faces* (1949). First, Shatner introduces us to Richard Imon, a professor of liberal arts at Regis University. Imon teaches "myths, cultures, and traditions," using *Star Trek* as a key vehicle for conveying to his students the ways in which myths help us to understand ourselves and the world around us. Imon's use of the theories of Campbell for this purpose then take Shatner to interview Robert Walter, the head of the Joseph Campbell Foundation, and it is Walter who provides the bulk of the theoretical understanding of *Trek* culture provided by this film.

Shatner appears to experience a revelation as Walter explains to him the way myths work, proclaiming with amazement late in the film that he suddenly now understands the significance of *Trek* fan culture as something that helps participants find meaning in their lives by providing an avenue toward "community, hope and love. It's fueled by the passions we fans feel for the ideals of *Star Trek*." The problem, of course, is that Campbell's theorization of myth is now outdated and rather simplistic, taking a universalist approach that ignores the material realities of specif-

ic historical circumstances and is underwritten by a right-wing individualist ideology that is very much at odds with that of the *Trek* franchise.
Moreover, what Imon and Walter convey in *Get a Life!* is an understanding of the mythic aspects of *Trek* fan culture so simplistic that it could
have been arrived at with no appeal to Campbell's theories at all. Indeed,
one wonders how Shatner could have so thoroughly failed to grasp the
mythic significance of *Star Trek* through all the years of his association
with the franchise—unless of course he is merely acting here, simply
pretending to be amazed at the supposed profundity of what he is hearing
from these learned experts.

There are, of course, far better conceptualizations available to help us
understand the true function of *Trek* fan culture. The portrayals of *Trek*
fans in the *Trekkies* films and in *Get a Life!* make clear that *Trek* fans
come in all shapes and sizes, can be all ages, and can come from all walks
of life. Variety is, in fact, a hallmark of *Trek* fan culture, but it is nevertheless an identifiable cultural phenomenon and one that clearly qualifies
as a "subculture" as defined by cultural theorists such as Dick Hebdige,
who emphasizes that the formation of subcultures tends to allow individuals who feel marginal to mainstream society to develop shared identities
that create a sense of belonging.

For Hebdige, subcultures (such as British punk culture) often carry a
subversive political charge—though he also emphasizes that, especially
as they become more and more successful, these subcultures tend to be
commercialized and drawn into the mainstream. For Hebdige, "youth
cultural styles may begin by offering symbolic challenges, but they must
inevitably end by establishing new sets of conventions; by creating new
commodities, new industries, or rejuvenating old ones."[9] In short, subcultures might initially be partly driven by a desire to oppose what is perceived as the dehumanizing and spiritually impoverishing power of the
capitalist system, but themselves ultimately tend to be appropriated by
that system and to become a part of it as merely another means of generating corporate profits.

It is certainly the case that the *Star Trek* franchise has generated substantial corporate profits for Paramount/CBS over the decades. It is also
the case that fan culture itself has generated considerable income for
some of those involved in it, outside the corporate mainstream of the
franchise. Indeed, *Trek* fan culture has become a very big business over
the decades and has no doubt contributed to an increasing commercializa-

tion of fan cultures as a whole over the years. Yet Trekkies (or Trekkers) have shown an unusual ability to maintain a distinctive identity that has prevented them from being fully appropriated by mainstream culture— probably because the science fictional basis of the *Trek* phenomenon has a built-in resistance to appropriation due to its inherently otherworldly setting.

In addition to the array of fan fictions mentioned above, *Trek* fans have produced a surprising amount of programming that essentially involves the creation of entire new fan-produced series and films, a phenomenon that has been largely enabled by recent advances in digital photography and computer-generated imagery. The recent rise of crowd-sourcing has also helped to produce funding for such efforts. Meanwhile, understanding how much of its income from the franchise derives from its energized fan base, Paramount has generally been quite cooperative in allowing nonprofit fan-produced "series" to use intellectual property from the franchise free of charge, often leading to quite sophisticated results, though such series in fact range from crude animated briefs to full-fledged, surprisingly professional-looking "television" episodes.

The three-part miniseries *Star Trek: Of Gods and Men*, released in 2007–2008, is a good example of such fan-funded and fan-produced work. Available as a free download from the official series website (and now available on YouTube at https://youtu.be/kFqAME7dx58), *Of Gods and Men* won the 2008 award for Best Web Production from the site SyFy Portal. Directed by *Trek* alum Tim Russ (who played the Vulcan Tuvok on *VOY*), this miniseries featured a number of former *Trek* actors, including Nichelle Nichols, Walter Koening, and Grace Lee Whitney from *TOS*. The same production team responsible for *Of Gods and Men* also created *Star Trek: Renegades*, a one-shot fan film (originally conceived as the beginning of a series) released on YouTube in August 2015 and featuring several actors who had formerly appeared in the *Trek* franchise, including Koenig, Robert Picardo, and Russ.

The most extensive *Star Trek* fan series ran intermittently from 2004 to 2008 as *Star Trek: New Voyages* and then from 2008 to 2015 as *Star Trek: Phase II* (picking up on Roddenberry's originally intended title for a series he saw as the successor to *TOS* in the 1970s). Designed as a direct extension of *TOS*, *New Voyages/Phase II* is linked to *TOS* in a particularly direct way, including episodes that are direct sequels to specific *TOS* episodes or that are based on fan fiction derived from *TOS*. However, the recent reboot of the *Trek* film franchise by J. J. Abrams has led CBC/ Paramount to begin guarding their material a bit more carefully in case they decide to use it in future films. Thus, a plan to base an episode of *Star Trek: Phase II* on an unproduced *TOS* script by Norman Spinrad in 2012 drew complaints from the CBS legal department and had to be canceled—as did plans to produce any future episodes as direct adaptations of preexisting works in the franchise, such as novels or comics. The third episode of the series, "World Enough and Time" (available on You- Tube at https://youtu.be/sJmpEo2-tok), was successful enough to win a 2008 Hugo Award nomination for Best Dramatic Presentation, Short Form—alongside episodes of such series as *Battlestar Galactica* and *Dr. Who*, the eventual winner. The series has struggled to produce more than an episode or so per year but remains officially in production as of this writing.

One of the most interesting products of *Star Trek* fan culture is the web series *Star Trek Continues*, which began appearing on YouTube and other online sites in May 2013. Partly funded with money raised through Kickstarter and Indiegogo campaigns, *Star Trek Continues* is a work of fan fiction that is set as an immediate sequel to *TOS*. Of all subsequent *Star Trek* series (commercial or fan-based), it is probably the one that most resembles *TOS*, though *Star Trek: New Voyages* might vie for that honor as well. *Star Trek Continues* consists of eleven episodes, released periodically on YouTube between May 24, 2013, and November 13, 2017. It features the same main characters as *TOS*, though of course with different actors. Series developer Vic Mignogna, who bears at least a passing resemblance to a young Shatner, plays Kirk, while Todd Haber- korn, previously known primarily as a voice actor, plays Spock. In one of the more interesting bits of casting, Scotty is played by Chris Doohan, the son of James Doohan, who played Scotty in *TOS*. The episodes have an obvious low-budget feel, but they are surprisingly effective—and the series as a whole does a superb job of replicating the look and feel of *TOS*, something that is furthered by the unusually generous attitude of the *Star Trek* franchise in allowing fan fictions to use its intellectual property.

Interestingly enough, *Star Trek Continues* premiered with "Pilgrim of Eternity," which is a direct sequel to one of the weaker (and sillier) episodes of *TOS*, the early second-season entry "Who Mourns for Ado- nais?" In the original, the *Enterprise* and its crew had encountered the Greek god Apollo, who (like all the Greek gods) turns out actually to have been a hyper-advanced alien. Here, Apollo returns—once again played by the same actor (Michael Forest), though the episodes were made nearly half a century apart. Indeed, Forest's availability to play the role was a key reason why *Star Trek Continues* began with this particular sequel, despite the weakness of the original episode upon which it is built. In another bit of clever casting that clearly shows the in-crowd, fan-oriented nature of the show, the episode also features a guest appearance by actor Jamie Bamber, who played Lee "Apollo" Adama on the Sci-Fi channel series *Battlestar Galactica* (2004–2009).

Finally, in addition to producing such original works (and in addition to the influence *Star Trek* itself has had on subsequent science fiction), *Trek* fan culture has itself been featured in a number of commercial films and television series—as in the example of the *Futurama* episode mentioned at the beginning of this chapter. For example, the highly popular CBS series *The Big Bang Theory* (on the air since September 2007) features several nerdy characters who are professional scientists—and who are also devoted *Trek* fans. Indeed, according to *The Big Bang Theory* Wiki, a product of *The Big Bang Theory*'s own fan culture, this series (which is in general filled with all sorts of references to popular culture) refers to *Star Trek* more than any other single cultural phenomenon. [10]

Star Trek fandom is such a well-known phenomenon that a number of commercial fictional works have been produced *about* the fan culture of *Star Trek*. For instance, the fiction film *Free Enterprise* (1998) details the misadventures of two young men in their late twenties trying to make their way in Hollywood. The nerdy Mark (Eric McCormack) and Robert (Rafer Weigel) are obsessed with pop cultural products such as film and comic books—but they are especially obsessed with *Star Trek*, particularly *TOS*. The two are actually depicted as having some success with women, despite their obsessions, though they are not really able to sustain a relationship because *Trek* culture in particular and nerd culture in general are depicted in the film as even more male-dominated than they are in the real world. Robert does briefly become involved with a young woman who is also into nerd culture, but his relationship ultimately fails as Claire (Audie England) leaves him due to his lack of real-world responsibility. In general, the film is undistinguished, but it does include one interesting wrinkle that occurs when the two of them become acquainted with their hero, William Shatner (played by himself). In this film, at least, Shatner is about as unsuccessful with relationships as his two young admirers, continually complaining in the film that his woman has just left him. He is also just as culturally obsessed as are Mark and Robert—in this case with the idea of producing and starring in a musical version of Shakespeare's *Julius Caesar*. Shatner indeed carries the film, portraying his haplessness with endearing good humor. The film ends happily, though. Claire and Robert get back together, and Shatner even gets a chance to perform part of his musical in the closing scene of the film, as the play is staged (informally) at last.

Probably the best-known fictional film inspired by *Trek* fan culture is *Galaxy Quest* (1999), a *Star Trek* spoof that draws heavily upon *Trek* fan culture and that has become a cult classic in its own right. The film focuses on a science fiction television show (also entitled *Galaxy Quest*) that has long been off the air but that still enjoys a loyal following among fans, who regularly attend *Galaxy Quest* conventions, where the principal actors from the series make appearances (and money). Comedian Tim Allen plays Jason Nesmith, the actor who leads the cast as Peter Quincy Taggart, the commander of the NSEA *Protector*, the starship around whose voyages the series was built. Taggart is transparently modeled on James T. Kirk, but the other crew members of the *Protector* do not correspond to individual characters from *TOS* so much as create a crew that has many of the overall characteristics of a *Trek* crew. British actor Alan Rickman stars as Alexander Dane, who played the ship's alien science officer, Dr. Lazarus. Perhaps Lazarus corresponds most closely to Spock in the *Star Trek* pantheon, but Dane's background as a Shakespearean actor (which causes him to feel that his role as a TV alien is beneath him) is more reminiscent of the background of Patrick Stewart. Particularly notable among the rest of the cast is Sigourney Weaver, herself something of an icon of SF film for her appearances as Ripley in the *Alien* franchise. Here, Weaver plays Gwen DeMarco, the actress who played Lt. Tawny Madison, the communications officer of the *Protector*. DeMarco's role in the original *Galaxy Quest* series seems to have been the provision of eye candy, her low-cut uniform designed to accentuate her breasts, a motif that clearly comments on the revealing costumes often worn by women in *TOS*.

Galaxy Quest the film begins as the actors from the series are attending a fan convention but are contacted there by a delegation of aliens who have been watching the series via television signals that leaked into space, misinterpreting the series as a record of real historical events. With their own planet threatened by dangerous alien forces, they have constructed a duplicate of the *Protector* and have now come to earth to recruit the original crew to help them man it. Thus, these aliens are a version of the fans who become so immersed in the *Trek* franchise that they seem to have trouble distinguishing fiction from reality. Much comic mayhem ensues, but of course Nesmith/Taggart and his crew ultimately succeed in saving the day—thanks partly to technical advice they receive from dedicated nerdy fans of the series, whose knowledge of the ship and its operations goes far beyond their own.

Galaxy Quest has become a favorite among *Trek* fans, despite the fact that it pokes a bit of gentle fun at their culture. Indeed, fans attending a *Star Trek* convention in Las Vegas in 2013 voted *Galaxy Quest* the seventh greatest *Star Trek* film ever made—at a time when there were already thirteen *actual* films in the *Trek* franchise.[11] Many of the actual *Star Trek* actors are reportedly fans of the film as well. The film was also well received upon its initial release, winning numerous awards, including a Hugo Award for Best Dramatic Presentation.

That a film based on *Star Trek* fandom could generate a significant fan base of its own (though of course the two fan groups overlap significantly) is still more proof of the strength of *Star Trek*'s impact on American popular culture—and of the devotion of *Star Trek*'s fans to the franchise. But the real proof of the power of *Trek* lies in its longevity and in the way it has remained an important part of American popular culture for more than half a century. That this phenomenon has, in more recent years, spread across the globe is partly a result of the globalization of popular culture as a whole in the past few decades. But it is also a testament to the global appeal of *Star Trek* and its vision of a utopian future for all. As planet earth faces the challenges of a very uncertain political, economic, and environmental future, that vision is now more appealing (and more important) than ever before. It is thus no surprise that the *Star Trek* franchise seems poised to remain a powerful force in popular culture as it moves into its second half century.

THE EPISODES

An Opinionated Compendium

Episode 1.0: "The Cage." First aired October 4, 1988. ★★★

"The Cage" was the initial (unsuccessful) *TOS* pilot, made in late 1964 and early 1965. Rejected by NBC, it did not air in its entirety until 1988, though footage from it was edited into the two-part, first-season episode "The Menagerie." In the original pilot, moribund brainiac aliens lure the *Enterprise* to their ruined planet in the Talos system, where they lead boring lives beneath a surface that was rendered uninhabitable long ago from the fallout of a planetary war. Jeffrey Hunter stars as Captain Christopher Pike (before the advent of Kirk), whom the Talosians hope to use as breeding stock to help them create a new human race that they can observe for their own entertainment. As a lure, they use the aging and disfigured human woman Vina (Susan Oliver), rendered as a sexy dream girl by the Talosians using the contents of Pike's own fantasies as a guide. In an iconic scene, Vina is at one point transformed (also based on Pike's fantasies) into a green-skinned Orion belly dancer writhing to the strains of Middle Eastern music.

Episode 1.1: "The Man Trap." First aired September 8, 1966. ★★★

In the first *TOS* episode actually to be aired, the *Enterprise* (now with its new captain) pays a visit to a remote planet ostensibly occupied only by archaeologist Robert Crater and his wife, Nancy, who are stationed there to study the ruins of a long-dead civilization. Complications arise because Nancy is an old flame of Dr. McCoy but even more because "Nancy" isn't really Nancy; she has been replaced by a deadly salt-sucking creature, the last of its species. The creature has the power to influence minds to make itself appear different ways to different people, thus extending a theme of the first pilot.

Episode 1.2: "Charlie X." First aired September 15, 1966. ★★

The *Enterprise* takes aboard a seventeen-year-old boy who turns out to have psychic powers that nearly do in the ship and its crew, especially given his level of immaturity and the level of his teenage lust for yeoman Janice Rand. In one of many examples of alien intervention in the series, the *Enterprise* and Yeoman Rand are saved by the super-powerful Thasians, who gave young Charlie his powers in the first place.

Episode 1.3: "Where No Man Has Gone Before." First aired September 22, 1966. ★★★

The second *Star Trek* pilot becomes the third aired episode, with certain odd effects, such as the fact that, without explanation and for one episode only, the *Enterprise* suddenly has a different ship's doctor and different uniforms for the crew, including pants for the female crew members instead of the now famous miniskirts. Meanwhile, the series continues its early emphasis on psychic powers, as Lt. Cmdr. Gary Mitchell (Gary Lockwood, who would become a familiar face on American TV) is hit by a cosmic cloud that causes him to gain near godlike powers, only to be defeated by Kirk in *Star Trek*'s first fistfight. Mitchell, incidentally, is the ship's pilot in this episode, with Sulu serving as the ship's physicist.

Episode 1.4: "The Naked Time." First aired September 29, 1966. ★★★

TOS returns to its regular continuity (and regular crew) with the fourth aired episode—and the first truly classic *Star Trek* episode. The *Enterprise* is in danger of crashing into a disintegrating planet, while a contagion picked up on the planet causes crew members to lose their inhibitions and begin to act out their fantasies. Best remembered for the scenes of a shirtless Sulu pretending to be a swordsman from the French Revolution era.

Episode 1.5: "The Enemy Within." First aired October 6, 1966. ★★★★

In another classic episode, a transporter malfunction splits Kirk into a good self and an evil self, somewhat along the lines of Jekyll and Hyde—and introducing the key motif of doubling that would feature prominently throughout the *Star Trek* franchise. The evil Kirk practically rapes Yeoman Rand. The episode also establishes that pesky transporter as a key source of problems for the ship's crew. In this case, the malfunctioning transporter also strands Sulu and a landing party on the surface of a dangerously cold planet, creating a typical *Star Trek* sense of urgency for dealing with the doubling of Kirk.

Episode 1.6: "Mudd's Women." First aired October 13, 1966. ★★

In the first comic *Star Trek* episode, huckster Harry Mudd traffics in women to serve as the wives of lonely men in outer space, especially rich miners. His efforts to rev up the attractiveness of his wares cause the male crew members of the *Enterprise* to go all gaga, generating most of the episode's comedy. Amid this comedy, however, the *Enterprise* is nearly destroyed. Again.

Episode 1.7: "What Are Little Girls Made Of?" First aired October 20, 1966. ★★★★

In this episode, we learn that Nurse Chapel signed on for a tour of duty aboard the *Enterprise* in order to search for her fiancé, scientist Roger Korby, who is lost somewhere in space. Believe it or not, they find him, but he is not quite what she expected. Meanwhile, the *Enterprise* is nearly conscripted in support of his plan to replace humanity with a race of superhuman android replicants, using ancient alien technology. This plan includes making an android double of Kirk (as well as of Korby himself), though one of the highlights of the episode is Korby's particularly well-constructed (and interestingly clad) sexbot Andrea, whose original model is unclear. This episode always hovers on the brink of campy silliness but never quite goes over, partly due to its thoughtful exploration of the question of just what it takes to be considered human.

Episode 1.8: "Miri." First aired October 27, 1966. ★★

In deep space, the *Enterprise* discovers a planet that appears to be an exact duplicate of earth—then the episode forgets about this intriguing premise altogether, never explaining it. Instead, the episode becomes another science-gone-wrong story with a dash of *Peter Pan* thrown in for good measure. Basically, it's a postapocalyptic cautionary tale, as a landing party led by Kirk, Spock, and McCoy discovers that all adults on the planet are long dead as the result of a pandemic caused by medical longevity research that backfired. The planet is thus inhabited only by half-feral three-hundred-year-old children, who stay perpetually young thanks to that same medical research—until they don't.

Episode 1.9: "Dagger of the Mind." First aired November 3, 1966. ★★

The *Enterprise* delivers supplies to a planet devoted to confining and treating the mentally insane. Unfortunately, the treatment facility has been taken over by a mad scientist who is using the inmates to experiment on the development of a mind-control device. Kirk nearly gets his mind blown by the device but manages to triumph—with the help of a friendly miniskirted lady psychiatrist from the *Enterprise* crew. The episode takes its title from *Macbeth* but otherwise has nothing to do with the Shakespeare play.

Episode 1.10: "The Corbomite Maneuver." First aired November 10, 1966. ★★★

In deep space, the *Enterprise* encounters a menacing alien who threatens to blow up the ship using his own highly advanced vehicle. Kirk saves his own ship on a bluff, a tactic he learned from playing poker. Meanwhile, the alien turns out not to be so dangerous after all, looking a lot like a seven-year-old earth boy, who is basically just lonely. Kirk agrees to leave a crew member behind to keep the alien company—and to pursue a program of mutual education and cultural exchange.

Episode 1.11–1.12: "The Menagerie." First aired November 17 and 24, 1966. ★★★

Cobbled together largely from footage from the unaired original pilot, this was the only two-part episode of *TOS*. Captain Pike has been horribly disfigured in an accident and now lives a life of suffering and pain, unable to speak or move. As one of his former officers, the ever-loyal Spock conceives a bold plan to take Pike back to Talos IV, which has been declared off limits on penalty of death due to the dangerous potential of the Talosians. But the Talosians have agreed to use their mind power to give Pike the illusion of a wonderful life with Vina, if only Spock can get him back to their planet, regulations or no regulations. On trial for his life for hijacking the *Enterprise* and programming it to head for the banned Talos IV, Spock uses images projected by the Talosians (actually footage from the pilot) to try to explain the situation in a way that will allow his plan to be carried out—and allow Spock to escape the death penalty.

Episode 1.13: "The Conscience of the King." First aired December 8, 1966. ★★

Another episode with a title from Shakespeare, this time from *Hamlet*—though the episode begins, oddly enough, as Kirk attends a performance of *Macbeth* in the company of scientist Thomas Leighton. Leighton has lured Kirk to his planet under false pretenses because he is convinced that one of the actors in the company that has come to the planet (the man who is starring as Macbeth in the opening) is in fact Kodos the Executioner, a former planetary governor who had conducted mass executions twenty years earlier. Kirk and Leighton are two of only three surviving witnesses who can identify Kodos—and Leighton is soon killed, leaving Kirk to pursue Kodos. Kirk delivers his essentialist view of womanhood: "Worlds may change, galaxies disintegrate, but a woman remains always a woman." The main woman in this episode, though, has some surprises in store, mostly delivered as the company performs *Hamlet* aboard the *Enterprise*.

Episode 1.14: "Balance of Terror." First aired December 15, 1966. ★★★★

Lots of new *Star Trek* mythology is introduced in this episode, the first in which Romulans appear, as well as the first one specifically to address the Cold War historical context of *TOS*, when "balance of terror" was a common catchphrase to describe the Cold War arms race. Here, after a bloody conflict employing "primitive" nuclear weapons, a century of uneasy peace has held in which the Romulan and "earth" territories (the idea of the "Federation" has yet to be fully developed at this point in the series) have been divided by a strip of space known as the "neutral zone," which seems to ignore the fact that space is three-dimensional. Now, however, a Romulan vessel, using their newly developed cloaking technology, crosses the zone and begins to demolish "earth" border outposts with a superweapon, also newly developed. We (and the crew of the *Enterprise* because the secretive Romulans have never been seen before) learn that the Romulans look exactly like Vulcans, and Spock speculates they must have split off from the Vulcans back before the latter put their savage and warlike ways behind them. This sets navigator Lt. Stiles off into a racist funk with regard to Spock. Despite the many Cold War echoes, though, this episode is really an update of a World War II submarine battle narrative, as the *Enterprise* and the Romulan vessel warily play cat-and-mouse with high stakes.

Episode 1.15: "Shore Leave." First aired December 29, 1966. ★★★

Worn out from their recent adventures, the *Enterprise* seeks a peaceful planet where they can have some R&R. They seem to find one, not realizing that they have happened upon an amusement park planet invested with advanced technologies that allow the thoughts of visitors literally to materialize before their very eyes. This lack of realization leads to considerable confusion and apparent danger, though the episode includes significant lighter elements as well, including a flirtation between McCoy and Yeoman Barrows. Kirk, meanwhile, has one of his most extended fistfights of the entire series—against a simulation of Finnegan, a fellow cadet who tormented him back at Starfleet Academy.

Episode 1.16: "The Galileo Seven." First aired January 5, 1967. ★★★

In his first command opportunity, Spock leads a group of seven crew members (including McCoy and a gratuitous beautiful Yeoman) who become stranded after their shuttlecraft (the first appearance of such a craft on *Star Trek*) crash-lands on a harsh planet while on a scientific mission—a promising premise marred by the incredibly cheesy aliens that attack them on the planet, but marred even more by the resentment shown toward Spock's authority by McCoy and the African American crewman Lt. Boma, resentment that borders on all-out anti-Vulcan racism. This one definitely shows McCoy at his worst.

Episode 1.17: "The Squire of Gothos." First aired January 12, 1967. ★

In one of the sillier episodes of *TOS*, Trelane, a seemingly all-powerful alien (a forerunner of the formidable "Q" of *TNG*, among others), lures the *Enterprise* to a planet he has created as a sort of game. He has also created an earth-like environment in which to host the crew so they can participate in familiar surroundings. The problem is that Trelane's knowledge of earth is hundreds of years out of date, so his costumes and the décor of the castle he has constructed are also anachronistic. His powers are thus clearly limited, but he still presents a real danger and is defeated only when his parents intervene and rein in what turns out to be their alien child, apologizing to Kirk for Trelane's bad behavior.

Episode 1.18: "Arena." First aired January 19, 1967. ★★★

In a conflict that appears to arise from a simple misunderstanding, a Gorn ship attacks an earth observation outpost that might inadvertently have been established in Gorn space. The *Enterprise* attempts to retaliate, chasing the Gorn ship into a quadrant dominated by the highly advanced Metrons. The Metrons abhor violence but nevertheless decide to settle the Gorn-human dispute by placing Kirk and the reptilian Gorn captain on a planet where they are supposed to battle to the death, essentially as gladiators. In a bit of confusing logic, the winner will be allowed to leave on his ship; the loser's ship will be destroyed. Kirk is no physical match for the powerful (but clumsy) Gorn but uses his wits to get the upper hand, then refuses to kill the Gorn, causing the Metrons to think there might be hope for humans after all, especially with a few thousand more years of advancement beyond their innate warlike tendencies. Apparently meant to be an anti-war episode, it is weakened by some muddled thinking—and by the fact that the Gorn is so clearly just a man in a cheap rubber suit.

Episode 1.19: "Tomorrow Is Yesterday." First aired January 26, 1967. ★★★★

In a fairly predictable (but often charming) time-travel episode, the *Enterprise* is inadvertently hurled back in time to the late 1960s; then the crew has to struggle to return to its own time, while at the same time avoiding doing anything that might change history with unpredictable (and possibly disastrous) results. Considerable drama ensues, sprinkled with an unusually large number of comic elements, accompanied by somewhat annoying comic music. As an added gag, the ship's computer has taken on a breathlessly flirtatious feminine personality, given to it while it was being repaired on a woman-dominated planet just before the events of the episode. Among other things, we are told in this episode that the *Enterprise* is operating under the authority of the "United Earth Space Probe Agency." It took a while to work out the Federation/Starfleet terminology that is now so well known to *Star Trek* fans.

Episode 1.20: "Court Martial." First aired February 2, 1967. ★★★

TOS moves into the courtroom genre—illustrating the way many episodes in fact participate in established TV genres other than pure science fiction. Here, an ion storm apparently leads to the death of an officer aboard the *Enterprise*. When Kirk's account of the events leading to this apparent death differ from the records of the ship's computer, the captain is suspected of malfeasance and court-martialed. His folksy lawyer has little luck defending him, until Spock steps in.

Episode 1.21: "The Return of the Archons." First aired February 9, 1967. ★★★★

A key episode in which *TOS* questions the whole idea of utopian societies, complicating its own seemingly utopian basis. The *Enterprise* visits a planet where the inhabitants seem to live in complete tranquility. They are, in fact, a bit *too* tranquil, perhaps like brainwashed members of a religious cult. Then suddenly all hell breaks loose as they blow off steam in a periodic "festival." Realizing that the behavior of the planet's inhabitants is being engineered by a powerful computer, Kirk decides to intervene, despite Spock's reminders about the Prime Directive of Noninterference.

Episode 1.22: "Space Seed." First aired February 16, 1967. ★★★★★

One of the best-known episodes of *TOS*, partly because it inspired the 1982 film *Star Trek II: The Wrath of Khan*. In the original episode, the *Enterprise* discovers a derelict earth ship, circa the 1990s, drifting in deep space. Aboard are dozens of humans in suspended animation, members of a super race produced by selective breeding back in the twentieth century. Their leader is Khan Noonien Singh, a superman who tried to take control of earth back in the 1990s but was forced to flee with his followers. Now he and his ambitions are reawakened.

Episode 1.23: "A Taste of Armageddon." First aired February 23, 1967. ★★★

The *Enterprise* delivers a Federation diplomat to a remote planet with which the Federation seeks to establish diplomatic relations. The officious diplomat causes all sorts of problems, but the real problem is that the planet is engaged in a five-hundred-year-long war with a neighboring planet, waging the war by computer simulation and thus eliminating property damage. The human damage is real, however; those on both sides designated by the computer as killed in the conflict are required to report to "disintegration chambers" within twenty-four hours so that their deaths can be carried out in reality. The *Enterprise* gets caught in the crossfire. A key episode in *Star Trek*'s portrayal of warfare as absurd, with obvious implications for the Cold War arms race.

Episode 1.24: "This Side of Paradise." First aired March 2, 1967. ★★★★★

The *Enterprise* visits an agricultural colony planet that deadly cosmic radiation has apparently rendered uninhabitable. Surprisingly, they find the colonists living in perfect health—and perfect bliss, thanks to the fact that plants on the surface produce spores that not only provide immunity to the radiation but also induce a state of permanent euphoria. The spores work even on Spock, who for once finds himself happy and in love. Kirk, however, decides to break up the party, feeling that human beings need challenges and conflicts and that they cannot fulfill their potential in perfect contentment, leaving them no reason to strive for more. An important example of the anti-utopian impulses that sometimes drove *TOS*—and a clear dose of skepticism concerning the summer-of-love mentality of the late 1960s—but with just a hint of complexity.

Episode 1.25: "The Devil in the Dark." First aired March 9, 1967. ★★★★

The *Enterprise* comes to the aid of a mining planet where the miners are suddenly being killed by some sort of deadly subterranean creature. The creature, a "Horta," turns out to be a silicon-based lifeform whose eggs are being inadvertently destroyed by the miners. It looks very much like a monster from a low-budget 1950s SF flick, but it is simply a mother protecting her young—yet one so different from humans that the miners are unable to recognize it as such. In a rather far-fetched move, Spock mind-melds with the Horta in an attempt to communicate. Big ideas meet small budgets in one of *TOS*'s most interesting explorations of Otherness, which makes it a strong episode, despite the near-ludicrous special effects and clumsy plotting.

Episode 1.26: "Errand of Mercy." First aired March 23, 1967. ★★★★

The first appearance of Klingons in *Star Trek* finds them in the process of launching an invasion against the Federation on the pretext that the Federation is disputing control of space that the Klingons regard as rightfully theirs. Meanwhile, the peaceful and seemingly primitive planet of Organia sits smack in the path of the invasion, leading to a confrontation on the surface of the planet between the occupying Klingons and Kirk and Spock. Echoes of the Cold War abound in this episode, but the Organians (as is often the case with alien races in the *Star Trek* universe) are not what they seem.

Episode 1.27: "The Alternative Factor." First aired on March 30, 1967. ★

A man fanatically devoted to the destruction of his anti-matter double draws the *Enterprise* into his quest, ultimately threatening the existence of both our universe and its anti-matter double. This episode features some high-concept science fiction, such as parallel universes and the interaction between matter and anti-matter. But poor execution ultimately reduces it to one of *TOS*'s most illogical and least satisfying episodes.

Episode 1.28: "The City on the Edge of Forever." First aired April 6, 1967. ★★★★★

McCoy accidentally injects himself with a drug that makes him delusional. He then leaps through a time portal and arrives in Depression-era New York. Back in the future, Kirk and Spock realize that McCoy has altered history, causing the twenty-third-century world they know to cease to exist—they themselves apparently continue to exist because they are in the vicinity of the time portal. They then follow McCoy into the portal in an attempt to prevent his interference in history. They succeed, of course, but only after Kirk has to make a very tough choice. This widely admired time-travel episode is filled with human interest, comedy, moral dilemmas, and meditations on the nature of history.

Episode 1.29: "Operation: Annihilate!" First aired April 13, 1967. ★★

The first season ends with an episode that is a bit too busy for its own good. Weird alien "things" have invaded a planet where Kirk's brother lives with his family; the things are gradually taking control of the planet's human inhabitants so they can use their bodies to build a fleet of spaceships to further their plan of galactic conquest. By the time the *Enterprise* comes to the rescue, Kirk's brother has been killed, though there is so much going on in the episode that the death seems a bit inconsequential and gratuitous. Kirk considers obliterating the entire population of the planet in order to stop the aliens, while McCoy and Spock (who has been inhabited by one of the creatures) struggle to find a better solution.

Episode 2.1: "Amok Time." First aired September 15, 1967. ★★★★★

TOS gets its second season off to a rousing start with this episode, a perennial fan favorite. Here, we learn that, every seven years, adult Vulcans depart from their logical ways and undergo a period of *pon farr*, during which they are driven by primitive and irresistible impulses to mate on their home planet. Though half human, Spock proves not to be immune, undergoing *pon farr* for the first time and returning to Vulcan, where his chosen mate, the beautiful T'Pring, is presumed to be awaiting their wedding. Unfortunately, T'Pring has other ideas, leading to serious and dangerous complications for both Spock and Kirk, who (along with McCoy) accompanies Spock to the "wedding." Some high drama ensues, but the real attraction of this episode is seeing the ultra-logical Spock suddenly driven by animal passions, even if the depiction of Vulcan culture here as ritualistic and dominated by tradition and ceremony really makes no sense given their high level of scientific and technological development. Vulcan gender politics don't appear to be very advanced, either. Despite the powerful position occupied by the aging T'Pau, we learn that Vulcan wives are apparently considered the property of their husbands. But, hey, they're aliens.

Episode 2.2: "Who Mourns for Adonais?" First aired September 22, 1967. ★

In an episode that makes no sense whatsoever, we learn that the Greek gods were actually ancient aliens, eventually driven away from earth by human ingratitude. The *Enterprise* runs into a ridiculous green energy hand in space that turns out to be a manifestation of the god Apollo, whom they soon encounter on a nearby planet. Apollo tries to make the crew his worshippers (because gods need worship) but is willing to settle for the love of space archaeologist Lt. Carolyn Palamas, much to the dismay of Scotty, who has also developed a thing for the beautiful lieutenant. Kirk, predictably, is having none of Apollo's pomposity, feeling that humans have long outgrown their need for "gods," though he does at one point, in an apparent nod toward religion that is unusual for *Star Trek*, proclaim that "the one god we have" is sufficient.

Episode 2.3: "The Changeling." First aired September 29, 1967. ★★★

In an episode that directly anticipates the first *Star Trek* movie, the *Enterprise* encounters an old space probe from earth that has merged with an alien probe and become artificially intelligent. It has also become extremely powerful and extremely dangerous. Luckily, the device mistakes Kirk for its creator, which gives him a leg up in trying to defeat it.

Episode 2.4: "Mirror, Mirror." First aired October 6, 1967. ★★★★★

In a crucial episode for true *Trek* fans, a freak transporter malfunction swaps Kirk, McCoy, Scotty, and Uhura with their doubles from a mirror *Enterprise* in a parallel universe. This particular parallel universe is a sort of evil twin of ours, and Kirk comes into immediate conflict with a ruthless, bearded Spock. But even this evil Spock remains logical, which Kirk hopes to use to survive the episode intact—and perhaps to change the whole parallel universe for the better. Evil Sulu is another highlight. This episode doesn't always make sense, but it's always great fun, which might be why it later became the inspiration for no less than five different episodes of *DS9*.

Episode 2.5: "The Apple." First aired October 13, 1967. ★★

Kirk and Spock head a landing party that beams down to a seemingly Edenic planet, only to discover that its innocent, childlike inhabitants are actually ruled by a powerful computer, Vaal, that forces them to do its bidding. Kirk, as usual, feels he must intervene, but in this case he has little choice, given that Vaal also launches a potentially deadly assault on the *Enterprise*.

Episode 2.6: "The Doomsday Machine." First aired October 20, 1967. ★★★★

In an episode packed with commentary on the Cold War arms race, the *Enterprise* encounters a giant, planet-killing device that has apparently wandered into the Milky Way from another galaxy. Kirk deduces that the device was designed as a deterrent, never meant actually to be used, but that it is now on the loose and must be stopped before it cuts a swath of destruction through the entire galaxy. A meddling and somewhat unhinged Starfleet commodore adds to the trouble—and to the Cold War allegory, suggesting that, with such weapons in existence, one unbalanced person in a high position could do untold damage.

Episode 2.7: "Catspaw." First aired October 27, 1967. ★

Advanced aliens from another galaxy threaten the *Enterprise* with seemingly magical powers, at times taking *TOS* into the realm of the then-recent Roger Corman cycle of film adaptations of the Gothic horror of Edgar Allan Poe. The aliens turn out, however, not to be so impressive without their technology.

Episode 2.8: "I, Mudd." First aired November 3, 1967. ★★★

In another skeptical treatment of the idea of a life with no troubles to confront or obstacles to overcome, Harry Mudd returns, backed by an army of androids from another galaxy. With Mudd as their main specimen, the androids decide that humans are too dangerously flawed to be allowed to run loose in the galaxy. So they decide to hijack the *Enterprise* and use it to launch a program of galactic conquest through which they plan to subdue human aggression by serving all the needs of humans, rendering them passive. (And that means *all* needs. As one of the female androids explains to a lustful Chekhov, "I am programmed to function as a human female.") Kirk, of course, objects to the plan, which he opposes with an amusing and rather creative plan of his own.

Episode 2.9: "Metamorphosis." First aired November 10, 1967. ★★★

Kirk, Spock, and McCoy lead a party that is taking Commissioner Nancy Hedford, an ailing Federation diplomat, back to the *Enterprise* for medical treatment. Suddenly their shuttle is drawn to a strange planetoid by a mysterious force encountered in space. There, they meet none other than Zefram Cochrane, the inventor of the warp drive, thought to have been dead for a century and a half. He's hale and hearty now, though, restored to vigor by the alien entity that brought the shuttle to the planetoid. Hedford, however, is fading fast—until the entity intervenes again. This episode anticipates Cochrane's key role in the 1996 film *Star Trek: First Contact*, though there are some inconsistencies in the portrayal of Cochrane between the two works.

Episode 2.10: "Journey to Babel." First aired November 17, 1967. ★★★★

The *Enterprise* is delivering a multispecies cohort of delegates to an upcoming conference to discuss the admission of the Coridan system to the Federation. This premise offers an opportunity to introduce two new alien races, the antennaed Andorians and the porcine Tellarites. Tensions run high due to animosity among the delegates—which seems rather inconsistent with the usual representation of the Federation as an organization filled with peace and harmony. Further tensions are caused by the fact that the Vulcan delegate to the conference, Sarek, is Spock's father—and a father with whom Spock has not spoken for eighteen years due to a disagreement over Spock's decision to enter Starfleet. To top it off, sinister forces are determined to sabotage the conference, hoping to trigger a war and then profit by selling dilithium to both sides.

Episode 2.11: "Friday's Child." First aired December 1, 1967. ★★★

Kirk, Spock, McCoy, and a doomed redshirt beam down to planet Capella IV, inhabited by a warlike, primitive, and highly patriarchal humanoid race. They hope to negotiate an agreement with the Capellans that will allow the Federation to begin mining the planet's rich mineral resources—only to find that a Klingon representative is already there on the same mission. Trouble predictably ensues in one of several *TOS* episodes that remind us of the importance of certain natural resources, even in this affluent future. In the case of Capella IV, the resource in question is the rare mineral "Topeline," which we are told is "vital to life-support systems of planetoid colonies." In general, though, the most valuable resource in the *Star Trek* universe seems to be the dilithium crystals that are the source of starship fuel, making clear that these minerals play much the same role in the twenty-third-century Federation that oil plays in our own present-day world.

Episode 2.12: "The Deadly Years." First aired December 8, 1967. ★

In what must be *Star Trek*'s most ageist episode (and what is certainly one of its most unbelievable), Kirk, Spock, McCoy, and Scotty are dosed with radiation that causes them to age at a rapid rate. Spock is a bit more resistant, of course, but the humans all quickly become not only physically weak but mentally incompetent due to age, unable to think clearly or remember anything. Meanwhile, with everybody else rendered feeble-minded by age, a Starfleet commodore (hopelessly inept as usual) takes command of the *Enterprise* in the midst of a Romulan threat, while Spock and McCoy race to find an antidote to the radiation before all is lost.

Episode 2.13: "Obsession." First aired December 15, 1967. ★

This episode gives us an interesting glimpse at Kirk's early career with Starfleet. Unfortunately, Kirk's Ahab-like obsession with a cloud-like alien creature that killed the captain of the ship to which he was first assigned eleven years earlier leads to such unbalanced (and unlikable) behavior in the present that it's all a bit unpleasant to watch.

Episode 2.14: "Wolf in the Fold." First aired December 22, 1967. ★

TOS takes on the murder mystery genre but not very successfully. Another Orientalist depiction of a relatively primitive society (complete with belly dancer) sets the scene for a series of murders of which Scotty is accused, but he is of course soon vindicated. Meanwhile, we learn that the real killer preys on women because it feeds on fear and women are more easily frightened than men.

Episode 2.15: "The Trouble with Tribbles." First aired December 29, 1967. ★★★★

TOS finally breaks the string of weak episodes that plagued the middle of the second season with one of its most charming and memorable stories. Seemingly lovable trilling fuzzballs turn out to have voracious appetites and high reproductive rates, with near-catastrophic results. Meanwhile, more tensions loom between the Federation and the Klingons, all once again made worse by the interference of a pompous Federation official. It's mostly all in good fun, though the Klingon-Federation aspect of the story does occasionally come close to veering into Cold War espionage drama territory.

Episode 2.16: "The Gamesters of Triskelion." First aired January 5, 1968. ★

Three brains in a jar capture Kirk, Uhura, and Chekov and transport them to their planet, where they keep captives from various planets to serve as gladiators for their amusement. One of the lamer and more nonsensical episodes of *TOS*, though it does offer an unusually large number of opportunities for Kirk to display his prowess at both seduction and hand-to-hand combat.

Episode 2.17: "A Piece of the Action." First aired January 12, 1968. ★★★★

One of best comedic episodes of *TOS*, though also an episode with a message about the dangers of interference in other cultures, this one finds the *Enterprise* visiting a planet where a previous Federation mission one hundred years earlier inadvertently caused the planet to build a global culture modeled on 1920s Chicago-style gangsterism. This premise allows the series to participate in still another pop cultural genre, as well as offering Kirk the opportunity to play comedy as an exaggeratedly swaggering gangster—and to engage in an unusually large number of fisticuffs, even for him.

Episode 2.18: "The Immunity Syndrome." First aired January 19, 1968. ★★★★

Spock at his good-of-the-many finest. The *Enterprise* encounters a giant amoeba in space that starts to suck the life out of the ship and its crew. The thing has already destroyed a Vulcan ship, so Spock has special reason to rise to extraordinary levels of heroism to combat it. Then again, no special reason is really needed because the space amoeba is starting to reproduce and threatens to spread its kind across the entire galaxy. A surprising amount of high drama for such an unlikely premise—and a surprising amount of sexual innuendo in an episode with such high drama.

Episode 2.19: "A Private Little War." First aired February 2, 1968. ★★

The *Enterprise* arrives at a primitive planet that McCoy discovers to be rich in materials needed for the manufacture of certain drugs. Luckily, the inhabitants, though primitive, are thought to be peaceful. When they turn out to be more warlike (and better armed) than expected, it comes as no surprise that the Klingons (who also want the medical materials) are involved. A thinly veiled Cold War allegory that casts the Klingons as evil Soviets attempting to win influence in the resource-rich Third World by supplying advanced weapons to the locals, while the Federation stands in for the peaceful Americans, who of course eschew such interference. Kirk and McCoy both manage to get shot with flintlocks, while Kirk manages to fall into the clutches of a beautiful native medicine woman—and to get in a fistfight with a ridiculous-looking giant unicorn-yeti-dragon thingy.

Episode 2.20: "Return to Tomorrow." First aired February 9, 1968. ★★★

Disembodied godlike super aliens borrow the bodies of Kirk, Spock, and Dr. Mulhall (a woman scientist) so they can use them to build permanent android bodies for themselves. Pure 1950s science fiction pulp that ought to be worse than it is but saved by the fact that it gives Kirk a key opportunity to speechify on the mission of the Federation, while giving Leonard Nimoy another chance to do evil Spock. Also adds a key bit of *Star Trek* mythology by explaining why there seem to be human-like races all over the galaxy.

Episode 2.21: "Patterns of Force." First aired February 16, 1968. ★★★

Hoping to bring the anarchic planet to order, John Gill, Kirk's old history instructor from Starfleet Academy, establishes a Nazi regime on the planet Ekos, with himself as führer. Then the whole plan gets hijacked by his evil understudy, who supports his schemes by launching a program of hatred against the neighboring planet of Zeon (read "Zion"). Kirk and Spock join the resistance in an attempt to save the day before Zeon is destroyed. Features some comments from Kirk on the inevitable failure of all systems based on leaders with absolute power, but the episode is possibly less unequivocal in its condemnation of Nazism than it should be.

Episode 2.22: "By Any Other Name." First aired February 23, 1968. ★★

In still another episode with a Shakespearean title, super-advanced aliens from the Andromeda galaxy take on human bodies so they can hijack the *Enterprise* and use it as part of their plan to conquer the Milky Way. Unfortunately for them, the bodies have minds of their own.

Episode 2.23: "The Omega Glory." First aired March 1, 1968. ★★★

In one of the most transparent Cold War allegories in all of *TOS*, Kirk, Spock, and McCoy contract a deadly contagion that forces them to beam down to a planet whose environment conveys immunity to the disease. Then they become mired in a local conflict that seems to be a continuation of a war from centuries earlier that somehow resembles the worst-case scenario of our own Cold War. Amid it all, the United States emerges as the paradigm of freedom and equality for the whole galaxy. Also lots of rather jumbled commentary on racism, Orientalism, and the Prime Directive in an episode that makes no sense whatsoever in a literal sense but is fascinating to try to untangle as an allegory.

Episode 2.24: "The Ultimate Computer." First aired March 8, 1968. ★★★

Starfleet decides to put an advanced computer in charge of the *Enterprise* as a test of its capabilities. But bad things always happen in *TOS* when computers are put in charge. For a series so dedicated to technological utopianism, *TOS* was oddly suspicious of computerization, perhaps most overtly in this episode. And for a series so dedicated to social utopianism, this episode seems to assume that the death penalty is the logical punishment for murder.

Episode 2.25: "Bread and Circuses." First aired March 15, 1968. ★★★

In what is essentially an alternative history narrative, Kirk, Spock, and McCoy beam down to a planet that is remarkably similar to twentieth-century earth but one in which the Roman Empire has survived until that time. Televised gladiatorial contests serve as obvious commentaries on televisual violence in our own world, while the pacification of slaves through the institution of medical and retirement benefits allegorizes the manipulation of populations through social safety nets on twentieth-century earth. But then the whole allegory collapses as Kirk and Uhura grow weirdly ecstatic over the expectation that the rise of Christianity will bring down the whole system, instituting an era of peace and love, just like it did on earth. One of the most maddening episodes of *TOS*, this one totters on the brink of brilliance, then collapses into silliness.

Episode 2.26: "Assignment: Earth." First aired March 29, 1968. ★★

The *Enterprise* once again travels back to the 1960s, this time on purpose. It is a mission of "historical research" to learn how earth managed to survive the "desperate problems" it faced back in 1968. Instead, they become involved in an attempt by advanced aliens to prevent the Cold War from going nuclear. Contains more than a dash of *The Day the Earth Stood Still*, plus a gratuitous black cat that turns out to be a sexy, seminude Cleopatra-esque Egyptian woman named Isis, perhaps suggesting that the ancient Egyptian gods were aliens. Some potentially interesting ideas but a bit of a mess.

Episode 3.1: "Spock's Brain." First aired September 20, 1968. ★

Alien women who've forgotten how to manage their technology steal Spock's brain and wire it in so it can run things for them. Almost certainly the most ridiculous episode in any *Star Trek* series. Even the actors seem like they can't believe what they're doing and saying, though DeForest Kelley certainly gives it his all. With this episode to begin the third season, it's little wonder that was also the last season.

Episode 3.2: "The *Enterprise* Incident." First aired September 27, 1968. ★★★

TOS does Cold War spy drama, as Kirk and Spock (without the knowledge of the rest of the crew of the *Enterprise*) execute a bold plan to steal one of the new Romulan cloaking devices. Meanwhile, Spock makes a connection with a beautiful Romulan commander.

Episode 3.3: "The Paradise Syndrome." First aired October 4, 1968. ★★

The *Enterprise* discovers still another planet that is almost just like earth and even has people and a society just like one on earth—in this case an idyllic Native American society. They also discover a reason why they keep finding such societies (seeding by an advanced civilization from long ago), apparently having already forgotten the similar reason they discovered in "Return to Tomorrow." The *Enterprise* races to save the planet from an approaching asteroid, while Kirk finds perfect contentment with a local Native American princess. Of course, the stereotypically childish innocents of her tribe think he is a god.

Episode 3.4: "And the Children Shall Lead." First aired October 11, 1968. ★

The *Enterprise* visits a scientific research outpost where all the adults have committed suicide, leaving behind a group of seemingly unfazed children. The children, though, have been possessed by a sinister force that hopes to hijack the *Enterprise* as part of its plan of galactic mayhem and conquest. By this point it is clear that the third season is in trouble.

Episode 3.5: "Is There in Truth No Beauty?" October 18, 1968. ★★

The *Enterprise* plays host to an ambassador from the Medusans—an energy-based race noted for its beautiful thoughts and for an appearance so disturbing that any human looking upon one goes dangerously insane. This premise opens the way for a potentially interesting exploration of what it means to encounter genuine Otherness and of the Keatsian equation between truth and beauty. That potential is not, alas, fulfilled.

Episode 3.6: "Spectre of the Gun." First aired October 25, 1968. ★

TOS explores still another genre, this time the Western, a genre that was one of the models for the series. Kirk, Spock, McCoy, Scotty, and Chekov find themselves transported into a simulation of 1881 Tombstone, Arizona, where they run afoul of the deadly Earp clan.

Episode 3.7: "Day of the Dove." First aired November 1, 1968. ★★★

Another energy-based alien super-being threatens the *Enterprise*. This one feeds on negative emotions, especially hatred and aggression, so naturally it tries to pit the *Enterprise* against Klingons to generate as many of such emotions as possible. Basically, this one is an allegorical tale about warmongers stirring up aggression for their own profit, with an added boost of anti-racist allegory as we see the *Enterprise* crew (including Spock) all start to turn into nasty bigots under the influence of the creature. Racism and war, the episode suggests, go hand in hand.

Episode 3.8: "For the World Is Hollow and I Have Touched the Sky." First aired November 8, 1968. ★★

From its title, one might expect that this one was written by Harlan Ellison. From its contents, it clearly wasn't. It does contain the very promising science fictional premise of a hollowed-out asteroid made into a generational starship, but unfortunately the people inside the ship are just another primitive culture built around ritualistic worship of a deity that turns out to be a computer—which has of course now malfunctioned. Enter the *Enterprise*.

Episode 3.9: "The Tholian Web." First aired November 15, 1968. ★★★

TOS at its most science fictional in a rip-roaring SF adventure involving overlapping universes, a mysterious ghost spaceship, a dangerous space plague, and menacing aliens, all rolled into one. Reminiscent of the science fiction films of the 1950s, down to the cumbersome protective suits worn by Kirk, Spock, and McCoy as they visit the derelict ship. All the crises are solved a bit too easily, but still good fun.

Episode 3.10: "Plato's Stepchildren." First aired November 22, 1968. ★★

Super aliens with vast mental powers once again threaten the *Enterprise* and its crew, which is pretty old hat by now, though these introduce the wrinkle of having based their civilization on that of the ancient Greeks, whom they had visited long ago. Remembered primarily because Kirk and Uhura share the first interracial kiss on American television in this episode, but that is less progressive than it sounds, given that they are forced to do it by the sadistic aliens, who are trying to get them to do as many degrading and humiliating things as possible. Some of the other things our heroes are forced to do put this episode high on the weirdness scale.

Episode 3.11: "Wink of an Eye." First aired November 29, 1968. ★★

Super-fast aliens invade the *Enterprise* and end up pulling Kirk into their time frame, where things move so rapidly they can barely be perceived at all by anyone operating at a "normal" speed. Then they try to conscript the ship's crew as breeding stock. Pure silliness.

Episode 3.12: "The Empath." First aired December 6, 1968. ★

Kirk, Spock, and McCoy get caught up in an experiment being conducted by super-advanced, bulgy-headed aliens, who are testing an empath to determine whether they should intervene to save her people from an impending supernova. But the aliens have themselves lost the very values they are seeking in the empath—until they get a lecture from Kirk.

Episode 3.13: "Elaan of Troyius." First aired December 20, 1968. ★★★

Another narrative in which the Federation and the Klingons vie for control of mineral resources (in this case, those crucial dilithium crystals) in a remote, backward solar system. This one, however, is spiced up by the fact that the *Enterprise* is delivering the title character (based, of course, on Helen of Troy but with a visual representation that seems more like Cleopatra) to a wedding with strong diplomatic implications. Sparks fly between Elaan and Kirk. Of course.

Episode 3.14: "Whom Gods Destroy." First aired January 3, 1969. ★★

As in "Dagger of the Mind," the *Enterprise* visits a planet designed to contain the criminally insane. And of course they find a lunatic in charge. This one is a former Starfleet captain with visions of grandeur and a Napoleon complex (indicated by the fact that the planet is named Elba 2). Also features another exotic dance by a green-skinned Orion woman, accompanied by music composed by Alexander Courage to sound as Oriental as possible, with the catchy title of "Arab Hootch Dance."

Episode 3.15: "Let That Be Your Last Battlefield." First aired January 10, 1969. ★

TOS goes for all-out heavy-handed allegory in an episode whose anti-hate, anti-racist message is all too clear, but which otherwise makes almost no sense at all. This is the one in which a half-white/half-black race battles to the death against a half-black/half-white race, leading to planetary destruction. Of course, the last surviving member of each race winds up on the *Enterprise*. This idea worked better when it was called "The Sneetches" and was written by Dr. Seuss.

Episode 3.16: "The Mark of Gideon." First aired January 17, 1969. ★★

The *Enterprise* visits a supposedly utopian planet on a diplomatic mission to try to get the planet to join the Federation. Refusing to allow anyone but Kirk to beam down to the planet, they have him beamed into a weird ghost-ship duplicate of the *Enterprise*, where he meets a beautiful young woman. As it turns out, the utopian conditions on the planet have led to overpopulation so extensive that life on the planet is a constant hell, and they hope Kirk will infect them with a disease that will kill off a big chunk of the population because they have too much love for life to do it themselves. A one-star nonsensical premise that gets two stars because the ghost ship is initially intriguing and because of the depiction of the frustration of Spock (the son of a diplomat) in dealing with diplomats from both the Federation and the planet as he tries to save Kirk.

Episode 3.17 "That Which Survives." First aired January 24, 1969. ★★

The *Enterprise* checks out a mysterious planet that turns out to be guarded by a super-powerful computer that has been left on the planet in the wake of the extinction (by a disease they themselves inadvertently created) of the advanced race that created and inhabited the planet. Thinking Kirk and his crew are invaders, the computer sets its sights on the *Enterprise*.

Episode 3.18: "The Lights of Zetar." First aired January 31, 1969. ★★

The *Enterprise* delivers an information systems expert, Lt. Mira Romaine, to install some new equipment on planetoid Memory Alpha, where the Federation has established a vast computer facility that houses all of the information known to them. Surprisingly, the computer is not the bad guy. Instead, the *Enterprise* and Memory Alpha are both attacked by still another group of disembodied aliens, who want to appropriate Lt. Romaine's body to allow them to live once again in corporeal form. Turns out Scotty wants the good lieutenant's body as well.

Episode 3.19: "Requiem for Methuselah." First aired February 14, 1969. ★★★

Flint, a super-smart immortal from earth, has established his own planetary refuge in deep space, just to get away from it all. Lonely, he constructs Rayna Kapec, a very realistic sexbot, for company, but Rayna seems uninterested in romance. So naturally, when Kirk, Spock, and McCoy come to the planet seeking a medical ingredient that can cure a plague that has struck the *Enterprise*, Flint decides to get Kirk together with Rayna so he can use his legendary sexual magnetism to get her jump-started. Both Rayna and Kirk fall in love, raising some interesting questions about just what it is that makes one human. Clearly inspired by Shakespeare's *The Tempest*, via the 1956 film *Forbidden Planet*.

Episode 3.20: "The Way to Eden." First aired February 21, 1969. ★

The *Enterprise* runs afoul of a gang of space hippies led by a middle-aged psychopath. Spock turns out to be surprisingly sympathetic to the hippies, but Kirk turns out to be a real Herbert. Then they hijack the *Enterprise* for their own purposes (something that happens surprisingly often in *TOS*), and suddenly they look very misguided. A not-very-flattering commentary on the 1960s counterculture and possibly the worst episode of *TOS* not called "Spock's Brain." Also the only episode of *TOS* that is essentially a musical. Unfortunately.

Episode 3.21: "The Cloud Minders." First aired February 28, 1969. ★★★★

The *Enterprise* visits a strictly segregated planet where the rich live luxurious lives of culture and contemplation, while the poor labor away (mostly as miners) on the surface below, intellectually stunted by conditions there. Kirk immediately decides he must intervene, especially as he has an emergency need for a mineral that lies in the mines, which the rebelling miners decide to withhold. A fairly heavy-handed allegory of class conflict and of the exploitation of poor workers by their rich bosses under capitalism. The episode completely ignores the crucial element of ideological manipulation, but it is a refreshing and radical statement by the standards of 1960s American television.

Episode 3.22: "The Savage Curtain." First aired March 7, 1969.
★

This episode starts out in an intriguing way when an entity claiming to be none other than Abraham Lincoln appears aboard the *Enterprise*. Then it quickly devolves into another gladiator episode in which still another capricious super alien decides to play games with lesser species for his own amusement and edification. Kirk, Spock, Lincoln, and the Vulcan hero Surak are assembled as a team representing "good," then set against a team of evil villains that includes, among others, Genghis Khan and an evil Klingon.

Episode 3.23: "All Our Yesterdays." First aired March 14, 1969.
★★★

The *Enterprise* races to rescue the population of a planet whose sun is going nova, even though it is not at all clear how they plan to evacuate an entire planet. When they arrive, however, they find that, except for a single librarian caretaker, everyone has already gone—using a problematic time-travel strategy that seems to ignore the usual concerns regarding time travel. Kirk, Spock, and McCoy inadvertently follow suit, leading to a number of interesting developments, including another case of Spock in love.

Episode 3.24: "Turnabout Intruder." First aired June 3, 1969. ★

The final season of *TOS* began in pure *Mystery Science Theater 3000* territory with "Spock's Brain." It returns there with "Turnabout Intruder," which draws on the pulp staple of a body swap as Kirk finds himself trapped inside the body of his psychotic ex-girlfriend, while the girlfriend occupies Kirk's body and tries to use it to take control of the *Enterprise*. Spock, Scotty, and the Kirk-in-a-woman are ordered executed by the fake Kirk—even though in this episode there is no death penalty in the Federation (except for violation of "General Order 4").

NOTES

INTRODUCTION

1. Quoted in Erik Barnouw, *Tube of Plenty: The Evolution of American Television*, 2nd ed. (New York: Oxford University Press, 1990), 300.

2. Uhura was given no first name in *TOS*, acquiring one only in the 2009 reboot of the *Star Trek* film franchise.

3. The embattled characters of *DS9* might seem to be an exception, but they are very much the exception that proves the rule. Placed in unusually harsh and demanding conditions far from the norms of life within the Federation, they sometimes compromise their usual values and act in less than ideally virtuous ways. Nevertheless, they continue to strive for the common good.

1. *STAR TREK* AND THE HISTORY OF *STAR TREK*

1. In fact, Kaiser Broadcasting Corporation, the first to syndicate the show to its chain of independent television stations, actually secured the rights to the series during its third season while it was still airing. Richard Block describes that process in Edward Gross and Mark A. Altman, *The Fifty-Year Mission: The Complete, Uncensored, Unauthorized Oral History of "Star Trek." The First 25 Years* (New York: Thomas Dunne Books, 2016), 232–233.

2. ABC tried the *Genesis II* concept one more time with still another pilot entitled *Strange New World*, which aired on March 23, 1975. Again starring Saxon (though the name of his character was changed), and with little participation from Roddenberry, this pilot once again failed to go to series.

3. Gross and Altman, *The Fifty-Year Mission*, 189.

4. Robert Greenberger, *"Star Trek": The Complete Unauthorized History* (Minneapolis: Voyageur Press, 2012), 81.

5. For an interesting account of the behind-the-scenes battles that marked the early years of *TNG*, see the 2014 documentary *Chaos on the Bridge*, written and directed by William Shatner, who interviews various principals involved in the series.

6. As I will note in chapter 4, the replicators of *TNG* were perhaps a more important technical advance, but they were really just an extension of the food synthesizers of *TOS* and relatively little was made of their appearance.

7. M. Keith Booker, *Science Fiction Television* (Westport, CT: Praeger, 2004), 94.

8. Quoted in Mark A. Altman and Edward Gross, *The Fifty-Year Mission: The Next 25 Years: From "The Next Generation" to J. J. Abrams: The Complete, Uncensored, and Unauthorized Oral History of "Star Trek"* (New York: Thomas Dunne Books, 2016), 426.

9. In general, the Cardassians are allegorically linked with the German Nazis of our world, while the Bajorans thus become Jews. Yet the explicit (and rather sympathetic) identification of the Bajoran resistance as terrorists suggests that there are ways in which the Cardassians can be associated, perhaps after the fact, with Israel, while the Bajorans are thus linked with Palestinians.

10. Ian Grey, "Now, *Voyager*: In Praise of the Trekkiest *Trek* of All," Rogerebert.com, June 11, 2013, http://www.rogerebert.com/balder-and-dash/now-voyager-the-least-beloved-star-trek-offered-some-of-the-franchises-strongest-feminist-messages (accessed September 19, 2017).

11. Tuvok is also black, further enhancing the multiracial feel of *Voyager*'s crew, which is probably the most diverse of any *Trek* crew, especially given the presence of the Maquis.

12. Given all of these strong female characters, it should come as no surprise that Jarrah Hodge found *VOY* to score the highest on the Bechdel Test of any *Trek* series ("How Does Your Favorite *Star Trek* Series Fare on the Bechdel Test?" The Mary Sue, September 1, 2014, https://www.themarysue.com/star-trek-bechdel-test/ [accessed September 20, 2017]). Applying the criteria of this popular test, Hodge found that that 86.9 percent of the episodes of *VOY* feature scenes in which two or more female characters talk with each other about something other than a man. By contrast, only 7.5 percent of the episodes of *TOS* passed this test.

13. This idea of going back to their Academy days to show how the *Enterprise* crew originally got together was not entirely new. Harve Bennett, the producer of several of the *Star Trek* films, had conceived a similar idea in the late 1980s but was unable to convince Paramount executives to go with the plan,

which was apparently heavily influenced by the 1986 film *Top Gun* (Altman and Gross, *The Fifty-Year Mission*, 752).

2. *STAR TREK* AND THE HISTORY OF AMERICAN SCIENCE FICTION

1. Darko Suvin, *Metamorphoses of Science Fiction: On the Poetics and History of a Literary Genre* (New Haven, CT: Yale University Press, 1979).

2. M. Keith Booker, "*Star Trek* and the Birth of a Film Franchise," in *Science Fiction Film, Television, and Adaptation: Across the Screens*, edited by J. P. Telotte and Gerald Duchovnay, 101–114 (London: Routledge, 2012), 110.

3. M. Keith Booker and Anne-Marie Thomas, *The Science Fiction Handbook* (Chichester, UK: Wiley-Blackwell, 2009), 40.

4. The 1958 film *The Brain Eaters* also resembles Heinlein's novel—so much so that he filed suit against the filmmakers. The suit was settled out of court.

5. Early predecessors such as *Tom Corbett—Space Cadet* (1950–1955) lacked the technical and budgetary resources to produce anything like effective science fictional narratives, though *Tom Corbett* (which ran briefly on each of the four networks then in existence) did make some effort.

6. For an overview of American science fiction television roughly through *ENT*, see M. Keith Booker, *Science Fiction Television* (Westport, CT: Praeger, 2004).

7. Eric Greene, *Planet of the Apes as American Myth: Race, Politics, and Culture* (Middletown, CT: Wesleyan University Press, 1996), 9.

8. Of course, the human women of *Planet of the Apes* are represented primarily by the taciturn (and scantily clad) Nova (Linda Harrison), just as the Yang women are represented by the similarly depicted (and clad) Sirah (Irene Kelly). Neither the film nor the episode really do much to promote equality for women.

9. Noted by David C. Fein, producer of the director's edition of *TMP*, in Edward Gross and Mark A. Altman, *The Fifty-Year Mission: The Complete, Uncensored, Unauthorized Oral History of "Star Trek." The First 25 Years* (New York: Thomas Dunne Books, 2016), 340.

10. Manu Saadia, *Trekonomics: The Economics of "Star Trek"* (San Francisco: Pipertext, 2016), 7.

11. Saadia, *Trekonomics*, 145.

12. Gross and Altman, *The Fifty-Year Mission*, 189.

13. Frederik Pohl, "The Politics of Prophecy," in *Political Science Fiction*, edited by Donald M. Hassler and Clyde Wilcox, 7–17 (Columbia: University of South Carolina Press, 1997), 10, 12. Roger Luckhurst has made a similar argument about the boom in politically engaged British speculative writing around

the beginning of the twenty-first century; he argues that the lack of respect given to science fiction, fantasy, and the Gothic has allowed these genres to "flourish largely below the radar" of the British cultural establishment ("Cultural Governance, New Labour, and the British SF Boom," *Science Fiction Studies* 30, no. 3 [2003]: 423).

14. De Witt Douglas Kilgore, *Astrofuturism: Science, Race and Visions of Utopia in Space* (Philadelphia: University of Pennsylvania Press, 2003), 1.

15. M. Keith Booker, "The Politics of *Star Trek*," in *The Essential Science Fiction Television Reader*, edited by J. P. Telotte, 195–208 (Lexington: University Press of Kentucky, 2008), 196.

16. Kilgore, *Astrofuturism*, 2.

17. Kilgore, *Astrofuturism*, 22.

18. See, for example, Andrew Ross on the dystopian turn taken by cyberpunk, especially in relation to the technological utopianism of the early Golden Age ("Getting Out of the Gernsback Continuum" in his *Strange Weather: Culture, Science and Technology in the Age of Limits* [London: Verso, 1991]).

19. See, for example, Andrew Liptak, "13 Science Fiction Writers on How *Star Trek* Influenced Their Lives," *The Verge*, September 10, 2016, https://www.theverge.com/2016/9/10/12847342/science-fiction-authors-star-trek-influenced (accessed March 27, 2018) for testimonials from a number of science fiction authors on the role of *Star Trek* in their lives.

20. For a somewhat darker recent use of *Star Trek* in science fiction, see "USS *Callister*," the first episode of the fourth season of the Netflix series *Black Mirror* (2017). Here, a programming genius creates a simulation of his favorite television series, *Space Fleet*, which is transparently based on *Star Trek*. Within the simulation, he can be all powerful and seek revenge on those he feels have slighted him in the real world. Interestingly enough, though, this episode turns out to be one of the few *Black Mirror* episodes that has a happy ending, suggesting the power of the utopian energies that resides within *Star Trek*.

21. Johnson Jerald, incidentally, had a recurring role in *DS9*, in which she eventually became Benjamin Sisko's second wife.

3. *STAR TREK* AND AMERICAN POLITICAL HISTORY

1. H. Bruce Franklin, "Vietnam, *Star Trek*, and the Real Future," in *"Star Trek" and History*, edited by Nancy R. Reagin, 88–108 (Hoboken, NJ: Wiley, 2013), 90.

2. This strong connection between *TOS* and the 1960s might be one reason why, when an exhibit called *"Star Trek* and the Sixties" opened at the Smithso-

nian Institution's National Air and Space Museum in 1992, it quickly became the most popular exhibit in the history of that museum (Franklin, "Vietnam," 88).

3. This message seems to have reflected the views of Roddenberry and was inserted into the episode over the objections of its writer, Harlan Ellison.

4. The first major attacks of the offensive occurred on the Tét holiday, the Vietnamese New Year.

5. Franklin, "Vietnam," 103.

6. Franklin, "Vietnam," 105–106.

7. The Academy Award–winning African American actress Whoopi Goldberg, who joined the cast of *TNG*, has been quite vocal about the influence of Nichols's portrayal of Uhura on her own life. She has also said that she wanted to be on *Star Trek* because it was the first vision she had seen that had "black people in the future" (Edward Gross and Mark A. Altman, *The Fifty-Year Mission: The Complete, Uncensored, Unauthorized Oral History of "Star Trek." The First 25 Years* [New York: Thomas Dunne Books, 2016], 154). In that same vein, Mae Jemison was inspired by Uhura to become the first African American woman to become a NASA astronaut. Jemison herself made a guest appearance on *TNG* in the episode "Second Chances" (May 24, 1993). See Jesse Katz, "Shooting Star: Former Astronaut Mae Jemison Brings Her Message down to Earth," *Stanford Today*, July–August 1996, https://web.stanford.edu/dept/news/stanfordtoday/ed/9607/pdf/ST9607mjemison.pdf (accessed November 5, 2017).

8. De Witt Douglas Kilgore, *Astrofuturism: Science, Race, and Visions of Utopia in Space* (Philadelphia: University of Pennsylvania Press, 2003), 22.

9. Daniel Leonard Bernardi, Star Trek *and History* (New Brunswick, NJ: Rutgers University Press, 1998), 68.

10. Anthony Shay details the long history of the American fascination with "exotic" dance forms such as belly dancing (*Dancing across Borders: The American Fascination with Exotic Dance Forms* [Jefferson, NC: McFarland, 2008]).

11. Ella Shohat and Robert Stam, *Unthinking Eurocentrism: Multiculturalism and the Media*, 2nd ed. (London: Routledge, 2014), 161.

12. Sexist stereotypes abound as well beyond Orientalist ones. At one point, Kirk quips to Spock that the women of Vulcan are the only ones in the galaxy who think logically.

13. M. G. DuPree, "Alien Babes and Alternate Universes: The Women of *Star Trek*," in *"Star Trek" and History*, edited by Nancy R. Reagin, 280–294 (Hoboken, NJ: Wiley, 2013), 281.

14. One might also compare here the conventional attitude shown toward marriage in the episode "Who Mourns for Adonais?" in which McCoy takes note of the promising (and beautiful) young space archaeologist Lt. Carolyn Palamas

(Leslie Parrish), observing that she will no doubt one day find a husband and then leave her Starfleet career behind her for domestic life.

15. Tom Hayden, "Port Huron Statement," *The Sixties Project*, http://www2. iath.virginia.edu/sixties/HTML_docs/Resources/Primary/Manifestos/SDS_Port_ Huron.html (accessed November 15, 2017).

16. Manu Saadia, *Trekonomics: The Economics of "Star Trek"* (San Francisco: Pipertext, 2016).

4. *STAR TREK* AND THE HISTORY OF TECHNOLOGY

1. Interestingly, communications satellites were first envisioned in 1945 by future science fiction master Arthur C. Clarke, who cowrote (with Kubrick) the screenplay for *2001* and wrote a novelization of the same story in parallel with the making of the film.

2. Deanna K. Kreisel, "Mr. Draper Goes to Town," *Kritik*, April 28, 2014, https://unitforcriticism.wordpress.com/2014/04/28/mad-world-on-kritik-mad-men-season-7-3-mr-draper-goes-to-town-guest-writer-deanna-k-kreisel/ (accessed November 24, 2017).

3. *TOS* ended its initial run on the cusp of this revolution. The first microprocessors were designed in 1969 and were finally produced in 1971.

4. *Mad Men* as a whole engages in a significant amount of dialogue with science fiction, including one moment—in the episode "Christmas Waltz" (May 20, 2012)—when one of the admen attempts (unsuccessfully) to sell a script to *TOS*. On *Mad Men* and science fiction, see M. Keith Booker and Bob Batchelor, *"Mad Men": A Cultural History* (Lanham, MD: Rowman & Littlefield, 2016), 103–117.

5. Brent McDonald, "Information Technology in *Star Trek*: Android vs. Android, iPads vs. PADDs, Facebook vs. the Borg," in *"Star Trek" and History*, edited by Nancy R. Reagin, 194–211 (Hoboken, NJ: Wiley, 2013), 194. For a spirited (but somewhat tongue-in-cheek) defense of the notion that *Star Trek* has directly inspired many technological advances in spaceflight, computers and electronics, and medicine, see the documentary film *How William Shatner Changed the World*, hosted by William Shatner.

6. Manu Saadia presents an eloquent argument for the notion that the affluent future as envisioned by *Star Trek* is indeed a possible one, thanks to the ability of technology to provide replacement for limited natural resources via "technology substitution" (*Trekonomics: The Economics of "Star Trek"* [San Francisco: Pipertext, 2016], 87–108).

7. H. Bruce Franklin, "Vietnam, *Star Trek*, and the Real Future," in *"Star Trek" and History*, edited by Nancy R. Reagin, 88–108 (Hoboken, NJ: Wiley, 2013), 89.

8. This episode is in many ways reenacted in the *TNG* episode "A Fistful of Datas" (November 9, 1992), which, by its very title, updates the allusive range of the *Trek* franchise to include Spaghetti Westerns. Here, Worf, Troi, and Worf's son, Alexander, enter a holodeck simulation of the Western mining town of Deadwood, South Dakota—site of the superb later HBO Western series *Deadwood* (2004–2006). As is often the case, the holodeck malfunctions, and the three adventurers barely manage to survive their visit.

9. Richard Slotkin, *Gunfighter Nation: The Myth of the Frontier in Twentieth-Century America* (Norman: University of Oklahoma Press, [1992] 1998), 633.

10. In fact, "Turnabout Intruder," the very last episode of *TOS*, stipulates that there is no death penalty in the Federation, except for violations of an undefined "General Order 4."

11. One might compare, though, the 1981 film *Evilspeak*, in which a nerdy kid, tormented by bullies, seeks bloody revenge by using his Apple II computer to summon up the evil energies of a medieval Satanic cult.

12. Stephanie Ricker Schulte, *Cached: Decoding the Internet in Global Popular Culture* (New York: New York University Press, 2013), 47.

5. *STAR TREK* AND THE HISTORY OF *STAR TREK* FANDOM

1. For a useful overview of this culture, see John Cheng, *Astounding Wonder: Imagining Science and Science Fiction in Interwar America* (Philadelphia: University of Pennsylvania Press, 2012).

2. On Palmer, see Fred Nadis, *The Man from Mars: Ray Palmer's Amazing Pulp Journey* (New York: Tarcher, 2013).

3. There is also an entire family of fan-generated stories that emphasize the *friendship* between Kirk and Spock, with no erotic intonations. These stories are generally known as "Kirk&Spock" stories or "K&S" stories.

4. See Maria Jose Tenuto and John Tenuto, "*Spockanalia*—The First *Star Trek* Fanzine," October 20, 2014, http://www.startrek.com/article/spockanalia-the-first-star-trek-fanzine (accessed December 9, 2017).

5. Edward Gross and Mark A. Altman, *The Fifty-Year Mission: The Complete, Uncensored, Unauthorized Oral History of "Star Trek." The First 25 Years* (New York: Thomas Dunne Books, 2016), 54.

6. In 1975, however, a disagreement among the original organizers led the New York conventions to split into two separate rival events held nine months

apart but each featuring William Shatner as a main draw. See Robert Greenberger, *"Star Trek": The Complete Unauthorized History* (Minneapolis: Voyageur Press, 2012), 69–70.

7. The film, of course, takes its title from the traditional designation given to dedicated *Trek* fans. The film also notes that many of the more serious fans prefer to be called "Trekkers," rather than "Trekkies," though the film itself takes no definitive position on the difference between these labels.

8. "Filk" music refers to science fiction–inspired folk music. The term was derived from a misprint of "folk" and has been an element of science fiction fan culture since being inadvertently coined by Lee Jacobs in the early 1950s. In fact, what is essentially filk music was written and performed by members of the Futurians fan group more than decade before the term was coined.

9. Dick Hebdige, *Subculture: The Meaning of Style*, rev. ed. (London: Routledge, 1979), 96.

10. See "Star Trek" in *The Big Bang Theory* Wiki: http://bigbangtheory.wikia.com/wiki/Star_Trek.

11. Interestingly enough, J. J. Abrams's *Star Trek Into Darkness* was named the worst *Star Trek* film, while *The Wrath of Khan* was predictably named the best. See Graeme McMillan, "Fans Name 'Star Trek Into Darkness' as the Worst 'Trek' Movie Ever," *The Hollywood Reporter*, August 13, 2013, http://www.hollywoodreporter.com/heat-vision/fans-name-star-trek-darkness-604978 (accessed October 22, 2017).

BIBLIOGRAPHY

Altman, Mark A., and Edward Gross. *The Fifty-Year Mission: The Next 25 Years: From "The Next Generation" to J. J. Abrams: The Complete, Uncensored, and Unauthorized Oral History of "Star Trek."* New York: Thomas Dunne Books, 2016.

Asimov, Isaac. "What Are a Few Galaxies among Friends?" *TV Guide* (November 26, 1966): 6–9.

Barnouw, Erik. *Tube of Plenty: The Evolution of American Television*. 2nd ed. New York: Oxford University Press, 1990.

Bernardi, Daniel Leonard. Star Trek *and History*. New Brunswick, NJ: Rutgers University Press, 1998.

Booker, M. Keith. "The Politics of *Star Trek*." In *The Essential Science Fiction Television Reader*, edited by J. P. Telotte, 195–208. Lexington: University Press of Kentucky, 2008.

———. *Science Fiction Television*. Westport, CT: Praeger, 2004.

———. "*Star Trek* and the Birth of a Film Franchise." In *Science Fiction Film, Television, and Adaptation: Across the Screens*, edited by J. P. Telotte and Gerald Duchovnay, 101–114. London: Routledge, 2012.

Booker, M. Keith, and Anne-Marie Thomas. *The Science Fiction Handbook*. Chichester, West Sussex, UK: Wiley-Blackwell, 2009.

Booker, M. Keith, and Bob Batchelor. *"Mad Men": A Cultural History*. Lanham, MD: Rowman & Littlefield, 2016.

Bradbury, Ray. *Fahrenheit 451*. New York: Ballantine, 1953.

Brunner, John. *Stand on Zanzibar*. New York: Doubleday, 1968.

Burgess, Anthony. *The Wanting Seed*. New York: W. W. Norton, 1962.

Cheng, John. *Astounding Wonder: Imagining Science and Science Fiction in Interwar America*. Philadelphia: University of Pennsylvania Press, 2012.

Collins, Suzanne. *Catching Fire*. New York: Scholastic, 2009.

———. *The Hunger Games*. New York: Scholastic, 2008.

———. *Mockingjay*. New York: Scholastic, 2010.

Cushman, Marc (with Susan Osborn). *These Are the Voyages: TOS Season One*. San Diego: Jacob Brown Media Group, 2013.

DuPree, M. G. "Alien Babes and Alternate Universes: The Women of *Star Trek*." In *"Star Trek" and History*, edited by Nancy R. Reagin, 280–294. Hoboken, NJ: Wiley, 2013.

Ehrlich, Paul R. *The Population Bomb: Population Control or Race to Oblivion*. New York: Ballantine Books, 1968.

Ellison, Harlan, ed. *Dangerous Visions*. New York: Doubleday, 1967.

Franklin, H. Bruce. "Vietnam, *Star Trek*, and the Real Future." In *"Star Trek" and History*, edited by Nancy R. Reagin, 88–108. Hoboken, NJ: Wiley, 2013.

Gibson, William. *Neuromancer*. New York: Ace, 1984.

Greenberger, Robert. *"Star Trek": The Complete Unauthorized History*. Minneapolis: Voyageur Press, 2012.

Greene, Eric. *Planet of the Apes as American Myth: Race, Politics, and Popular Culture*. Middletown, CT: Wesleyan University Press, 1996.

Grey, Ian. "Now, *Voyager*: In Praise of the Trekkiest *Trek* of All." Rogerebert.com. June 11, 2013. http://www.rogerebert.com/balder-and-dash/now-voyager-the-least-beloved-star-trek-offered-some-of-the-franchises-strongest-feminist-messages. Accessed September 19, 2017.

Gross, Edward, and Mark A. Altman. *The Fifty-Year Mission: The Complete, Uncensored, Unauthorized Oral History of "Star Trek." The First 25 Years*. New York: Thomas Dunne Books, 2016.

Harrison, Harry. *Make Room! Make Room!* New York: Orb Books, 1966.

Hayden, Tom. "Port Huron Statement." *The Sixties Project*. http://www2.iath.virginia.edu/sixties/HTML_docs/Resources/Primary/Manifestos/SDS_Port_Huron.html. Accessed November 15, 2017.

Hebdige, Dick. *Subculture: The Meaning of Style*. Rev. ed. London: Routledge, 1979.

Heinlein, Robert A. *The Puppet Masters*. New York: Doubleday, 1951.

Hodge, Jarrah. "How Does Your Favorite *Star Trek* Series Fare on the Bechdel Test?" The Mary Sue. September 1, 2014. https://www.themarysue.com/star-trek-bechdel-test/. Accessed September 20, 2017.

Huxley, Aldous. *Brave New World*. London: Chatto & Windus, 1932.

Katz, Jesse. "Shooting Star: Former Astronaut Mae Jemison Brings Her Message down to Earth." *Stanford Today*. July–August 1996. https://web.stanford.edu/dept/news/stanfordtoday/ed/9607/pdf/ST9607mjemison.pdf. Accessed November 5, 2017.

Kilgore, De Witt Douglas. *Astrofuturism: Science, Race, and Visions of Utopia in Space*. Philadelphia: University of Pennsylvania Press, 2003.

Kreisel, Deanna K. "Mr. Draper Goes to Town." *Kritik*. April 28, 2014. https://unitforcriticism.wordpress.com/2014/04/28/mad-world-on-kritik-mad-men-season-7-3-mr-draper-gocs-to-town-guest-writer-deanna-k-kreisel/. Accessed November 24, 2017.

Lewis, Michael. "You're Doing It Wrong: Cause and Effect in *Star Trek*'s Histories." In *"Star Trek" and History*, edited by Nancy R. Reagin, 109–124. Hoboken, NJ: Wiley, 2013.

Liptak, Andrew. "13 Science Fiction Writers on How *Star Trek* Influenced Their Lives." *The Verge*, September 10, 2016, https://www.theverge.com/2016/9/10/12847342/science-fiction-authors-star-trek-influenced. Accessed March 27, 2018.

Luckhurst, Roger. "Cultural Governance, New Labour, and the British SF Boom." *Science Fiction Studies* 30, no. 3 (2003): 417–435.

McDonald, Brent. "Information Technology in *Star Trek*: Android vs. Android, iPads vs. PADDs, Facebook vs. the Borg." In *"Star Trek" and History*, edited by Nancy R. Reagin, 194–211. Hoboken, NJ: Wiley, 2013.

McMillan, Graeme. "Fans Name 'Star Trek Into Darkness' as the Worst 'Trek' Movie Ever." *The Hollywood Reporter*. August 13, 2013. http://www.hollywoodreporter.com/heat-vision/fans-name-star-trek-darkness-604978. Accessed October 22, 2017.

Nadis, Fred. *The Man from Mars: Ray Palmer's Amazing Pulp Journey*. New York: Tarcher, 2013.

Penley, Constance. "Feminism, Psychoanalysis, and the Study of Popular Culture." In *Cultural Studies*, edited by Lawrence Grossberg, 494–500. London: Routledge, 1991.

Pohl, Frederik. "The Politics of Prophecy." In *Political Science Fiction*, edited by Donald M. Hassler and Clyde Wilcox, 7–17. Columbia: University of South Carolina Press, 1997.

Pohl, Frederik, and Cyril M. Kornbluth. *The Space Merchants*. 1953. New York: St. Martin's Griffin, 2011.

Reagin, Nancy R., ed. *"Star Trek" and History*. Hoboken, NJ: Wiley, 2013.

Ross, Andrew. "Getting Out of the Gernsback Continuum." In his *Strange Weather: Culture, Science, and Technology in the Age of Limits*. London: Verso, 1991.

Saadia, Manu. *Trekonomics: The Economics of "Star Trek."* San Francisco: Pipertext, 2016.

Said, Edward W. *Orientalism*. New York: Vintage-Random House, 1979.

Schulte, Stephanie Ricker. *Cached: Decoding the Internet in Global Popular Culture*. New York: New York University Press, 2013.

Shay, Anthony. *Dancing across Borders: The American Fascination with Exotic Dance Forms*. Jefferson, NC: McFarland, 2008.

Shohat, Ella, and Robert Stam. *Unthinking Eurocentrism: Multiculturalism and the Media*. 2nd ed. London: Routledge, 2014.

Slotkin, Richard. *Gunfighter Nation: The Myth of the Frontier in Twentieth-Century America*. 1992. Norman: University of Oklahoma Press, 1998.

Spinrad, Norman. *Bug Jack Barron*. New York: Walker & Company, 1969.

"Star Trek." *The Big Bang Theory* Wiki. http://bigbangtheory.wikia.com/wiki/Star_Trek. Accessed December 17, 2017.

Suvin, Darko. *Metamorphoses of Science Fiction: On the Poetics and History of a Literary Genre*. New Haven, CT: Yale University Press, 1979.

Tenuto, Maria Jose, and John Tenuto. "*Spockanalia*—The First *Star Trek* Fanzine." October 20, 2014. http://www.startrek.com/article/spockanalia-the-first-star-trek-fanzine. Accessed December 9, 2017.

Weitekamp, Margaret A. "More Than 'Just Uhura': Understanding *Star Trek*'s Lt. Uhura, Civil Rights, and Space History." In *"Star Trek" and History*, edited by Nancy R. Reagin, 22–38. Hoboken, NJ: Wiley, 2013.

FILMS CITED

Altman, Robert, dir. *Buffalo Bill and the Indians, or Sitting Bull's History Lesson*. United Artists, 1976.

——, dir. *McCabe & Mrs. Miller*. Warner Bros., 1971.

Badham, John, dir. *WarGames*. United Artists, 1983.

Brooks, Richard, dir. *The Professionals*. Columbia Pictures, 1966.

Burke, Martyn, dir. *Pirates of Silicon Valley*. TNT, 1999.

Burnett, Robert Meyer, dir. *Free Enterprise*. Regent Entertainment, 1998.

Cameron, James, dir. *The Abyss*. Twentieth Century Fox, 1989.

——, dir. *The Terminator*. Orion, 1984.

Cimino, Michael, dir. *Heaven's Gate*. United Artists, 1980.

Coolidge, Martha, dir. *Real Genius*. TriStar, 1985.

Fleischer, Richard, dir. *Soylent Green*. MGM, 1973.

Forbes, Bryan, dir. *The Stepford Wives*. Columbia Pictures, 1975.

Glaser, Paul Michael, dir. *The Running Man*. TriStar, 1987.

Godard, Jean-Luc, dir. *Alphaville*. André Michelin Productions, 1965.

Guillerman, John, dir. *The Towering Inferno*. Twentieth Century Fox, 1974.

Hill, George Roy, dir. *Butch Cassidy and the Sundance Kid*. Twentieth Century Fox, 1969.

Hughes, John, dir. *The Breakfast Club*. Universal, 1985.

——, dir. *Sixteen Candles*. Universal, 1984.

——, dir. *Weird Science*. Universal, 1985.

Jones, Julian, dir. *How William Shatner Changed the World*. Allumination Filmworks, 2005.

Kanew, Jeff, dir. *Revenge of the Nerds*. Twentieth Century Fox, 1984.

Kershner, Irvin, dir. *The Empire Strikes Back*. Twentieth Century Fox, 1980.

Kubrick, Stanley, dir. *2001: A Space Odyssey*. MGM, 1968.

——, dir. *Dr. Strangelove or: How I Learned to Stop Worrying and Love the Bomb*. Columbia, 1964.

Landis, John, dir. *Animal House*. Universal, 1978.

Lucas, George, dir. *Star Wars*. Twentieth Century Fox, 1977.

Marquand, Richard, dir. *The Return of the Jedi*. Twentieth Century Fox, 1983.

McLeod, Norman, dir. *Horse Feathers*. Paramount, 1932.

Menzies, William Cameron, dir. *Invaders from Mars*. Edward L. Alperson Productions, 1953.

Neame, Ronald, dir. *The Poseidon Adventure*. Twentieth Century Fox, 1972.

Nygard, Roger, dir. *Trekkies*. NEO Motion Pictures, 1997.

——, dir. *Trekkies 2*. NEO Motion Pictures, 2004.

Parisot, Dean, dir. *Galaxy Quest*. DreamWorks, 1999.

Penn, Arthur, dir. *Little Big Man*. National General Pictures, 1970.

———, dir. *The Missouri Breaks*. United Artists, 1976.

Schaffner, Franklin, dir. *Planet of the Apes*. Twentieth Century Fox, 1968.

Scott, Ridley, dir. *Alien*. Twentieth Century Fox, 1979.

———, dir. *Blade Runner*. Warner Bros., 1982.

Shatner, William, dir. *Chaos on the Bridge*. Wacky Doodle Productions, 2014.

Siegel, Don, dir. *Invasion of the Body Snatchers*. Walter Wanger Productions, 1956.

Spielberg, Steven, dir. *Close Encounters of the Third Kind*. Columbia, 1977.

Thompson, J. Craig, dir. *The Truth Is in the Stars*. Ballinran Entertainment, 2017.

Truffaut, François, dir. *Fahrenheit 451*. Universal, 1966.

Whale, James, dir. *Frankenstein*. Universal, 1931.

Wilcox, Fred M., dir. *Forbidden Planet*. MGM, 1956.

Wilder, Gene, dir. *The Woman in Red*. Orion, 1984.

Wise, Robert, dir. *The Day the Earth Stood Still*. Twentieth Century Fox, 1951.

INDEX

2001: A Space Odyssey, 13, 38, 48, 52, 96, 97, 104, 178n1

The Abyss, 42
Alien, 60
androids and robots, 5, 19, 44, 106, 117. *See also* artificial intelligence; computers
Apple Inc., 104, 110, 111, 114, 179n11. *See also* computers
artificial intelligence, xxii, 61, 104, 105–107. *See also* androids and robots; computers
Asimov, Isaac, 43, 52, 53, 56, 125; *Foundation Trilogy*, 54
astrofuturism, xix, 38, 58–59

Behr, Ira Steven, 21
Big Bang Theory, 139
Black Mirror, 176n20
Blade Runner, 60
Booker, M. Keith, 38, 174n7, 175n2, 175n3, 175n6, 176n15, 178n4
The Borg, 19, 20, 28, 29, 41, 42, 178n5
Braga, Brannon, 63, 64
Brave New World, 57, 118
Bug Jack Barron, 57

capitalism, xx, 19, 71, 87, 90, 92, 94, 110, 120, 121, 129, 131, 136, 171
Close Encounters of the Third Kind, 13, 60

Cold War, xix–xx, 9, 40, 42, 47, 49, 53, 56, 65, 68–69, 71, 112, 148, 153, 157, 162, 163; absurdity of, 70, 71; and the arms race, 50, 57, 69, 70, 152, 157; and espionage drama, 160, 165; and the space race, xix, xx, 45, 58, 59, 95, 99, 101; and utopianism, 84; *See also* *Vietnam War*
comics, xviii, xxiii, 1, 10–11, 13, 33, 61
computers, xii, xxii, 132; suspicion of, 61, 96–97, 104, 105–110. *See also* androids and robots; Apple Inc.; artificial intelligence
cyberpunk science fiction, xix, 60, 61, 176n18

The Day the Earth Stood Still, 42, 47, 70, 164
Demon Seed, 109
Dr. Strangelove, 71, 112
dystopian imagery, 47–48, 60, 105; in *Genesis II*, 6; in *Star Trek: Deep Space Nine*, 25, 40. *See also* cyberpunk science fiction

Ellison, Harlan, 11, 39, 46, 53, 56, 177n3

Fahrenheit 451, 47–48
Ferengi, 24, 25, 26, 118, 121
Forbidden Planet, xvi, 52, 170
Franklin, H. Bruce, 65, 67–68, 99, 176n2

ABOUT THE AUTHOR

M. Keith Booker is professor of English and director of the Program in Comparative Literature and Cultural Studies at the University of Arkansas. He has written or edited more than forty books on literature and popular culture. His books include *Drawn to Television: Prime-Time Animated Series from* The Flintstones *to* Family Guy (2006) and *Historical Dictionary of American Cinema* (2011). Booker is also the coauthor of Mad Men*: A Cultural History* (2015) and *Tony Soprano's America: Gangsters, Guns, and Money* (2017), both published by Rowman & Littlefield.